Breaking Through the Plate Glass Window— Prophetic Fragments

Breaking Through the Plate Glass Window— Prophetic Fragments

On Doing Justice and Loving Kindness in a Time of Reckoning

MICHAEL GRANZEN

Preface by Traci C. West
Introduction by Chris Hedges

*With Reflections from
Lorna Goodison, Richard Fenn, Mike Gecan,
Karen Hernandez-Granzen, and Archainge Antoine*

 CASCADE *Books* · Eugene, Oregon

BREAKING THROUGH THE PLATE GLASS WINDOW—PROPHETIC
FRAGMENTS
On Doing Justice and Loving Kindness in a Time of Reckoning

Cascade Books
An Imprint of Wipf and Stock Publishers
199 W. 8th Ave., Suite 3
Eugene, OR 97401

www.wipfandstock.com

PAPERBACK ISBN: 978-1-7252-9457-8
HARDCOVER ISBN: 978-1-7252-9458-5
EBOOK ISBN: 978-1-7252-9459-2

Cataloguing-in-Publication data:

Names: Granzen, Michael, author. | West, Traci C., 1959–, preface. |
Hedges, Chris, inroduction. | Goodison, Lorna, reflection. | Fenn, Richard
K., reflection. | Gecan, Michael, reflection. | Hernandez-Granzen, Karen,
reflection. | Archainge, Antoine, reflection.

Title: Breaking through the plate glass window—prophetic fragments : on
seeking justice and compassion in America / Michael Granzen ; preface by
Traci C. West ; introduction by Chris Hedges ; with reflections by Lorna
Goodison, Richard Fenn, Mike Gecan, Karen Hernandez-Granzen, and
Antonie Archainge.

Description: Eugene, OR : Cascade Books, 2022 | Includes bibliographical
references.

Identifiers: ISBN 978-1-7252-9457-8 (paperback) | ISBN 978-1-7252-9458-5
(hardcover) | ISBN 978-1-7252-9459-2 (ebook)

Subjects: LCSH: Granzen, Michael. | Presbyterian Church (U.S.A.)—Clergy—
Biography. | Presbyterians—United States—Biography.

Classification: BX9225.G72 A3 2022 (paperback) | BX9225.G72 A3 (ebook)

05/09/22

Karen Hernandez-Granzen "The Kin-dom Coming in the Joyful Worship of the
God of All People" from Intercultural Ministry: Hope for a Changing World ed-
ited by Grace Ji-Sun Kim and Jann Aldredge-Clanton, copyright © 2017 by Judson
Press. Used by permission of Judson Press.

This book is dedicated to my daughters,
Mikaella Julia Granzen and Olivia Danielle Granzen,
and to the gracious disrupters of their generation.

And Jesus said to his disciples:
"Gather up the fragments,
that none shall be lost."

JOHN 6:12

Contents

Preface

Traci C. West

There are questions that I wish Christian white men who offer progressive social change leadership would investigate about their own formation. For these leaders and others, a durable commitment to creating social change inescapably involves one's own capacities and stamina. An investigation of one's formative life experiences can provide clues about how personal resources that enable this kind of leadership are acquired and nurtured. In the work of addressing white racism, for instance, there are questions to be explored about how to stay with the struggle beyond the moments of focused public attention to certain racist crises. Then, how does one persevere in spite of disparaging criticism and disdain for white race traitors from one's own community? Or, exactly how does one sustain a refusal to give up when feeling overwhelmed by conflicting, competing anti-racist interests and perspectives? To cultivate an enduring commitment requires effort deeper than posing the right questions and demands more than outward facing, publicly articulated political analysis. It also relies upon vulnerable, reflective, inward facing self-understanding that can tap into flourishing reservoirs of tenacity, replenish them, and filter out detritus that excuses inaction. To be counted as someone who will remain committed matters for building necessary forms of solidarity. It signals trustworthiness.

When I, a black woman Christian activist/scholar, initially encounter leaders who are progressive Christian white men in our shared work of addressing racism, I admit that sometimes I feel uncertain about their trustworthiness. I find myself annoyed and resentful if they seem too self-congratulatory or demanding of my praise for merely being willing to raise questions about the problematic nature of white racism. I am reticent if they seem to be passing along to me all of the specific tasks that are involved in devising strategies to name, address, and redress the consequences of white racism. At the same time, I am also suspicious if they seem to be too tightly controlling or certain of their sole possession of the answers that will supposedly resolve issues of racism.

Eventually, my willingness to trust them always has something to do with how they show up in the midst of the turmoil and risks of this antiracism work and do so again and again. More importantly, because of our political and ecological interdependence, I must invest in solidarity work with some of them and others in order to jointly respond to the urgent need for human freedom and wholeness in the face of entrenched opposition that white racism poses. My training ground has mainly been in my long-standing anti-racist work on ending gender violence and abuse and insisting on LGTBQIA+ equality in church and society. It has taught me too well how the emotional costs resulting from communally sanctioned harm require mutually galvanized fortitude and trust and directly rely upon the emotionally mature formation of leaders who dare to challenge racist heteropatriarchies.

Breaking Through the Plate Glass Window illustrates trustworthiness. Michael Granzen offers fierce honesty about how his own longings, traumas, and emotional growth have been formative in what it means to seek justice in times of reckoning. Who must you befriend, stare down in a confrontation, or mobilize for the struggle? How might your international travel instructively both disorient and orient your understanding of racialized violence? This account details a pursuit that is never overly determined by certainty but tarries in vulnerability and evolving wisdom drawn from experiential and conceptual learning.

Personal histories of social learning and emotional and spiritual formation are of course shaped by broad racialized community histories. Dominant communal narratives about racial relations in the past and their imprint on the present can forcefully erode trust and destroy even the possibility of anti-racist solidarity if they are left uninterrogated. So there are patterns of white racism within particular communal histories that I wish Christian white pastor-scholars who offer progressive social change leadership would uproot. I do not mean that I wish for more commemorations in Christian worship services during black history month that point out the courage of heroic anti-racist figures while leaving out the details of the white racist practices and people that made all of that anti-racist courage and heroism so necessary. I do not mean that I wish for sorrowful historical references to displaced Indigenous nations of people, dehumanizing Southern slave plantations, or segregated Southern public buses. They omit any mention of the role of Christian faith, Scriptures, pastors, and congregations in maintaining those practices that have upheld white supremacy through-out US history. There are particular situations of Christianized local tradi-tions of white racism that need to be disturbed by white Christian leaders in their particular local contexts. What does it mean, for example, for white leaders committed to progressive social change in northeastern regions of the United States to situate contemporary racist practices in the histories of their own communities, especially the life and legacies of their own church communities?

To all who pass by them, church windows traditionally project a sym-bolic message of localized space that is marked off as sacred for those who belong inside and evidence transparency that allows the sacredness to shine outwardly as a witness to the rest of world of Christian virtuosity. The church buildings to which the windows are attached represent a long tradition of safeguarding Christian respect for human moral worth. It stretches back to the birth of Christianity in the ancient Mediterranean world and supports contemporary claims of divine sanction for this territorialized morality. *Breaking Through the Plate Glass Window* refuses to uncritically accept any such conventions. The idea of the window functions as a metaphor for the opportunity taken in these essays for the excavation of racist histories. We are guided not only to peak through the glass in order to see inside and rec-ognize the racist local history of Christianity in Elizabeth, New Jersey, but also to break through it and reject the false veneer of racial virtuousness at-tributed to white Christianity. Dominant expressions of Christianity under scrutiny here share the spotlight with one of the other assumed preservers of respect for moral behavior and worth in local community life—law en-forcement. Uprooting established narratives of moral virtuousness within the local histories of church and policing with truths about actual practices denies their innocence and exposes the lie that they are unencumbered by situational and patterned influences of white supremacy. Focusing on the particularities in the communal histories of these institutions breaks apart their traditionally projected image as religious and state pillars of moral stability and discipline that infuse local community life with the values of justice and respect for human worth and rights.

I crave confrontations of racial innocence sometimes claimed by Christian white pastor-scholars and others who offer progressive social change leadership. This claim may not be overtly asserted but, instead, a subtle assumption of white entitlement is to position one's self as detached from any direct relationship to the lived impacts of racism. Claims of in-nocence by these leaders can emerge when an inverted version of "not in my back yard," conveying the message that problems of blatant racism do not occur in my (liberal) backyard, combines with a form of presentism. In this configuration, the progressive response to racism is stuck in the present, willfully rejecting the significance and adaptations of historical patterns of white racism that inform current sociopolitical attitudes and everyday institutional practices in one's liberal ethos.

I remember when I attended a Black Lives Matter protest and rally in a predominantly white, small New Jersey suburban town near my home. I was pleasantly surprised by the size of the crowd. It comprised hundreds of mostly white marchers across a spectrum of age groups. The racially diverse speakers, especially the youth and young adults, inspired us with their sincerity and articulate urging of our commitment to address racism. At one point toward the end of the event, one of the speakers spoke of "our" local police who were standing outside of their cars during the rally portion of the event. Earlier a large contingent of police cars, including a few from neighboring towns, had flanked the marchers along their short four to five square block route and now awaited the conclusion of the rally. The speaker pointed to them, thanked them for their cooperative work with the organizers, and generally praised the protection that they had provided. As I looked at the predominantly white crowd enthusiastically applauding in response to these comments by the speaker, it seemed that everyone around me presumed that we were protesting racist police practices in troubled places elsewhere, not here in our suburban New Jersey community. At that moment, I could not help but feel extremely alienated from the rest of the crowd.

I recalled multiple instances in past years in which a black male member of my family had been stopped and questioned for driving while black by officers from predominantly white local police departments of adjoining towns near my home. The reasons that the officers stated for stopping and questioning him were spurious, such as for driving too slowly (28 mph in a 30 mph zone), or for driving late at night (they asked where he was going at 11 PM). Occasionally, after being stopped by a police officer and required to show his driver's license and insurance card, he had to respond to especially inane questions such as, "Why do you have so many books in your backseat?" He would patiently respond by explaining to the police officer that he was a graduate school professor and researcher and thus needed to read many books. Fortunately, no ticket was ever issued, nor any escalation to violence by the officers ever occurred during those frequent traffic stops.

The unpredictability and possibility of white racist state violence arbitrarily exercised by the police remains a fearful reality. But only with attention to historical patterns might the persistence and significance of that reality be truthfully revealed. Ignoring history protects white entitlement to claim innocence and eliminates our ability to grasp the systemic nature of racist state intimidation and violence. In the following pages of *Breaking Through the Plate Glass Window*, we are not allowed to avoid the pattern of repeated, terrorizing acts of white brutality that occur. The account begins with New Jersey's eighteenth-century practices of slavery through to corrupt and racist police tactics that include 1990s beatings of black teens in its city of Elizabeth. This analysis confronts the claims of white innocence, the moral disciplining of the broader society that takes place through historical patterns of white racist state violence, and the role of Christian religiosity in sustaining them both.

In this book, we learn through an array of fragments of experientially based revelations and visionary thought. The fragments provide multiple carefully crafted lenses of insight. Cumulatively, they map out a model of moral leadership needed to create progressive social change. The map includes personal narratives of formation and leadership, documented communal histories of state and church practices that sanctioned racist violence, and the voices of leaders whose testimonies of courage augment the notion of solidarity that pervades this text. I am grateful for this method of cohesively arranged fragments. This approach serves as a reminder of incalculable fragments left behind in the costs for targeted communities to their minds, bodies, and spirits, as well as to their collective trust of the state. Mostly, they are costs for which there will never be any accountability. It is also a method that extends an invitation to readers to ask their own questions about their leadership capacities, to find the historical narratives that keep in place patterns of white racist terror committed by public officials, and then seek to uproot them. Finally, as we are beneficially immersed in understanding the process of unraveling systemic racism, we are kept aware of the fragmentary or partial nature of that understanding. Therefore, this approach makes possible ongoing recognition of the need for more discovery of how intersectional, entangled systems of power related to gender, sexual orientation, and other markers of social identity are always operative in shaping racist dynamics of power.

Breaking Through the Plate Glass Window is the project that I wish for because of the myriad of ways Michael Granzen demonstrates radical disruptions of religious and historical narratives of white innocence and communal calcifications of white racism. His disruptiveness joins together with an enduring spiritual commitment to human becoming that tangibly and adaptively generates political interventions to match the adaptability of white racist harm.

Introduction

Chris Hedges

WHEN MICHAEL GRANZEN AND I graduated from Harvard Divinity School nearly four decades ago, the liberal church was already in crisis. Numbers were declining. Congregations were aging. Revenue was dropping. Seminary enrollment was dropping, and many were closing or dramatically reducing staff and tenured faculty. The response of the institutional church, as Reinhold Niebuhr understood, was to search for ways to perpetuate itself rather than hold fast to the demands of the Christian gospel. Fearful of alienating its more conservative members, it fled from the kind of overt social activism that made the church a vital part of the anti-war movement and the civil rights movement. It reconfigured the idea of spirituality into a how-is-it-with-me introspection that mirrored the cult of the self that defines the consumer society. It remained silent, in the name of tolerance—a word Martin Luther King never used—as the Christian Right, which should have been vocally condemned as heretical, sacralized the worst strains of white supremacy, capitalism, and imperialism. You do not need a master of divinity degree from Harvard to realize that Jesus did not come to make us rich. Administrators and church leaders, abandoning the poor in our internal colonies in decayed post-industrial America with white flight, chased after elusive and futile schemes for church growth and the newest fad to upgrade digital platforms.

The leaders of these church institutions, by abandoning the core tenants of the gospel, exacerbated the decline. Liberal denominations lose about a million members a year. In 2019 alone, 4,500 churches were closed. The prophetic voice of the church, the only thing that gives it relevance and can renew its spiritual life, has been largely ignored or silenced.

This decline, and the complicity of many church administrators in the decline, is what makes Michael's book relevant and important. He remained true to the call to minister to those the theologian James Cone calls the "crucified of the earth."[1] These were poor people of color, those in our jails, detention centers, and prisons, and immigrants living in fear of arrest and deportation in depressed urban communities. These communities lack the resources to maintain the aging, often cavernous church buildings left behind by white flight or sometimes raise the money to pay an adequate salary for their pastors. But here, as Michael points out, is where the embers of the real church lie. This ministry, which Michael profoundly reflects upon, is an act of faith. It does not prioritize financial solvency and growth over the commitment to stand alongside the oppressed. And it reminds us that when we truly stand with the oppressed, we will, in the end, be treated like the oppressed.

Michael understands, as Paul Tillich writes, that all institutions, including the church, are inherently demonic. Reinhold Niebuhr in his classic work *Moral Man and Immoral Society*, which Michael and I read with one of Niebuhr's former students, Professor Coleman Brown, when we were undergraduates at Colgate University, asserts that no institution can ever achieve the morality of the individual. Institutions, Niebuhr warns, to extend their lives when confronted with decline, will swiftly betray the stances that ostensibly define them. Only individual men and women have the strength to hold fast to virtue when faced with the threat of death. And decaying institutions, including the church, when consumed by fear, swiftly push those endowed with this moral courage and radicalism to the margins or from their ranks, further rendering themselves obsolete.

The self-identified religious institutions that thrive preach the perverted "prosperity gospel," the message that magic Jesus will make us rich, respected, and powerful if we believe in him. Jesus, these heretics claim, is an American capitalist, bigot, and ardent imperialist. These sects selectively lift passages from the Bible to justify the unjustifiable, including homophobia, war, racism, Islamophobia, and supporting the death penalty and political demagogues such as Donald Trump. There are more students—1,660—at the evangelical Gordon-Conwell Theological Seminary alone than at the divinity schools and seminaries of Yale, Harvard, Union, Vanderbilt, and Chicago, combined. The Christian faith—as in the 1930s under Germany's pro-Nazi Christian church—is being distorted to sanctify nationalism, unregulated capitalism, and militarism. The connecting tissue of the assault on the Congress on January 6, 2021, was this species of Christian fascism. And

---

1. Cone, *The Cross and the Lynching Tree*, 165. Also see Cone, *God of the Oppressed*.

one of the greatest failings of the liberal church is that by not denouncing these sects—the radical message of the gospel necessitates confrontation—it has tacitly given them religious credibility. These heretical sects have been lavishly funded since the early twentieth century. The wealthy elites and industrialists were determined to crush the social witness movements that found their origins in the liberal church. These ruling elites promoted and funded a brand of Christianity—which is today dominant—that conflates faith with free enterprise and American exceptionalism. The rich are rich, this creed goes, not because they are greedy or privileged, not because they use their power to their own advantage, not because they oppress the poor and the vulnerable, but because they are blessed. And if we have enough faith, this heretical form of Christianity claims, God will bless the rest of us too. It is an inversion of the central message of the gospel.

Radical Christians led the abolitionist movement, were active in the Anti-Imperialist League, participated in the bloody labor wars, fought for women's suffrage, formulated the Social Gospel—which included a huge effort to carry out prison reform and provide education to prisoners—and were engines in the civil rights and anti-war movements. Norman Thomas, a longtime leader of the Socialist Party of America, was a Presbyterian minister. These radicals were not always embraced by the church hierarchy, which served as a bulwark of the establishment, but they kept the church vital, alive, and prophetic. They made it relevant and important to the oppressed, the poor, and to working men and women. Radicals, like Michael, were and remain its hope.

The loss of an array of prophetic religious voices on the national scene such as Phil and Daniel Berrigan, William Stringfellow, Rabbi Abraham Heschel, Dorothy Day, and Martin Luther King Jr. left the liberal church as morally bankrupt as the rest of the liberal class. James Baldwin, who grew up in the church and was briefly a preacher, said he abandoned the pulpit to preach the gospel. The gospel, he knew, was not heard most Sundays in Christian houses of worship. And today with most ministers wary of offending their aging and dwindling flocks—counted on to pay the clergy salary and the bills—this is even truer than when Baldwin was writing.

The church is also, of course, a victim of the disintegration of the civic associations that, as Alex de Tocqueville observed, are vital to the maintenance of a healthy democracy and the common good. Robert Putnam in his book *Bowling Alone* chronicled the broad disengagement from political and public life. He lamented, correctly, the loss of this "social capital." Those who no longer join parents' organizations, gardening and historical clubs, or fraternal orders, who do not show up at town hall or city council meetings, also no longer attend church. There is little, given this cultural malaise—much of it driven by the constant availability of entertainment through the internet and electronic devices—that the church can do to blunt the public's retreat from public space.

Michael, drawing on his decades ministering in depressed communities, reminds us that if the church is to survive as a social and cultural force, clergy and congregants *must* leave church sanctuaries to minister in prisons, schools, labor halls, and homeless and women's shelters. They must, as Michael did in his church in Elizabeth, New Jersey, organize night basketball leagues and participate in grass-roots movements such as the anti-fracking struggle, the fight to raise the minimum wage, and efforts to stem police violence. Yes, this focus will make it hard to financially maintain the massive and largely empty church edifices, and perhaps even the seminaries, but it will keep Christianity alive.

William Stringfellow, who worked as a lawyer in Harlem in the 1950s and 1960s, in his book *My People Is the Enemy*, wrote of the church:

> The premise of most urban church work, it seems, is that in order for the Church to minister among the poor, the church has to be rich, that is, to have specially trained personnel, huge funds and many facilities, rummage to distribute, and a whole battery of social services. Just the opposite is the case. The Church must be free to be poor in order to minister among the poor. The Church must trust the Gospel enough to come among the poor with nothing to offer the poor except the Gospel, except the power to apprehend and the courage to reveal the Word of God as it is already mediated in the life of the poor. When the Church has the freedom itself to be poor among the poor, it will know how to use what riches it has. When the Church has that freedom, it will be a missionary people again in all the world.[2]

Stringfellow, who influenced Michael's ministry, repeatedly warned Christians, as well as Christian institutions, not to allow the fear of death to diminish the power of Christian witness. Faith becomes real on the edge of the abyss. "In the face of death," he wrote, "live humanly. In the middle of chaos, celebrate the Word. Amidst Babel, speak the truth. Confront the noise and verbiage and falsehood of death with the truth and potency and efficacy of the Word of God."[3]

The liberal church needs to ask for forgiveness. It looked the other way while the poor and working men and women, especially those of color, were ruthlessly disempowered and impoverished through de-industrialization,

2. Stringfellow, *My People Is the Enemy*, 102.
3. Stringfellow, *An Ethic for Christians*, 142.

the abolition of welfare, and austerity. The church and liberals were as silent about the militarization of police and the massive expansion of mass incarceration as they once were about lynching. The liberal church refused to confront and denounce the destructive force of corporate power. It placed its faith in institutions—such as the Democratic Party—that had long ceased to function as mechanisms of reform. The liberal church, mirroring the liberal establishment, busied itself with charity, multiculturalism, and gender-identity politics at the expense of justice, especially racial and economic justice. Although the mainline church pays lip service to diversity, it has never welcomed significant numbers of people of color or the marginalized into their sanctuaries. The Presbyterian Church, for example, is 90 percent white. The liberal church, like the Catholic Church, pushed to the margins or sought to discredit Liberation Theology, which called out the evils of unfettered capitalism, white supremacy, and imperialism. The retreat from radicalism—in essence the abandonment of the vulnerable to the predatory forces of corporate capitalism—created the spiritual void filled by protofascist movements that have usurped Christian symbols and provided a species of faith that is, at its core, a belief in magic.

Fear has driven many church and seminary leaders into the hands of those the gospel condemns as exploiters of the poor and the oppressed. They have turned their backs on Christian radicals, those like Michael who alone can infuse new life into the church. The institutions believe alliances with the powerful and the wealthy will save them. They are wrong. They are selling their soul. Once they stand for nothing, they become nothing. Michael's book is a prophetic warning, a clarion call to the Christian community to return to a life of faith, to hold fast to the radical call of the gospel, to bear the cross. Only then will we find our spiritual strength, our purpose, our renewal, and our faith.

SECTION I

Biographical Fragments

Write by telling the truth. In your own voice.
We cannot heal from what we do not name.

CLIMBING THE MOUNTAIN

During my years living in Boston, I'd go hiking in the White Mountains with my minister friend, Dave. The wild beauty of the granite rock and cold streams were healing. At one point, we decided to climb the highest mountain four times, in spring, summer, fall, and winter. After finishing up our church work late Sunday afternoon, we'd drive up on Route 91 and camp in a small tent near the base of Mt. Washington. At dawn, we'd hike up to the summit. But you can't live on the mountain. We'd return by dusk and drive home to the city. We were both in our late twenties and in good shape.

Sometimes we'd run up the mountain. More often we'd walk and talk. One morning, we started a conversation on bulldozer theology. The presupposition of bulldozer theology is that life is like a slow (or sometimes fast) moving bulldozer. You avoid the bulldozer if you can, for as long as you can. But eventually it will get you. There is no escaping. Life will run you over. Bulldozer theology begins then with certain questions: How do you get up? Do you want to get up? Where is God? What really counts? This is true for both individuals and communities.

We ran to the mountain three times, in spring, summer, and fall. Even in summer the summit was cool and windy. Autumn was a rare beauty. Spring was gorgeous but treacherous with the snowpack melting. Dave once fell through the melting snow up to his shoulders. An icy subterranean river ran under him. I grabbed his arms and pulled. "Deliver us, O God, from Sheol," he cried. We always returned by dusk.

The last time we climbed Mt. Washington was on December 30. The temperature was minus 20 degrees. We had crampons, ice axes, and a strong rope that connected us. We hired a guide from Eastern Mountain Sports. The mountain in winter was extremely icy with biting wind and snow. We had a covenant that if one of us slipped and fell, the others would dig their axes into the ice and hold on for dear life. At about 2:00 PM, I could faintly hear, through the wind and snow, the weather station machinery on the top of the mountain. I wanted to go on. But the weather was getting worse and it would soon be dark. They persuaded me to turn back. Thank God, we barely made it home.

The first section of this book is about life after the bulldozer runs you over. How do you get up? How do you live with others who don't understand or don't want to understand? How do you keep climbing the mountain in spite of the bulldozer? "The world breaks everyone," wrote Ernest Hemingway, "and afterwards many are strong at the broken places."[1]

The gift of courage or faith is a many-splendored thing. Faith is not so much about agreeing with doctrine but a dynamic, active, seeking, questioning, trust in God. It is creative appropriation of an open past. It includes both audacity and humility. William Stringfellow connects faith from a Christian perspective with history and biography. He turns the metaphor of bulldozer theology on its head, focusing on the unrelenting grace of God. He writes:

> Biblical faith is distinguished by its redundant insistence upon the presence and vitality of the Word of God in common history; and Christians particularly confess that the involvement of the Word of God in the life of this world becomes most conscientious, comprehensible, and intentional in the event of Jesus Christ.[2]

Stringfellow continues, "I believe, biography (and history), any biography and every biography, is inherently theological, in the sense that it contains already—literally by virtue of the Incarnation—the news of the gospel

1. Hemingway, *A Farewell to Arms*, 249.
2. Stringfellow, *A Simplicity of Faith*, 20.

whether or not anyone discerns that. *We are each of one of us parables.*"[3]
And yet our biographies and histories are complicated by fallen creation,
principalities, and powers.

> What I am discussing is how the living Word of God is impli-
> cated in the actual life of this world, in all its tumult and ex-
> citement, ambiguity and change, in the existence of the nations
> and principalities, human beings and other creatures, and every
> happening in every place and every moment. This world is the
> scene where the Word of God is; fallen creation—in all its scope,
> detail, and diversity—is the milieu in which the Word of God is
> disclosed and apprehended; Jesus Christ verifies how the Word
> of God may be beheld by those who have sight and hearing to
> notice and give heed to the Word of God (John 1:1–14).[4]

Stringfellow appropriates this approach in relation to his work in East Harlem (*My People Is the Enemy*), his experience of severe illness and spiritual
awakening (*A Second Birthday*), and in lamentations and gratitude for his
lover and friend, Anthony (*A Simplicity of Faith: My Experience of Mourning*). He concludes:

> Every biography is significant for the knowledge it yields of
> the Word of God incarnate in common life, whether or not the
> subject of the biography is aware of that significance of his or
> her own story. Vocation is the name of the awareness of that
> significance of one's own biography. To have a vocation or to be
> called in Christ means to discern the coincidence of the Word
> of God with one's own selfhood, in one's own being, and its most
> specific, thorough, unique, and conscientious sense.[5]

Stringfellow is a master in weaving together the intersection of biography and theology from the point of view of Christian faith. His books have
stirred up hope in many, including myself.

In writing these fragments, I appropriate some of my own experience
in trauma and transformation, anguish and hope. I do so in part because
the self is often glossed over in relation to our public lives. We learned that
in the last presidency, "private pain equals public cost." Like some, I grew
up in a family that experienced dysfunction and grueling divorce; there was
mental illness, including a parent diagnosed with schizophrenia; and there

3. Stringfellow, *A Simplicity of Faith*, 20.
4. Stringfellow, *A Simplicity of Faith*, 21.
5. Stringfellow, *A Simplicity of Faith*, 21.

was great love. The love abides, yet it needs to be guided by practical wisdom and strengthened in courageous community.

Whatever our families of origin, I think it decisive to develop and sustain communities of character and compassion, praise and dispraise, that welcome the poor and include mentors, friends, lovers, strangers, and "work-out" partners. Some are more consciously connected to the Word (grace) of God, some are more seeking and doubting. By the fruits ye shall know them, within and without. A few of us need a "therapy" dog. My first dog was the beagle Charlie Brown, then the dog of my teenage years, Charlotte, and finally, the best dog of all, Charlie. This book could be subtitled *Travels with Charlie*. Charlie means freedom. In his eyes you could see "the whole creation groaning in longing for adoption, for transformation . . ." (cf. Rom 8:22).

In the second section, I draw upon fragments of historical reflection. This is an exploration of the principality of white supremacy, state-based violence, and exploitation of the poor in New Jersey: the collective bulldozers, so to speak. It asks the question: How did the Confederate flag get in the front window of the Presbyterian church on Lincoln's birthday? Some of the white terrorism that happened on January 6, 2021, at the Capitol is prefigured here. The church was ironically the canary in the coal mine. Yet there is grace hidden in judgment. We cannot heal from what we do not name.

Acknowledging my own limitations, I partner in the third section with others. I am grateful for Karen Hernandez-Granzen, Lorna Goodison, Richard Fenn, Mike Gecan, and Archange Antoine. I thank Traci C. West and Chris Hedges for their gracious introductions. Their voices are strong and wise; I commend their prophetic fragments to you.

I thank those who offered comments on the manuscript: Karen Hernandez-Granzen, Lorna Goodison, Chris Hedges, Daniel Abramson, Miriam Shaw, Christopher Michael Jones, Todd Royer, Christina Orsini Broderick, Edie Cheney, Brooks Smith, Ellen Gallagher, Gladys Valverde, Kiko Denzer, Scott Spencer, Daniel Cattau, Sara Cullinane, Dave Good, Dave Johnson, Wanda Lundy, David Clohessy, Lisa Masotta, and James Livingston. Special thanks to editor Charlie Collier and the excellent team at Cascade. It takes a village to write a book.

This approach does not seek to pull it all together like a systematic theology or ethics. As Paul wrote, "We see in a mirror dimly" (1 Cor 13:12). On an existential level, the task is for each of us to "gather up the fragments that none shall be lost" (John 6:12). And keep walking. Keep moving on the path.

GEORGIA ON MY MIND

I was born in Ft. Benning, Georgia, in April 1958, in the red soil of the Jim Crow South. My parents were from Brooklyn and the Bronx. My father, Roderick, was the first one in his family to go to college, Fordham University and then Georgetown Medical School. He was training as a young resident at Ft. Benning. My mother, Doris, who never graduated from a four-year college, remembers counting the cockroaches crawling on the wall as she waited for the army doctor to induce labor because he was hungry and it was getting late for dinner. She had coins thrown in her face shortly after by an angry white woman when Doris, a Northerner, spoke up for her friend, who happened to be Black, for the money that was owed her for cleaning the woman's house. My mother and her friend bent down and picked up the crumpled bills and coins scattered across the front steps as the woman cursed and slammed the door shut. My father was getting his hair cut in a local barbershop nearby and overheard men talking in low voices about bombing a synagogue in Atlanta. It was the summer of 1958. I asked my father what he said. He told me the barber had a razor to his throat.

Four months later, Roderick and Doris drove north, with their new country beagle, Charlie Brown, and three-month-old child, Michael, through the Shenandoah mountains to Mt. Vernon, New York. One note concerning the journey north: during the first hot August morning, the beagle was pacing and slathering drool from the back seat upon said mother and child. Fr. Roderick pulled the car over to the side of the road. He took out his shiny black doctor's bag and injected the dog with a shot of tranquilizer. Charlie Brown slept the whole rest of the way north to the George Washington Bridge in New Jersey.

I learned later during the Black Lives Matter movement in the summer of 2020 that Ft. Benning was named after a Confederate general. I had known it was the base for the School of Americas, when I drove back—the only time—with my friend Dave Johnson from Harvard Divinity School the summer of 1986 after I was ordained in South Boston. We drove down in my shiny new Toyota with green and white Massachusetts license plates. On the way, we saw a sign for white-water rafting and pulled down a dirt road to ask the price of going on the Chattahoochee River near where the movie *Deliverance* was filmed. We could barely understand the thick Georgia accents of the three white men who looked over slowly at our car. "Well," one man finally said, "we're all booked up for today. But you all come back now. And next time, you bring Ted Kennedy. He knows about water."

I

Southie Will Go

ON GRADUATING HARVARD AND ENTERING SOUTH BOSTON

I had a dream one night. I woke up at 3 a.m. and wrote down these words. "Build a home (for the Spirit to dwell); Find life partners (be-truthed); Get a dog (for vigilance); Be irreverent (real) in your reverence."

I met Valerie Russell when I was preparing to graduate in 1985. She was teaching urban ministry with George "Bill" Weber. She was a Black woman of fierce love and truth telling. My friend Chris Hedges was taking the class with me. More about Chris later. Valerie gave me an "A" and offered me a job to work for City Mission Society of Boston (CMS) when I graduated. She was building a salty team, she said, for doing justice in the city.

Valerie and I met every month at Joyce Chen for spareribs. Along with the appetizers came morsels of wisdom. "If love isn't being served," she said quoting Nina Simone, "you've got to learn to leave the table."

"The one thing a minister has is integrity," Valerie told me. "Don't lose it."

She introduced me to her friend Peg Jacobs. Together we edited the journal *Mighty Waters*. The subject was the institutional church and doing justice. After a while I suggested we change the name to *Tiny Trickle*.

Valerie knew William Stringfellow from her work at Riverside Church in New York. She invited him to speak to the staff and volunteers shortly before I arrived.

He is reported to have asked them,

"Who is your enemy?

What is your relationship with them?

Do you pray for them?"

After a few months, Valerie suggested that I get my head examined. She knew that children of a parent with schizophrenia were 2.5 times more likely to have anxiety disorders than other people. Along with this, she said, seek out good friends. Valerie was a matchmaker. She introduced me to Scott Spencer and Robina Winbush by the elevator in the CMS office at 14 Beacon Street. They both became lifelong friends. Until Robina died from a heart attack in a NYC airport, which was not unlike Valerie's death.

Valerie helped me find a good psychotherapist, Tom, in North Cambridge. I'd park my car and walk the ten minutes along the big houses on Brattle Street to his dark brown house on the corner. It developed into Tuesdays with Tom for four years. It was like getting an undergraduate degree in psychotherapy, but harder. We entered into the existential fire of memories, trauma, dreams, subterranean Irish emotions, hard reflection, mourning, and here and there, glimpses of healing. Actually, it got worse before it got better.

Interpretation of things getting worse was problematic. I had a brief period when the traumatized child or self was being released, out of his Harry Potter closet, so to speak, and he began spilling thoughts and emotions of desperation. I had a dream that the riptide was sweeping me out to sea. I was terrified. I wanted to stop treading water, stop the pain. I saw a man standing on the shore. He told me to keep going, to swim, to trust the current. The waters would take me, he said, to a whole new place. Who was that one standing on the shore?

Tom helped me see that repressed thoughts and emotions of the traumatized child were coming out. Don't be distracted or concerned overmuch, he said. Focus on our therapeutic work together, on the task of bringing the split-off fragments of psyche into the light of consciousness. Truth and compassion were at work in the mourning and individuation. The desperate thoughts and hopelessness will pass, he told me.

I started reading about depth psychology. I read a lot of Karen Horney and Carl Jung, Sigmund Freud, Heinz Kohut, and existential psychologist Hannah Kolm. The destructive rage of Medusa was being transformed through the mirror of analysis, said Tom. It was transformed with the sword of truth-love, guided by critical reflection.

Here was the mirror—where was my sword?

Hannah Kolm wrote that we are held by a therapeutic covenant, commitment to the safety and integrity of healing from both sides in counseling. Could I trust Tom? Who else? Could I trust Valerie? Healing happens over time in the context of mutual covenants of truth and love with friends, lovers, counselors, mentors. We are "be-truthed" to each other, in the best sense of the word, giving our existential truths with compassion. There are mutual covenants with God and each other in communities. And there are inclusive civil-social-political covenants in nations. Always covenants are in historical context. What happens when the covenants are broken?

Valerie had been through intense therapy. She told me, at one point, she hit rock bottom. She would take long walks each day with the trees. Her only friends, she said, in her year of loneliness were the willow trees. They would weep together.

There is freedom in hitting bottom, in seeing that you won't be able to save or deliver others or even yourself, relief in reaching the place of great unknowing.[1]

During this time, I took a friend to an Al-Anon meeting in late September. We went to First Church in Cambridge on a Tuesday evening. I heard vulnerability, honesty. Not isolation. At the break, someone said she had made fresh bread. It was on the table next to me. I just had to reach over—and break it open. It was the bread of healing. Later I realized the day was September 29, the "Feast of Michael the Archangel and All Angels."

I kept coming back. I went to meetings in snow storms. I went to meetings in Watertown, in Somerville, in Boston. Going to meetings was like training for and running the marathon, only with Al-Anon. I met Stringfellow fans at one Saturday meeting, we had coffee afterwards at a diner.

One day I was walking through Harvard Square—at the very bottom, the nadir. I saw a skinny woman I recognized from Al-Anon. I barely knew her name. I couldn't sleep. I could barely work. I was hurting bad. She recognized me and looked over. "Michael we are in the garden of agony right now." There was a silence amidst the noise around us.

"One day," she said, "we will meet in another garden."

I began to walk, then run on paths along the Charles River. Travels with Charlie. I began working at Fourth Church in South Boston, in the spring, so I'd run by the sea. I'd see the New England tides rise and ebb. Sleet and rain washed over my head and down my back. I felt my soul, a dry husk, was being watered to new life. A green life that was not yet.

1. Lamott, *Help, Thanks, Wow,* 13; adapted.

I'd go to L Street gym in South Boston to change clothes, lift weights, then run for an hour. One early spring day I sprinted back, the last mile, racing an older Southie man against the biting northeast wind to L Street. We began to sprint harder, harder, finally with everything we had to our invented finish line, the L Street doors. We hit the doors in a perfect tie. The other guy looked over at me. "You know, I didn't need that!"

I smiled for the first time in a long time.

Running became a moveable feast for meditating, listening, crying out. I began to train for marathons, New York and then Boston.

Judith Herman has written in *Trauma and Recovery* how there must be a habitation of safety claimed for the traumatized self out of which this self begins to speak, giving voice to the unspeakable. The crushed part of ourselves begins to be awakened, brought to life, welcomed home—the un-lived life is being lived. This can't be forced. Yet it can be discovered, trusted, embraced, entered into with others.[2]

"Let being be," said one friend.

I was hungry; I wanted to be healed. I began to go to weekly Communion services at Society of St. John the Evangelist (SSJE) on Tuesdays, at five. I read that T. S. Elliot once came forward there to receive the Communion. He was so overwhelmed by Christ's presence he fell forward prostrate on the floor and wept.

I decided to have a three-day retreat at SSJE. The first day would be calming down. The second day would be for discernment. The third day was for joy.

On my first day, I met a man named Bobby from Florida.

We talked for hours after lunch. He had been sexually abused as a child. He tried to kill himself several times. He said he came to meetings, then he came to. Then he came to believe. He said he had been twelve stepped by a guy who had been twelve stepped by AA founder, Big Bill Wilson.

"Michael," he said, "we are sometimes our own worst enemies. Letting go of self and surrender to God is at the heart of recovery. And it has deeper levels. The breakthrough is letting go of self-will. But it does not happen without a miracle. It is you, your self-will that is keeping you from sleeping, Michael. You need a miracle."

I met Lorna soon after in Harvard Square. I was walking down Brattle Street. She was a Jamaican poet visiting Cambridge for the year as a Bunting Fellow. She wanted directions to Harvard Divinity School. It was not easy to tell her the way on the old winding cow paths. I said I'll show you.

---

2. See Herman, *Trauma and Recovery*.

Our exquisite conversation began on the way to HDS and grew and blossomed into a God friendship. It was joyous, tears, truth, and healing.

I cried a river that year. I cried hope and listened to the One on the shore. I began to sleep again. And gradually, amidst the ebbs and flows of life, thoughts of despair and desperation passed. Thank God, for Coleman, for Valerie, for Tom, for Lorna Goodison and other friends who were (and are) steady, truthful voices, covenantal partners amidst the raging waters. As Anne Lamott writes, "We are haunted by our failures and mortality. And yet the world keeps on spinning, and in our grief, rage, and fear a few people keep on loving us and showing up."[3]

I discovered in my own way and time there is an underground River of healing. As we begin to immerse ourselves in this River, with our whole being, hope meets us. As we surrender our will to the higher will, in spite of ourselves, we become more fully alive. And though it may get worse at first, as we persevere with others through self-hate and anguish, there are breakthroughs, wonders, miracles.

Another way of understanding this is glimpsed in words given by my friend and mentor Coleman Brown:

> Self-clarification, transformation of our lives begins with the decision not to fight against our failures, not to run away from them or conceal them, but to bring them into the light; and this decision enables us to confess. None of us can truly and thoroughly confess as long as we judge, condemn, excuse or praise ourselves. In doing that we shall repress or forget the most important part of our life and therefore never discover the truth.
>
> But if our desire to be honest can become greater than our desire to be good or bad, then the terrific power of our failures will become clear, and behind the repeated failure—and the hostility that surrounds it—the old forgotten fear will turn up: the fear of being excluded from life; and behind the fear, the pain—the pain of not being loved; and behind this pain of loneliness, the deepest and most powerful and hidden of all human desires: the desire to love, to give oneself, and to be part of the living stream that we call human unity.
>
> And when that love is discovered behind hostility, hostility [begins to] disappear. The transmutation of power is brought about by the discovery of truth. But truth cannot be taught in words. It must actually be experienced within our hearts. Furthermore, it cannot be experienced without confession, and

---

3. Lamott, *Help, Thanks, Wow*, 92.

confession needs a confessor who becomes a friend through suffering, fear, anxiety, anguish and pain.[4]

Community means shared gift, freely giving and freely receiving in the gift of the Spirit. Healing of trauma, I discovered, is a way of life, a moveable feast with others and Other who is Infinite Compassion. Tuesdays in Cambridge, running by the River, truth-telling in twelve step meetings, the grace of friendship. They are green pastures giving rest and rejuvenation, stirring the dry soul into green life, new life.

As Irenaeus wrote, "The glory of God is a human being fully alive."[5]

BEGINNINGS AT FOURTH CHURCH, NEW POSSIBILITIES

In my deepest wound I saw Your glory, and it dazzled me.
—Augustine of Hippo[6]

As a self in the journey of recovery, I began Christian ministry in January 1986 at Fourth Presbyterian Church in South Boston. Guest preaching there led to a call as part-time pastor while still working at CMS. Emily Chandler was my predecessor. She was a fellow graduate of Harvard and a woman of fire and truth telling. God has blessed me with many such women in my life.

Bob and Joanie showed up at the door one morning during my first week. They rang the bell. "Hi Pastor Mike—we were wondering, can we hold an AA meeting here? There are no meetings on this side of town. But there's a ton of addiction in the neighborhood."

They asked for one meeting a week. Soon there were three: Alcoholics Anonymous, Narcotics Anonymous, Overeaters Anonymous.

I sat in on some meetings. I remember hearing one woman say she lost her job, she lost her children, then she lost her sanity. At Mass Mental she got down on her knees and turned it over, surrendered her will and her life to God. Now she was beginning again, getting up on her feet—living with a new purpose, friends, and God consciousness she never could have anticipated.

This was a vision for us all.

---

4. Kunkel, *In Search of Maturity*, 3–9.

5 Irenaeus, *Against Heresies*, IV:20.7, quoted in Coffin, "A Politically Engaged Spirituality."

6. Quoted in Rohr, *Everything Belongs*, 166.

A man in the neighborhood complained about the lack of parking on the street because of the AA meetings. I said, "Come in and see. Hear how people's lives are being changed, turned around."

He said he wanted his parking space.

When I left the church five years later, he walked over to my car.

"There's a new regime here now, Michael. We'll get them out."

I remember feeling out of control. I got in my car. I prayed the serenity prayer. I called church leaders.

The groups are still meeting at the church in 2022.

ORDINATION

> Paul found himself buried under the fragments of his knowledge and his morals. But Paul never tried to build up a new, comfortable house out of the pieces. He lived with the pieces. He realized always that fragments remain fragments, even if one attempts to reorganize them. The unity to which they belong lies beyond them. It is grasped, but not face to face. How could Paul endure life which lay in fragments? He endured it because the fragments bore a new meaning. The power of love transformed the tragic fragments of life into symbols of the whole.[7]

Four months into my work in South Boston, Coleman Brown preached at my ordination service at Fourth Presbyterian Church. Valerie gave the charge. It was 95 degrees that day with no air conditioning. It was the first ordination at Fourth Church anyone could remember.

At the service were persons who were homeless, Rick, Pete, Mark.

At the service were my divorced parents, father Roderick and mother Doris.

There were good friends Gabrielle, Young Mi, Ellen, Andrea, David, Wayne, and Kiko.

There were church leaders Phyllis, Bill, Angie, Laughlin, Libby.

I didn't know it then, but several future leaders—Ruth, Eleanor, Margaret, Helen, Frank, Erma—were present that day just out of curiosity.

Coleman had pastored an urban Presbyterian church in Chicago where Martin Luther King Jr. had visited and preached. He was the university chaplain and professor at Colgate University, a man of holy fire, with lightning in his eye. Along with Valerie (whose manuscript I do not have), he was the right person to speak that day.

7. Tillich, "Knowledge through Love," 112–13.

Michael, it's a good sign: see how many people for whom you are more important than the Boston Celtics.

But it's not, perhaps, a good sign that the preacher from Colgate is not known for short sermons.

I want immediately to say how thankful I am to be here this afternoon—with this congregation with whom I had the privilege to worship this morning and who have been so cordial; with others from the community who visit today; in the company of this presbytery, and clergy, and lay people from other churches; with family and friends of the one to be ordained (some of them very special friends of mine); to be here with an old and unbeatable friend from an inner-city church I served in Chicago—and now a new friend of yours, Michael; to be here with my beloved wife and son; and to be here with you, Michael, my dear friend—this is a goodly company, and I am filled with thankfulness.

We are, in fact, surrounded by a great cloud of witnesses.

There will be those of us who may find what I preach this afternoon platitudinous. I preach this afternoon with a real and justified sense of inadequacy. I have been gone from the urban ministry for eighteen years. Moreover, I confess before you all and the one to be ordained I have been reading a book called *Ministry Burnout.*

I asked myself, "How shall I preach at the ordination of Michael Granzen to the Ministry of the Word?"

With St. Paul I say, "I am not ashamed of the Gospel" (Rom 1:16). And an answer came to my question: "How are you to preach? You are to preach with compassion. With compassion."

We're all sinners and we're all gonna die. To face one of those realities—and for some of us this afternoon one or both of those realities is very present—to face one of those realities is enough to drive us out of our right mind; and both seem unbearable.

So how to preach? With compassion—because we're all sinners (and we all know, deep down, that we are, even after we've discovered neurotic or patriarchal or other socially induced inner sources of self-condemnation). We're all sinners. And we're all folk on our way towards death, the death of this body and of this achingly familiar identity which—with all its fuzziness and its defects and tribulations—can mean so much to us. We're going to lose ourselves and what's worse we're going to lose each other.

A kind of common sense of compassion sometimes wells up in us for one another when we lose (even if just for a while) our dryness and our defensiveness and our judgmental spirit and our self-preoccupation, and we recognize our common condition and the humanity of our neighbor.

How much more grasp on us does that compassion have when the gospel sinks home to us.

Oh, we should recognize the ways we corrupt the compassion of the gospel into "cheap grace" and moral cowardice and sentimentality. And those of us who have learned to recognize how widespread is the taint of ideology, and how subtle "bad faith" can be, have special sentry-duties to stand, I know: but let even those occupying those stern posts remember that the gospel is compassion, upsetting and transforming the very judgment of the world, including that judgment which earnest Christians and post-Christians might pronounce (whatever our various labels, liberal or conservative, liberationist, feminist, or evangelical, neo-orthodox or radical).

We can only preach with compassion if we remember who we are and how it is with all who hear the gospel. With compassion and with humility. For what one of us is in any way equal to, commensurate with (as some might say), leave alone remotely worthy of the scandal of the gospel—the word from God and by God to us—that "your sins are forgiven," yours and mine? Lay that burden down. Lay that burden down.

As for death—"the last enemy to be destroyed is death," but destroyed (1 Cor 15:26). "Death is swallowed up in victory" (1 Cor 15:54).

Thanks be to God who gives us—gives us, you know, the special sentries among us and just ordinary burnt-out, vulnerable, wounded, defensive, doubtful, often bitter and self-serving people—people like me and, perhaps, like you (whatever post we occupy)—thanks be to God who gives to us the victory over sin and death, gives to us the victory through our crucified sovereign Jesus Christ, whose very power to change us is compassion.

Some of us preach, literally, from pulpits—as, Michael, you do and will. But all of us—whether from pulpits or picket lines, in parlors or bedrooms or supermarkets, from our places of work and leisure (seekers, believers and doubters; ordained or not)—all of us are always preaching with our lives.

I learned that from my children I think. For the momentous preaching which our lives convey—unavoidably convey; for the necessary preaching to which God calls some of us in the ministry of the Word: preach—with compassion.

Now I've come a ways with what I want to say this afternoon, but I confess—I've still got a ways to go.

There are rules about preaching, honed by experience, tested by trial. I try to honor those rules; and I hope, Michael, that you will too. Yet today—as you, my sisters and brothers of the clergy, already sense—I violate some of the rules. I wanted to start by giving thanks for all of us (and to bring some greetings as well). And then I wanted to say what I believe God has tried to tell me all my adult life and may have begun at last to get through to me about how, how we are to preach our sermons— and our lives. "I desire mercy and not sacrifice," says the Lord (Matt 9:13). Go, learn how to be compassionate, Jesus Christ says. Learn how to be compassionate.

But the sermon critic—and I'm one too—can say the sermon was more like a catalog—and that will have to do: First "this," and then "that." And then "another thing."

But even through a catalog, gifts may be found; at least, they may be pointed out.

So keeping always in mind that we are all to be thankful for each other, and that we are all sinners and going to die, and that we all are called to learn how to be compassionate by the common sense of our humanity and by Jesus Christ our Lord, I want to say something about our use of words.

I want, for a moment, especially to address the members of the Fourth Presbyterian Church.

I don't want you worrying each other or Michael Granzen too much about swelling the membership rolls of the church. If that happens, praise God. But in small churches, growth can be one of those "fixations" which Michael mentioned in his sermon this morning. The issue is not growth but faithfulness. You already know that.

And the next thing I'm going to say you already know, too—but it's well to be reminded of it at an ordination. Don't make too much of it, if you and the minister differ on, say, whether to put in new toilets or not; or because he went off to a retreat or a consultation or something when a bazaar was being held. (I know bazaars help raise money for pastors' salaries.)

And I know it's human to have a strong opinion about— what was it?—toilets. And those who worked the bazaar wore themselves out, and next year the minister—we'll hope—can drop in on that.

But let us all keep in mind what drives the Holy Spirit out of the community of faith: it is scandal—but not the glorious scandal of the gospel about which St. Paul writes (that your sins, and mine, are forgiven! That death is not going to have the last word over you or over me!), not the glorious scandal of the gospel; not the scandal of notorious sinners coming into the congregation (after all, the rest of us are just not so notorious), but the scandal of pettiness—and indulging our over-sensitive feelings—and mountains made out of molehills: that is what drives out the Spirit.

And so I come back to the words we heard from the letter of James—and I speak not only to the members here, but to the visitors and, yes, very much to my fellow clergy: "The tongue is fire . . . every kind of beast can be tamed, and has been tamed . . . but no human being can tame the tongue—a restless evil, full of deadly poison. With it we bless God, and with it we curse each other, who are made in the likeness of God" (see Jas 3:6–9).

How do we curse with our tongues? I'm not talking of oaths we may mutter watching the Celtics lose (a rare occasion, I realize). The frequency of four letter vulgarities is not even what I have in mind. Rather, what I have in mind is gossip, both personal gossip, and gossip by groups about other groups. We curse each other—with gossip.

Now those who are gossips have the same promise of forgiveness—of generous acceptance by Christ as those who have become thieves or adulterous, or liars. And the word holds, "Whoever is without sin among you, cast the first stone"—at the one who gossips (see John 8:7).

We all have delighted in passing on malicious information or fantasy (if only we knew) about someone or another group. After all, gossip is exciting. It quickens our blood. We feel lost passions. It gives release to resentment and irritation; to frustration; and boredom. Women gossip. Men gossip. Conservatives gossip; radicals gossip. The old gossip; but so do the young.

And sometimes when we gossip we destroy children's parents, and children, yes, and families and ministers (and fellow clergy) and others in the church of God; yes, we destroy the churches, and, all unknowingly, we destroy ourselves.

Gossip can become as addictive as heroin or alcohol. We have Alcoholics Anonymous and Gamblers Anonymous. (I hope there may be chapters meeting in this church.) I'm serious when I suggest that some of us need "Gossips Anonymous" so that our tongues may be tamed.

All of us do well to pray for the conversion—of our tongues.

Most gossip is neither innocent nor trivial. A good test, of course, is simply would I speak thus about that person (or those persons) in the presence of someone who loves them: Would I speak that way about them in the presence of God?

Let us instead learn how to pray. Prayer—that's the next thing.

A person whose dear friend had died—albeit a troublesome friend—wrote, "I need another afternoon with her, to sit among spring flowers and listen to her fears"—and listen to her fears.

How shall we find the freedom to spend an afternoon in the presence of others or another and, with love, listen to their fears?

We are entered into an age, I believe, where we must learn to pray or die.

Those who would live the good life must learn to pray. Those who would make peace must learn to pray. Those who would make it a world fit for children must learn to pray; those who claim they love children must learn to pray.

Those who would become themselves must learn to pray. Those who would forget themselves must learn to pray. Those who would resist injustice—racism and sexism and national priorities that sacrifice the lives of the poor for extra vacations for the rich—those who would resist must learn to pray. Those who would hope must learn to pray. And those who would be happy—must learn to pray.

We must learn to pray, not as a way to become pious or to indicate our piety. (The nub of Jesus' teaching about piety seems to be: hide it [see Matt 6:5–6]). Not learn to pray as a way to piety—but as a way to life, a way to life instead of death.

But someone says quietly to herself, to himself (someone ordained as likely as anyone else), "I can't pray—I can't pray any more. The words go up to the ceiling and drop aimless, harmless, dead."

"I need another afternoon with her, to sit among spring flowers and listen to her fears."

Will you let such words, but words of your own—such as those—pierce your heart?!

Then you shall have begun to pray. For never are your real words aimless, harmless, or dead. Your question is whether or not you can dare approach your real words, the words in your heart.

Prayer begins in receiving your own real words.

But prayer is more. "The Spirit—the Spirit intercedes for us with sighs too deep for words" (Rom 8:26). The Spirit takes up our praying. "O God," cries the Spirit deeper than our own spirit, "this poor failure at prayer has nothing left—no hope or faith or joy. Raise from the dead the words and the life of this one." God's own cry on our behalf.

Therefore, we can be directed to pray. Pray for other people. Try that again. Hold others in prayer. Those of you who keep lists or have special directories—pray for those on your lists, and in your directories—even name by name by name.

Pray for those you love. Pray for those you feel uncomfortable with.

Pray for the one who has let you down so terribly.

Pray for the SOBs in your life. We all know what SOBs are. Admit in anguish and anger, and with any humor you can find, that they are, for you, indeed SOBs, but pray for them—not necessarily that you will feel differently about them, not necessarily that they'll change—but that God will be their good God, their good God and yours. Pray for the SOBs in your life—and maybe somewhere, someone will be praying for you in the same way.

Admit your hatreds, but pray. Cry out that you have been let down, but pray. Admit you are uncomfortable—but pray. Don't take those you love for granted any more—pray for them.

And I said that those who would make peace, who would make it a world fit for children, who would resist injustice must learn to pray.

But—someone wants to cry out: prayer is no substitute for work!

No, indeed it is not.

But work is no substitute for prayer!

Prayer is the transformation of our work. Prayer brings our work from death to life.

I believe God can accomplish great if hidden things through us all. We do not—any of us—know how to pray as we ought. But the Spirit helps us in our weakness—takes up our prayers; makes a home in us, sticks with us, and intercedes for us—yes, with sighs too deep for words.

It's been my assumption throughout that we are all sinners and sufferers. Whether we're pastors or church agency people, homemakers or homeless, steamfitters or unemployed, lawyers or computer programmers, students or teachers makes no difference; no difference whether we're women or men; lesbian, gay, or straight; married or single. The life of each one of us could be a novel—or a TV soap opera—if the story were disclosed and told right. The sins and sufferings of those of us gathered here right now, this afternoon, are enough to break the heart of God.

And God's heart is broken—and God assures us that where sin, and, yes, death abound, there life and grace, yes, and love the more abound (see Rom 5:20).

Our sins and our sorrows and the power of death are where either we break into despair or we break into Christ's new life. Our sins and our sorrows are where all our great gifts are hidden, above all the gift of our compassion, the gift of our love.

So I am coming on in now. Catch the points again: Thanks for everybody here this afternoon—and for those who are not here and—yet who are.

Compassion . . . that's the main point isn't it? To learn compassion. How. To be. Compassionate.

So tame your tongues. Together, let us give up gossip.

Instead . . . pray your own real words. The Spirit makes a home in us, intercedes for us and brings us back to life.

And now include Michael Granzen in your love even more than ever you have before.

But love one another in the congregation, in the presbytery, in the struggles. Love one another—in joy and in sorrow, in success and in conflicts and failure.

Indeed, your love—"tough love," at times—but your love for one another will be as important to Michael Granzen as loving him directly. That will be to make the gospel credible to him, to make a believer of him—and give him joy and power in his ministry—that we love one another!

But don't do that with condescension as if you "had it together." Let us learn to love one another as fellow-sinners and sufferers, on our way to die—even as we are. Let us love one another as God loves each of you—and loves me.

Remember Jesus' haunting question, "When the Son of Man comes, will he find faith?" When Christ comes, will Christ find faith? (see Luke 18:8).

When the battle of life is over and our work is done and we are fully revealed in the presence of God, will there be found in us faith and hope and love? That is Jesus' question.

Even so, come, Lord Jesus![8]

After ordination, midweek Bible study began. We used the *Transforming Bible Study*, written by Walter Wink.[9] The theme was unmasking and naming our enemies within and without in God's humanity. Jesus' teaching on the splinter and beam was a central text (i.e., Matt 7:3–5).

The Bible study grew from five to twenty to forty. We had to break into small groups. Wednesdays began to exceed in size the Sunday worshipping community. One man told us he thought the honest give-and-take dialogue,

---

8. Brown, *Our Hearts Are Restless*, 179–86.

9. Wink, *Transforming Bible Study*.

hard questions, and earthy prayers of the Bible study far exceeded his experience of Sunday worship, which focused on proclamation. We listened. Participatory singing, improvisational joys and concerns, and community meals were soon added to Sunday worship. For worship to have integrity, it must reflect the diversity and experience of its community.

One Sunday during the period of "joys and concerns," a woman announced she was one year sober, and the congregation burst into applause. After church, an old timer, Phil, took me aside.

"You are way over the line. This no longer resembles our church. This is—unPresbyterian!"

I had learned from my experience in recovery to not react, but breathe and respond. I waited.

"Phil, so when would you think it appropriate to applaud in church?"

He thought for a moment. "Well maybe at the end of World War II. And, then, just maybe."

The applause continued, and Phil kept protesting.

He would welcome and escort people to their seats on Sunday morning. He was the maitre d' of the congregation. He loved people, he loved worship, and he loved tradition. It took him a while, but eventually he learned to love people and worship more than tradition. Not without resistance.

He offered to play the entire 1933 green hymnal so I could become better acquainted. He would play five hymns each Wednesday morning, so I could then pick two for the evening Bible study. I did this for two weeks and then opted out.

There was a moment soon after at a session meeting in June. A woman from AA wanted to join the church. Her name was Shirley. She wore heavy pock marks and scars on her face. She talked slowly in a thick working-class Boston accent. We spoke with her and then I asked three questions, "Who is your Lord and Savior? Do you trust in him? Will you give of yourself to Christ's church wherever you may be?"

She answered in the affirmative. And then left the room.

A motion was made and seconded to receive her by affirmation of faith. I asked for questions and discussion. Phil spoke up. I don't remember much of what he said, but his closing words were, "We don't want people like this joining our church. It will change who we are."

There was a stunned silence.

"Phil, if you want the church to be a country club then change the name and get a country club director. But this is a church. You were at my ordination. Shirley has answered the required questions. She comes to the Bible study and Sunday worship. She affirms she is a disciple of Jesus Christ. Any other questions or discussion?"

I don't remember what was said next, but the session voted seven to one to receive Shirley as a new member. When she came back into the room, there was an awkward silence. One woman took off the cross from her own neck and put it on Shirley.

The next morning, I was sitting alone in my tiny office. I could barely close the door with all the books. There was a knock. Phil stood high above me, all six foot two.

"Good morning. I do have a question. Do you want me to punch you in the face before or after we talk?"

"Well, why don't we talk first."

We spoke for over an hour. Then we went to lunch. It was the beginning of a beautiful friendship.

At a later session meeting, Phil said he would give the church a significant sum of money to restore and paint the whole building if he could pick the colors, including painting the front doors red. He liked that color.

The session voted unambiguously against it.

Five years later, when I was leaving Fourth Church to go to Iona, I went up to Phil by my car at the edge of busy Fourth Street. It was the last time I would see him.

"Well, Phil," I said, "You've given me a lot of advice during my time here."

"Yes, Michael. And you didn't listen to one damn bit."

We embraced.

Years later, when I was visiting Boston for the American Academy of Religion's Annual Meeting, I drove over to Fourth Church. It was a grey November afternoon in Southie. The salt air blew in from the sea. Phil had been dead now for many years. The church had bought a second adjacent building on Vinton Street for youth ministry. Teenagers—Black, brown, and white—flowed up and down the stairs like a river, talking together. I walked over to the front of the building where Phil and I had bid goodbye. I looked over. The church stood out now with fresh white paint against the grey sky. The doors were all bright red.

ON BEING HOMELESS

> As they were going along the road, someone said to him, "I will follow you wherever you go." And Jesus said to him, "Foxes have holes, and birds of the air have nests, but the Son of Man has no-where to lay his head." (Luke 9:57)

I was watching the Red Sox pregame show on our little black-and-white TV in Fields Corner, Dorchester, while sipping Progresso minestrone soup for dinner. I got a phone call from a fellow Harvard Divinity student, Stewart. He couldn't make it to the Phillips Brooks House planning meeting that night at Harvard. Could I go and convene the undergraduates? I hesitated; it was a cool night, the Red Sox were playing the Yankees, my two favorite teams. I'd have to take the Red Line. I said yes.

When I arrived an hour or so later, there was a group of ten undergraduates gathered in a circle. They wanted to start a shelter for the homeless that winter in Harvard Square. Who would volunteer, where would we hold it, how much would it cost? I said it would probably cost about $15,000 or so for the beds, blankets, food, and coffee. While we talked, one student opened up his wallet, scribbled something and stepped forward; he handed me a check for $30,000. He later told me he was tithing his allowance from his dad, a Manhattan art dealer, which was $300,000 for that year.

The shelter opened in September at University Lutheran Church in Harvard Square. It was run by Harvard undergraduates, graduate students, and church volunteers. I supervised the volunteers for Tuesday nights. After 10 PM, we learned to give the residents not coffee but sleepy time tea. I met some great characters in that shelter: Pete, John the Champ, Mark. I connected with Mark the night when a major fight was erupting. I attempted to calm folks down, to no avail.

Finally, John the Champ, all 250 pounds, stood up in his red underwear, "Everyone shut the fuck up! Go to sleep!" They did.

We couldn't sleep, so Mark and I started talking quietly. He was Jewish. He grew up in Wappinger Falls, New York. His father had died when he was very young. He fought with his stepfather and was thrown out of the home. He was about twenty-two.

I tried to help Mark find permanent shelter. He would call me collect and we would have long conversations about Christianity and Judaism. Mark left finally to stay with his brother in Georgia. They fought. Mark connected with a radical Muslim group in Atlanta. He called me collect. I could hear chanting in Arabic. "Michael, if they knew I was Jewish, they'd probably kill me. But they have good food." From there he went to the Georgia State Mental Institution. He tried to cut his wrists. He ran away to Atlanta and in desperation began begging for bus fare back to Boston. A wealthy Jewish banker stopped. He listened to Mark's story. While they were speaking, the banker's rabbi came by. The rabbi stopped and listened. He offered a prayer to God for this living miracle.

The banker took him home. Mark gave the banker my number and the banker called me. We arranged for Mark to go to Beth Israel Hospital for two weeks. He received a mental health diagnosis and was given a so-cial worker who got him assigned to subsidized housing in Central Square Cambridge. The banker paid for everything. The only problem, Mark had a few weeks before he could get into the subsidized apartment. Could he stay with me? It was a vulnerable moment; we didn't want him to go backwards and fall through the cracks on the dangerous streets of Boston.

I persuaded my two roommates to give it a try. It started out pretty well, but then the weeks stretched on. Mark loved yogurt. He would some-times eat my roommate's yogurt. Finally, they both confronted me. This was their apartment, too. They'd had enough, it was time for Mark to go.

I said, "Listen, God is with the homeless. In fact, God is homeless. Mark could be—God."

There was a pause.

"Mark is God?"

They threatened to move out. So I agreed to have Mark stay in the basement, just for the last few nights, by the furnace on a spare bed. In Boston, many triple-deckers have three separate compartments in the base-ment, each with a separate furnace and dusty storage area for their corre-sponding apartment. Mark was in the central one, as we lived on the middle floor. With three furnaces, it was an extremely dark and sooty place. Two professional women in their thirties lived above us on the top floor. That night, around 11 PM, unbeknownst to me, one of them went down to the basement to do her laundry. She heard singing in the dark.

"Who's—there?"

"It's Mark, Michael's friend. I'm staying with him for the weekend."

Eileen came up stairs and banged on my door.

"If this is how you treat your friends, I definitely don't want to be your enemy!"

Mark found affordable subsidized housing and a support group near Central Square, Cambridge. He called me every year for decades to con-tinue our hard conversations about Judaism and Christianity. He told me not long ago that his neighborhood had gentrified, that he was now living among millionaires. They had put him at risk again. He said his subsidized apartment was bigger than the millionaire's condo next door.

The rabbi's prayer in Atlanta had been answered. But unfinished.

The folks in the homeless shelter in Harvard Square were overflow-ing as homelessness was growing across the city and nation under Reagan's "war on the poor." With the $30,000 from the wealthy Harvard student, we opened a second shelter at a Lutheran Church near Central Square. Henri Nouwen was among the volunteers. But then one of the homeless men broke in and stole all the afghans from the Ladies Knitting Group. The shelter was immediately closed. We decided to buy tents and sleeping bags with the leftover money and set up a "tent city" protest for affordable housing at the Boston Common. Ray Flynn had just been elected mayor, running on a progressive agenda for Boston. He was politically vulnerable. Homeless people from the shelter and Harvard Divinity students spent over a week camped out on the Common, marching in protest through the financial district at the noon hour.

"What do we want?"

"Homes!"

"When do we want them?"

"Now!"

We had caught the city by surprise. There were fifteen thousand homeless people in Boston and the numbers were growing. Flynn didn't want to publicly arrest the two hundred people in Tent City, especially the Harvard students. But as international tourists and spring arrived, the mayor wanted these unruly people off the Common. Talks were begun with representatives from the mayor, the governor, and the Fund for the Homeless. Stewart Guernsey, along with delegates from Tent City, led the negotiations. A large triple-decker in Boston was promised, along with funds for renovating the building into transitional housing for the homeless. This became "Family House" on Dakota Street in Dorchester.[10]

This was just a morsel of bread. There are now over 580,000 homeless people in the nation, a city the size of Boston.[11]

In the years since, predatory capitalism in America has decimated the poor. In spite of initiatives like Family House and the excellent Project Nehemiah in New York, there is chronic homelessness and poverty.

"The child without shoes and without a home, made proper answer to the cruel-minded person, a religious person, too, who asked the child, 'But if God loved you wouldn't God send you shoes and a home?' The child replied, 'God told someone, but the one God told, forgot.'"[12]

There need to be a thousand Project Nehemiahs across the nation of building safe affordable housing for all people. Such morsels should be multiplied through agency, protest, and organizing into whole loaves for the homeless.

10. Witcher, "Tent City Group Departs with Hope for a Home," 61; Witcher, "Dorchester House Is Helping Homeless Find the Way Back," 17.

11. See Fessler, "HUD: Growth of Homelessness was Devasting."

12. Brown, *Our Hearts Are Restless*, 61.

ON BEING ARRESTED

We entered the John F. Kennedy Federal Building in Boston at 5:30 PM just before closing time. The police asked us to leave, but we sat down. Then one by one we were handcuffed and brought in small groups to an elevator which took us downstairs to large underground cells in the basement. The cells had been constructed along with the building in the 1960s. There was a long tunnel from one cell to the basement of the Charles Street Jail.

Police began treating some protestors roughly. I saw one policeman slam a protestor against the elevator door. As camera crews on the outside began filming this violence through the plate glass windows, police horses were brought in to force the photographers away from the windows. Several large horses mounted by police galloped around the building in widening circles. Some of the journalists outside were thrown to the ground. The whole scene looked surrealistic, like a Goya painting.

In the basement we were finger printed, photographed, and booked. There were small groups from churches. I heard people singing hymns. I saw Dan Buttry from Dorchester Temple Baptist Church reading his Bible. At three in the morning, a federal judge was brought to the building. We were taken in clusters up the elevator to the twentieth floor to appear before the judge. Howard Zinn, the WWII veteran, teacher, and activist, was on the elevator with me. As we came before the judge, Howard stood and spoke forcefully about the purpose of our civil disobedience. President Reagan was escalating illegal support for the Contras in Central America. This was an unjust and dirty war of regime change. The money spent on America's military-industrial complex should be used to help the poor and homeless. This action was calling the nation to account before a higher law.

If you're going to get arrested, it's good to get arrested with 558 other people. We were released on our own recognizance at 5 AM, agreeing to appear in court the following month. I went outside into the cool morning and joined friends for an early breakfast. I was thankful to be alive and free.[13]

ON MOURNING AND METANOIA

Do good, resist evil. Persevere with Christ . . . into what is real.

Amy had a secret. I didn't know this. She was eighty and would invite me to her home for Lithuanian suppers before the Bible study. We would pick up other ladies on the way to the Bible study and later drive them home. They became the Go-Getter's woman's group. They were mostly widowed

---

13. Gelbspan and Tracy, "Hundreds Arrested in Boston Protest," 21.

women who were now coming into their own. Every Wednesday, Amy and I would talk over supper, then pray.

I would lift up fragments of what she shared. Awkwardly, imperfectly. Then we would sing from Amy's childhood Lutheran hymnal. We did this for six weeks. Each week while I prayed, Amy would cry. Then we would sing. As the weeks went by, she began to sob. In my last week, she shared a deep secret from her childhood. I prayed. She wept. We sang.

"If ever I needed thee, I need thee now."

Years later after I had moved to Elizabeth, when Amy was dying at Boston City Hospital, she left a phone message for me. She sang the song.

Ralph had fought in North Africa in World War II. He was now in the hospital with multiple problems. He wanted out. He wanted to ride his bicycle again by the waterfront. He shared words with me about driving a Sherman tank with General Patton in the North African desert. The tank became stuck on a cliff edge, Germans were all around. He was the driver and had to slowly back the tank off the cliff. One mistake and he and his crew would fall to their death on the rocks below. He said he did it very slowly, while praying, by God's grace. I said maybe he had to pray again for the grace and courage to get off this cliff. Somehow, he got off this second cliff, too.

Ruthie was dying. Her daughters were coming to say goodbye. Her nickname was the General. She was a natural leader like none other.

I said to her, "Turn it over, Ruthie, God won't let you down now." She smiled.

"I sure hope not."

Amy, Ruth, Ralph—together they taught me what really counts in life, and in ministry. For ministry is simply life in intensity. As William String-fellow wrote, "In the face of death, live humanly. In the middle of chaos, celebrate the Word. Amidst Babel, speak the truth. Confront the noise and verbiage and falsehood of death with the truth and potency and efficacy of the Word of God."[14]

ON BEING CHURCH AND WALKING DOWN HARD PATHS

God's grace will lead us by running waters, down stony paths, and through valleys. You never walk alone.

14. Stringfellow, *An Ethic for Christians*, 142.

What we do with others, we do in history, shaped by our social group and vocation. Much has been written about the history of South Boston. The Pulitzer Prize–winning book *Common Ground*, by J. Anthony Lukas, is one outstanding source. Since then, several other books on South Boston and the Bulger brothers have been published.[15]

The South Boston Information Center was an organization founded in opposition to the desegregation of schools in South Boston. When I walked by their office near the church, the people inside seemed to always be wearing sunglasses, even on cloudy days.

One morning during my first year at Fourth Church, I received a phone call from Rick and Toby Gillespie-Mobley. They were the new Black pastors at Roxbury Presbyterian Church. We had started out together. As we talked, I learned that the South Boston and Roxbury churches had once been one. This year was the one-hundredth anniversary of Roxbury's founding as a separate church. The idea emerged to hold a unity walk from Roxbury to South Boston in late September, then worship and break bread together. A minister friend, Alice Hageman, suggested we bring both sessions together to do the planning themselves. That was decisive. We met every Wednesday evening through the summer. We read Scripture, we prayed, we laughed, we ate together. By late August there was unity. We were called by God to do this walk from Roxbury to South Boston. We did it.

The Monday afterwards, an article came out on the metropolitan front page of the Boston Globe: "A Walk of History, Healing," by Diana Alters:

> Some 40 men, women, and children who walked from Roxbury to South Boston yesterday, holding helium filled pastel balloons and singing hymns, were celebrating history for two reasons.
>
> Members of the Roxbury Presbyterian Church were commemorating the time 100 years ago when their church opened its doors. Before that, Roxbury residents had walked each Sunday to the Fourth Presbyterian Church in South Boston.
>
> "It sort of got cold walking to South Boston," said Reverend Frank Miller, minister emeritus of the Roxbury church. "They didn't believe in taking the tram because of the Sabbath." The nearly two mile trek of the mostly black congregation to a white congregation in South Boston was also historic because it was one way to signal an end to discord between the two communities, participants said.

15. Lukas, *Common Ground*. See also Lehr and O'Neill, *Black Mass*; Carr, *The Bulger Brothers*; MacDonald, *All Souls*.

"Five years ago we might not have done this," said Reverend Toby Gillespie-Mobley, co-minister with her husband, Rick, of the Roxbury church.

"It shows that in Christ there is unity, regardless of race, color or creed," said Gillespie Mobley, who wore a long dress and shawl to imitate clothing worn in 1886 and she walked with her four-year-old daughter, Samantha.

The exuberant group, dressed in long skirts, morning coats or striped jackets with straw bowlers, sang, "We've Come This Far by Faith" and other hymns as they walked from the Roxbury Presbyterian Church, on the corner of Woodbine and Warren Streets toward South Boston.

They drew the curious to door-steps and windows as they passed, escorted by two Boston police cruisers. On Dorchester Street in South Boston, an informal escort of freckle-faced youngsters on bicycles pedaled with them to the corner of Vinton Street, where the churchgoers released the balloons into the air.

Members of Fourth Presbyterian waited outside their church. "This is like a homecoming event," said Laughlin McMillan of South Boston as he stood smiling.

Elders in the . . . South Boston congregation met with elders of the Roxbury church during the summer to plan the event, according to Reverend Michael Granzen, pastor of the South Boston church.

"Our folks are really excited about it. At first, they were a little apprehensive," Granzen said. "It's both historic and healing, but between two communities that have experienced a lot of division."

Granzen said some members "weren't sure how the neighborhood would react." During the summer, however, members of the congregations got to know each other well, and the apprehension dissipated.

After the walk, the congregation celebrated during a joint service at Fourth Presbyterian. Reverend John Macinnes, director of the office of ecumenism for the Boston Archdiocese, also attended the service as a representative of Cardinal Bernard Law.[16]

The next morning, I went into my tiny office at church. There was a new message on the answering machine. I pressed the button. It was the voice of Whitey Bulger, the organized crime boss and leader of the Winter Hill

16. Alters, "A Walk of History, Healing."

Gang. Bulger's name was later put on the FBI's "Ten Most Wanted Fugitive" list as number two, just behind Osama Bin Laden.

"Reverend, we're gonna blow up your church!" I learned later this was his signature threat. He used the exact same words with the owners of the nearby liquor store when they resisted selling it to him. I called one elder, who immediately came in to my office.

"You don't know what these people are like, what they'll do." His hands were shaking.

I called the Boston Police. Two men arrived from the bomb squad wearing bulky suits and carrying explosive detection equipment. I told them the threat was given in the future tense. I didn't think there were any bombs on the premises. Nevertheless, they searched all through the church, under the pews, and outside. One man turned finally and said, "Well, it's all clear of bombs." I thanked him.

The good news was the article put us on the map. The bad news was the threat of violence. The word got out that we were welcoming people, all kinds of people, to our church. Some folks liked that, others did not.

I connected with a group of nuns and activists living on the edge of the Southie community. These included Father Tom Clark, Sister Sue Murphy, and Sister Margaret Lanen. Field education students called from Harvard Divinity School and wanted to work with us.

One friend provided an introduction to John Waco Hurley, the Grand Marshall of the St. Patrick's Day Parade. She said it was important to connect with him, this would help. I had lunch and four beers one afternoon with him at Amhrein's Pub. I wasn't used to drinking four beers. I opened up about my Irish grandmother, Lilly O'Hara. He told me about his heart attacks. As he was leaving, he turned and said, "If you're in trouble, son, give me a call."

I had a cup of coffee with an old Jesuit priest, Fr. Martin, who was friends with Whitey Bulger's brother, State Senate President William Bulger. He told me to watch my back. These one-on-one meetings seemed to help. The twelve-step meetings for young adults at the church were increasingly visible, four nights a week, packed to overflowing. The larger Southie community saw this. As one resident told me, "The meetings are scratching where people are itching." When I'd go walking along the waterfront now, sometimes with my collar on, random people would call out, "Hey, Father Mike!"

Two years later, the NAACP filed a lawsuit to desegregate public housing in South Boston. Some of the Catholic Churches began hosting meetings, "Southie Against Forced Housing." You could see the bumper stickers appearing on cars and in stores.

A few of us gathered to plan a response. There were about a dozen or so nuns, priests, minister types. Some people wanted to write a resolution in favor of desegregating public housing and publish it in the newspaper. A nun brought up the Fourth Church walk with the Roxbury Church. We decided to hold a large interfaith gathering on Pentecost at St. Monica's Catholic Church, two blocks from Fourth, with food afterward. We would organize two more services at other locations in the city with the same theme of praying for shalom and racial justice in Boston.

We decided to invite local city councilor Jim Kelly to our planning meeting. He was publicly opposed to the Pentecost service in South Boston. When he arrived, he took off his sunglasses and looked around. His anger was real.

"I challenge anyone of you to give me one good reason to have this service in South Boston."

"Councilor, I'll give you two." I couldn't help myself.

"Worship of God is a good thing. We need to pray together for South Boston. And second, as Dr. King said, many of us are afraid of each other because we don't know each other. Breaking bread together will begin to break down the walls between our communities so there will be less fear."

These words seemed only to infuriate him.

"Disgusting! I can't stand when people come into our neighborhood and look down their long, arrogant, religious noses and tell us what to do!"

The old Jesuit priest, Fr. Martin, stood up.

"Jimmy, he's one of us. He lives and works here."

Kelly hesitated for a moment.

"Reverend, I'm sorry."

The meeting continued for another hour. When Kelly got up to leave, he looked around the room to take in our faces, then over at Rev. Joe Washington, who was Black and the mayor's representative.

"I just want you to know, there is one person at this table, who will betray you."

He slammed the door shut. There was silence.

Someone said, "Is it I, Lord?"

The story of what happened at St. Monica's Church is told in an article I wrote for *Housing Matters*, called "Unity in Diversity."

In May 1988, neighborhood churches and public housing tenants in Boston responded to racism and discrimination in public housing with a series of interfaith worship services. As the pastor of the Fourth Presbyterian Church in South Boston, I was part of the group called the Combined Religious Communities (CRC) that organized and invited people from all parts of the city to come together in an interracial prayer service to demonstrate the "richness of our diversity, and the strength of our unity."

As in many situations, the background to graceful action was law and ethics in crisis. Since the mid-seventies, the Boston Housing Authority had been covertly keeping people of color from living in three very large public housing development projects in South Boston. Over the years, a certain "common sense" developed in South Boston—Black people could work there, but they couldn't live there. The almost complete absence of Black families in the community of 35,000 was evidence alone of this.

In 1987, HUD issued a report criticizing the city of Boston for using the tenant selection process to discriminate against minorities. While for over a decade the city has been under court order to desegregate its public housing, out of approximately 2,500 units of public housing in South Boston there was not a single unit occupied by a Black family. Soon after the report came out, HUD found that the Boston Housing Authority (BHA) was discriminating against minority applicants for public housing. The NAACP initiated a legal suit against the BHA on behalf of those who had been discriminated against.

Boston's Mayor Flynn announced in the fall of 1987 that the city would comply with the HUD mandate, and Black families would soon be moved into public housing in South Boston. Yet both publicly and privately, a number of groups had been aggressively enforcing what they saw as "Southie's" way of life and "neighborhood integrity." Among those most vocal was a group called the South Boston Information Center, formally led by Boston city councilor Jim Kelly. The Information Center quickly organized an "information" meeting where hundreds of people angrily denounced Mayor Flynn for what they referred to as "social engineering." Their rallying cry became "forced housing," an allusion to the forced busing of the early seventies. Rumors were spread that elderly people would be evicted for the incoming families. A thick air of fear began to pervade the neighborhood. Old wounds and bitterness rose to the surface, threatening to break into ugly manifestations of violence.

A COLLECTIVE RESPONSE

In early February 1988, clergy and leaders from several churches in South Boston, Roxbury, Mattapan, and Dorchester gathered together in South Boston to discuss how we might respond collectively to the situation. Unanimously, we agreed that what we could do well was to hold a large interfaith, interracial service at a local church to pray for peace in the integration process. The hope was that a visible gathering of diverse people in this setting would show our "strength in unity," and that through the planning of the service, we could also work within our own congregations for greater understanding of racial reconciliation and harmony.

PLANNING THE WORSHIP SERVICE

As plans for the service evolved, CRC came to include over twenty representatives from the Black Muslim, Buddhist, Roman Catholic, Baptist, Methodist, Presbyterian, and United Church of Christ denominations. Meeting weekly for several months, CRC consciously sought to include more people in the planning process and to reach out to local public housing tenants and tenant organizers.

In shaping the service, CRC chose not to have elected officials or professional politicians speak on behalf of their own agenda nor to invite Cardinal Law, who might dominate the event with the media. Rather, we saw public housing tenants, neighborhood clergy, laypersons, and local folks who were directly involved and at risk come together to speak and participate.

The service itself was slated for the afternoon of Pentecost at Saint Monica's Catholic Church in South Boston, located in the midst of two of the housing projects which were to undergo integration. It was also chosen because it had been a site of several angry meetings sponsored by the information center, which were not representative of the church's position on integration of public housing.

Meanwhile, Boston City Councilor Kelly, who represents South Boston, came out against the service and attempted to convince people that it should be held in a more "neutral" location than South Boston. We invited Counselor Kelly to a planning meeting to try to include him and the information center in the event. Although Kelley came, meaningful dialogue failed. The process, however, of including those who disagreed became personally transforming, as we learned how to pray for and love our enemy.

Ironically, Kelly's attempt to relocate the service peaked the curiosity of the local media, who then picked up on the story despite our earlier press conference which was only attended by one media representative.

THE SERVICE

On the day of the service about a hundred hecklers gathered outside the church taunting those who went in. There were police sharpshooters on roofs to protect those who attended. For the approximately six hundred persons who walked the gauntlet outside, the inside of the church truly seemed like a sanctuary. The first hymn, "Blessed Assurance," was literally shouted out, releasing the pent-up tension. Included in the hour-and-a-half-long service were songs, prayers, meditations, Scripture readings, and testimonials. One woman, Chew Chin, a Cambodian immigrant, spoken in a heavy accent, "When I first came here, I was very afraid, but now I am not afraid."

Rev. John Borders from the Morning Star Baptist Church, whose parishioners were among the first Blacks moving into the South Boston projects, also spoke: "Racial understanding is not something that we find, it's something that we must create. The ability of Blacks and whites to work and live together, to understand each other, will not be found ready-made. It must be created by the fact of contact."

City counselor Rosario Salerno praised the service in a letter to area churches, "Only broad-based community endeavors such as this can counter the fear and misinformation which perpetuates racism in our city."

Mayor Ray Flynn said, "There was a real feeling of coming together, of unity in the city. This day was one of most important days in the history of Boston."

Some people commented on how similar the service was to the mass rallies held during the civil rights movement in the South. It provided a forum in the midst of real and potential violence for people to overcome their fear and isolation, draw mutual strength and encouragement, sing their deepest spirituals and songs of freedom, and dream together of a better day.

In the weeks that followed, while some local papers attacked the sponsors of the service, calling the clergy "betrayers," many Boston TV stations and newspapers editorialized in favor of the service and the integration process. Surprisingly, there was a greater consensus for civil rights in the city that had first been thought, and the worship service brought that out.

In the two years after the service in South Boston, CRC held more services in 1988 at First Church in Roxbury and Mount Olive Temple Baptist Church in Mattapan. As of September 1989, twenty-three Black families moved into public housing in South Boston. Area churches supported the families moving in with visits and material help. The process, however, was far from complete.

LESSONS LEARNED

With such unfinished business concerning racism in Boston and in this country there are a number of lessons to be learned, in particular for churches seeking to help create conditions for a more diverse and just public housing and urban community.

The churches can do certain things well, when they do them with integrity. One of them is worship. In the midst of unrest, neighborhood worship focuses our community less on our own egos and more on the source and end of life. As such, worship becomes a way to overcome fear, self-righteousness, and violence—those things which poison our common life and paralyze creative action. This insight was at the heart of the civil rights movement.

For the sake of their own lives, churches must be "response-able." The curse of contemporary organization is bureaucracy and evasion. This culture paralyzes goodwill by subtly displacing directness and decision with distance and resolution. "Let others do it," becomes the prevailing attitude. When the churches respond to real situations in direct ways that involve getting messy and taking risks, self-transcendence occurs—divisions are overcome. This occurs within a congregation as well as within a broader community. AIDS, drugs, urban violence, homelessness, and the resurgence of racism are all overwhelming problems that have arisen, unanticipated by many, in the last decade. The question in the face of them is not whether we're right or wrong in our resolutions, but whether we act and then learn from our mistakes—whether we are responsible.

Our task is one of justice with compassion. With tremendous rage and defensiveness present in race relations in Boston and the nation, our public language and example make a difference. If our worship service had been a self-righteous gathering of scornful outsiders, the likelihood of violence would've been great. Public expressions of self-righteousness and violent rhetoric are not helpful, whether expressed from the right or left. Law and ethics need grace as an ally in changing the heart and society. Therein the churches have a particular role to play. To take a stand for justice with compassion on a daily basis, in continually ambiguous and dangerous situations—this is our task.[17]

There is one important addition to this story. On the day of the Pentecost Service, my friend Scott Spencer was the designated leader for Fourth Church along with Jeff McArn. Scott is now pastor at Woodridge Congregational Church in Cranston, Rhode Island, and Jeff is university chaplain at Hamilton College in Clinton, New York. At the time both were lay leaders at Fourth. A year before the event, I had committed to performing a wedding for two good friends in New York City. The large ceremony would be over by noon, so there was plenty of time to fly back to Boston for the 4 PM service.

17. Granzen, "Housing Matters," 6–7.

Of course, in my twenty-nine-year-old naivete, I didn't realize you can't be in two places at once. I assumed the large wedding would go off as planned; it did not. The ceremony was delayed, then unexpected thunderstorms kept the plane stuck on the tarmac for two hours. As I waited in my seat on the runway at LaGuardia there was absolutely nothing I could do—but turn it over to God and the leadership at Fourth.

Back in South Boston, a dozen or so Fourth leaders gathered with Scott in front of the church to walk the three blocks to St. Monica's. They knew they would have to walk through a gauntlet of angry protestors, some of whom were spitting and cursing at those attending. There were police sharpshooters on the roofs. As the Fourth flock waited for more folks to arrive, suddenly a dark car appeared at the intersection. It was Jim Kelly. His window was down and he looked over at each of them, long and hard, just as he had done at the planning meeting. Scott said it was intimidating. Kelly then drove on, looking scary, but defeated.

The group hesitated. Dottie Lockhart, a seventy-five-year-old saint of the church, who had grown up in the neighborhood, stepped forward. "What are we waiting for?" Dottie asked. She grasped her Bible in her wrinkled hands and led Scott, Jeff, and the others down the street and through the gauntlet. When they came to the entrance of St. Monica's, the ushers told them there was no seating available except in the front pew. They were led around to the back entrance and then upstairs through a hallway to the front of the sanctuary. As they looked down the pew there were the Roxbury Presbyterian Church leaders with whom they had walked and prayed two years earlier. There were hugs and embracing. The Holy Spirit was present.

In the service, Dottie Lockhart got up and read the Scripture, "'And it shall come to pass in the last days,' says God, 'that I will pour out my Spirit on all flesh; your sons and your daughters shall prophesy, your young men and women shall see visions, your old men and women shall dream dreams'" (Joel 2:28).

Dottie was on television that night. According to Dottie, her son, a police officer who lived on the first floor of her triple decker, saw her on the evening news. He had not known she would be in the service. He came running upstairs.

"Mom, are you crazy? What were you doing there?"

"Son, I was just reading my Bible."

After the service I had lunch with Fr. Al Puccini who was the head priest at St. Monica's Church. He was a courageous man. He told me that because his church hosted the Pentecost service, a boycott was organized against their weekly bingo. This made a dent in their income, but it lasted only a year. The people eventually tired of walking the longer distance to St. Augustine's bingo.

The following November, I was invited to preach at the ecumenical Thanksgiving service in South Boston:

> I would like to talk tonight about the gift of trust in God which, involves denying ourselves, taking up our crosses and following each day. This suggests a whole-hearted faith, a radical letting go and letting God which is an affront to the spirit of the times. To illustrate what this means and the context in which we hear it, I will tell a story about a man who went into the wilderness late in life to discover if there really is anyone up there. For six days he fasted, meditated and asked the question, "Is anyone up there?" He received no answer.
>
> Finally on the seventh day he decided to climb a mountain in the wilderness and ask the question from the top. So, he climbed up and up—but right before he got to the top he slipped, and fell, and slid down, down to the edge of the abyss. He grabbed hold of a shrub, and with his body dangling over the edge he decided, well, this is a good time to ask the question.
>
> "Is anyone up there?"
>
> "Yes," was the answer.
>
> That's a good start, he thought to himself.
>
> "What must I do to be helped?"
>
> "Let go. Let go," was the reply.
>
> Well, he looked down, and could not see bottom.
>
> He looked up again.
>
> "Is anyone else up there?"
>
> In many respects this is our situation as a community and as individuals; it is the context for us tonight. We and those around us want another way, any other way, than trusting finally in God, in God's mercy. For we are afraid of losing control, of losing our lives.
>
> So we hold on, clutching our shrubs with all our might. And we become crippled by dread, fear, defensiveness.
>
> Of course, we have good reasons to hold on, particularly as people of the twentieth century, a time of great change. For underlying the age is a tremendous fear of emptiness, a fear that no one will catch us as we fall.
>
> This comes out in our literature. Recently, I read two books in particular which are representative of our age.
>
> One was *All Quiet on the Western Front*, about WWI and the suffering and tragedy and devastation of a whole generation

of young men. In the book, the narrator is a cynical but honest voice with whom we grow familiar and even friendly, as he tells us of the insanity, violence, and death happening around him.

At the end of the book, it says simply: "He fell (he fell) in October 1918 on a day that was so quiet and still on the whole front, that the Army report confined itself to the single sentence: all quiet on the western front."

What happens in that quiet, that silence? We are left with a question.

The other book was *Night* by Elie Wiesel. It is an autobiographical story of the Holocaust, which increasingly I see cannot be explained or analyzed away but which must be simply faced. There is an overpowering image in the middle of the book. Wiesel and the other inmates have been hardened by what is happening around them and by the frequent executions of prisoners who are caught trying to escape. On this particular day, a boy, around twelve years old, has been caught apparently organizing an escape. The prisoners are ordered to the main yard to watch his hanging. Yet unlike the others who curse defiantly at the Fascists, this young man is absolutely silent as he goes to his death. And in silence he is hanged. The hardened prisoners begin to break down and weep. In the midst of this, Wiesel hears someone ask, "And where is God now?" We are left with a question.

The situation of the twenty-first century is one of a question, one of an underlying fear of emptiness, of the abyss below and beyond the suffering.

It is the very hour in which the Christ speaks to us tonight. "If anyone would come after me, let them deny themselves, take up their cross and follow me."

These words point to the real meaning of trusting the void beyond the void, of letting go and letting God.

First, deny yourself.

This suggests a turning away from the self and the attachments of the self. Freud uses the term fixation to describe the way human beings become attached to objects of the world. As the baby becomes attached to its mother's breast as the source of security, so adults can become fixated on money, power, social group, and other finite securities. Jung speaks of addiction (the scourge of our day) as simply a low-level longing for God which has gone awry.

Jesus is saying, give up your fixations of self and fix your gaze on God. That's the beginning of trust. Give up those things which get in the way, and look God-ward.

Second, take up your cross. This can have different nuances. I would interpret it to mean, as you trust you will encounter pain, adversity, even threats of destruction but don't stop trusting, keep going. For God's ways are not our ways. God is doing things in God's time and God's way. We are not promised success, but something much, much more.

Jesus asks each of us to take up our cross, to turn towards it and not away. Can you sense where the cross is in your life, in the life of this community? This is the very place where we are being asked to turn and trust God.

There are personal crosses to bear, such as reconciliation with our friends and neighbors. This is not an easy or quick cross. It may involve facing deep-seated anger and grief. It may involve learning to forgive another whom we can't even begin to think about forgiving right now. It may involve walking through the valley of deep darkness to a whole new place. The journey is not without laughter, it is not without pain—it involves trusting someone.

The mystery of the cross is this: if we die with Christ, we shall also live with Christ.

And there are larger collective crosses to bear here and now in this city. There are powers that would have us believe that the whole earth is not meant to be a place of openness and equality for all God's people. There are principalities that tell us the means of life—housing, food, health care, jobs, education—are not meant to be distributed fairly to all God's children. Be not deceived, there are those who profit from homelessness, economic inequity, racism, and militarism.

We live in a time of great change—the old is passing, the new has not yet come. The change is bringing old wounds to the light. It is forcing people to decide on whom they can rely for security and hope. The question is: Will we break into despair—or into God's new life? Will the wound be the vehicle by which the old voices of racial idolatry and false security are heard or will it be the agent of the Gospel, the good news that our sins are forgiven, and that death, the last enemy, is defeated, swallowed up in victory . . . for all people . . . black, white, latino, asian, jew, gentile, gay, straight, seeking, believing, doubting.

The challenge of the hour is to be patient and persevere through a period when the new possibilities are not always in sight, to sow seeds of hope where there is despair, faith where there is doubt; to take up our crosses daily (it really is a daily thing) which go against the grain of the world—challenging the rules of Egypt (literally in Hebrew *mitzrayim*, "the tight, confining place") in order to obey the voice of God. For we do not belong to Mitzrayim, we belong to God.

If anyone would come after me, let them deny themselves, take up their cross—and follow me. The last two words are decisive. Follow connotes dynamic, living, in movement, being part of a movement that we are not in control of.

Follow "me."

Who is asking us to give up our fixations, to follow in spite of all?

The One who watches our back.

The One who gives hope in spite of despair.

The One who died on another mountain—called Golgotha—for us all.

And leads us to new life.

Jesu—God with us.

ON LEAVING FOURTH CHURCH

The human is a fragment and a riddle to the self. The more we experience and know that fact, the more we are really human. Fragments remain fragments, even if one attempts to reorganize them. The unity to which they belong lies beyond them; it is grasped through hope. The power of love transforms tragic fragments into symbols of the whole.[18]

Before leaving this earth, I believe there are certain errands or tasks we are called to do, however incomplete and imperfect. Each morning we may ask, "What do you want me to do for you today?" There are signs when you sense a task is coming to an end. I had been at Fourth Church for almost five years and loved the people and community. Yet in my running dialogue—within and without—I began to discern hints that staying longer might undermine what God's grace had accomplished. Like Emily Chandler, I trusted that someone might come to lead Fourth to higher ground.

It's hard to turn back from reaching the summit, to accept incompletion. But the goal is to leave the community with fragments of hope rather than the opposite. Let it go, I mean all of it, the good, the bad, the beautiful, and ugly, into the dying and rising grace of Christ. Trust in the place of resurrection. Let God complete what we cannot complete.

18. Tillich, "Knowledge through Love," 108–9; adapted.

Rumi speaks of gradually becoming unglued from places and things. At a session meeting at Fourth Church in June, I announced my decision to leave at the end of the year. I was being called to work at the Iona Community in Scotland and trusted God would send them the right person to follow. They were in good hands. There were some tears. Bill offered a higher salary. Phyllis finally rose and spoke, "Michael, we love you, we bless you."

I felt the blessing in my heart. And still do.

I did not know it at the time, but a man with extraordinary gifts, the Rev. Burns Stanfield, would come a year later to lead Fourth Church to much higher ground, closer to the summit.[19]

Saying goodbye is practice for the last goodbye. Elizabeth O'Connor wrote,

> When we are still very young we can feel and see in ourselves the hints of our dying. Nature too instructs us. I think about this as I watch the leaves on the trees outside my windows. Some fall when they are still green, others go down in a brilliance of color, still others when they are withered, and then there is that last brown one that clings to a bare branch through the whole of winter. Though I may wish to be the flaming leaf, only one thing is clear about my dying: I am not supposed to know the way it will be. Mine is simply to practice saying yes to life and yes to death and to whatever comes with one or the other. Each day the practice of surrender, each day the practice of letting go.[20]

Each day running to the mountain. One day I will die there.

---

19. See Dawson, "Practical Theology."
20. O'Connor, *Cry Pain, Cry Hope*, 48.

2

The Iona Paradox

Consider what is going on in the depths of the self, community, and society.

Boston had been about opening up to dialogue with the other, including the self and community—both fragments of light and night—through prayer, protests, marathons, messiness. And meetings. "All real living is meeting," said Martin Buber.[1] Yet did he mean presbytery meetings, city hall meetings, neighborhood meetings? Where was the depth, the divine, in that dialogue?

I discovered that dread is the toxic ingredient that distorts the soul, both individual and collective. Anxiety within, at what we may be stuffing—rage, hate, guilt, Eros and Thanatos. And anxiety without—threats of humiliation, rejection, death—not only to self, but to loved ones. Fears are engendered by this dread of suffering and nothingness.

Oppression of self and others often follows from this dread.

Yet the prophetic fragment in the midst of fear: in quietness and confidence shall be your strength, in returning and rest shall be your strength.

The better way to deal with anxiety and grief is through prayer, silence, friendship, community, practices of metanoia and mourning. To double-down on forgiveness and courageous community. To learn to trust the spring of life, that it will well up in you.

With the self there are cookie-cutter categories of being which distort profoundly, often unconsciously, more than folks realize versus the true self

---

1. Buber, *I and Thou*, 11.

which is rising strange and eccentric. As Valerie said, "The more people become themselves, the more they become eccentric. Good eccentric."

I discovered in Boston a certain mysticism and eccentricity that was a gift and a challenge.

This was present when running along the sea, as the tides ebb and rise.

This was present when riding my bicycle along the river surrounded by green trees, immersed in nature.

This was present in early morning solitude, with cup of coffee, in a lonely place, on the roof of a triple-decker.

This was present when joining with others in truth telling in a twelve-step community.

And this was present when walking along stony paths of tough love.

But what about life together in contemplative community at a beautiful place guided by Celtic worship, prayer, and silence?

Emily Dickinson tells it:

> He fumbles at your Soul
> As Players at the Keys
> Before they drop full Music on—
> He stuns you by degrees—
> Prepares your brittle nature
> For the Ethereal Blow . . .[2]

I wanted more holy fire, the Ethereal Blow, sooner rather than later. I went to Iona for intensity of contemplation.

THE IONA PARADOX

I found I had less and less to say, until finally, I became silent, and began to listen. In the silence I heard the voice of God.
—*Soren Kierkegaard*[3]

After leaving Fourth Church, I spent the winter and spring on a small (one-by-three-mile) rocky island in the Atlantic Ocean off the coast of Scotland—Iona. St. Columba first brought Christianity from Ireland in the 560s, which he then used as his base to evangelize Scotland and Scandinavia. Since then, various monastic communities, crofters, fisherman, seagulls, and Presbyterians have inhabited this bleak but beautiful isle.

About fifty residents and guests lived, worked, and worshipped at the retreat center when I was there.

2. Dickinson, "The Master."
3. Kierkegaard, *Writings*, XVIII:11–12.

Iona contains some of the oldest black surface rock on the earth and some of the worst weather. Huge storms with gale force winds would blow in from the north Atlantic and rage for days. I learned to walk bent over to compensate for the fifty-mile-per-hour gusts. Occasionally, the driving sleet, snow, and rain would stop and there would be a brief period of calm and "brightness." We'd run outside to savor the weak horizontal light. Sometimes amidst our "sun dance" there were even wee glimpses of rainbow. But mostly it was absolutely the worst weather I have ever seen.

During one five-day storm, the ferry from the island of Mull was cancelled for the week, and we had to live off food stocks: endless tea, oatmeal (with salt, not sugar), thick stale bread, and old yellow pudding. When I grew weary of caffeinated tea and asked for the herbal variety, the locals laughed, "The Yank wants Herb tea!" Later in the month when I came down with the inevitable flu and was bedridden, friends somehow found and brought me fresh green salad with a slice of tomato—a miracle!

Three times daily we trudged though the darkness and cold and gathered to worship in the abbey. There was no heat and only candlelight (my job was to light the candles, so I better not be late). There was no organ, just the sound of the wind howling outside. I remember singing with that small company, "O Come, O Come Emmanuel, to ransom captive Israel, who mourns in lonely exile here . . . Rejoice, Rejoice, Emmanuel shall come to thee O Israel."

Strangely, the severity of weather and life seemed to contribute to the warmth of the Spirit and community. Acknowledging the existential darkness allowed the light to truly shine. Why is that?

I believe the Iona Paradox can be stated as follows: the more we acknowledge our hurt and brokenness, the more we may receive the divine-human light. And the inverse is equally true: the less we acknowledge our hurt, fear, and hostility (and project it onto others), the less we are open to the true light of forgiveness, justice, and joy. In the very things that we ignore, reject, and even despise as dirty and strange, God's incarnate light and presence is shining deep in the flesh.

In other words, God is in the wound. The prophet was right, "The people who walked in deep darkness have seen a great light; those who have lived in a land of deep darkness—on them light has shined" (Isa 9:2).

THE IONA CONTRADICTION

There was an event that occurred near the end of my time at Iona that was revealing. Every Friday morning there were "community meetings," mostly these were informal social gatherings over tea and biscuits. On this particular Friday morning after worship an official announcement was made by the wardens regarding the new lounge which was opening at the MacLeod Youth Center. In the Iona community there were three-year volunteers, one-year volunteers, and six-month volunteers, like myself.

It was announced during tea that only the three-year and one-year volunteers could henceforth use the new lounge "because of their greater commitment." The six-month volunteers would therefore be excluded. Most of the six-month volunteers were in their early twenties, and worked very hard cooking in the kitchen and cleaning rooms.

You could see their crestfallen faces. There was a gasp. I was the only American in the room, and couldn't help but raise my hand. I said every morning we pray that justice and mercy should kiss, but they're not kissing in Iona today. I said this was unfair, that all the volunteers should be included, or no volunteers should be included.

There was a stunned silence. And then the Scottish treasurer, Ken said, "Aye, I'm with the Yank on this one!" There was an uproar, especially from the younger volunteers. The wardens said they would reconsider and get back to us. A week later they changed their decision.

There is still time to change the road we're on.

A SURPRISING GIFT

I woke up in radical amazement. I wrote to my friend Lorna:

> Thomas Merton appeared in my dream! It was him! He was fully alive, intellectually magnetic, a youthful countenance. We were traveling—waiting in line in an upper room for a doctor. I recognized him. There was awesome silence. I found the courage to speak. I told him I go sometimes to SSJE on retreat. He said he knew the place, beautiful building, those Episcopalians have wealth. I understood he was telling me that it is really about the infinite love of God and this love in the heart. There was silence. I pointed upwards and then to my heart. He smiled. Then he told me he had a gift for me—he gave me a walking stick, an Irish walking stick. He said it would help me keep my rhythm, my step as I walked. He demonstrated.
>
> I thanked him for this gift and for his tremendous witness in his writings to the love of God. Then as we were preparing to depart on our separate journeys, I reached out to embrace him and he disappeared. A force field of love filled my whole being. I began to weep with joy.

I went out into the pouring rain filled with gratitude and awe walking down the path with the staff.

I woke up trembling at the infinite love of God. I realized Merton had died suddenly and unexpectedly. I didn't know what this meant. . . preparing me to be ready to move on when God calls. The walking stick is beautiful and mysterious . . . like a shepherd's crook . . . like a baseball bat for getting hits . . . like a writer's pen for going public . . . a holy staff . . . raising the staff up to God is for healing.

Lorna wrote back, "Maybe it is a shillelagh . . . You'd better accept it. We your friends need your help."

ON CROSSING THROUGH BROKEN WALLS

As the wild irises blossomed in May, I completed my six months at Iona and decided to travel to Germany. The wall was coming down in Berlin, so I wanted to go and break off a piece, and then travel into East Germany to Wittenberg and see the church where Luther posted his ninety-five theses.

I connected with a friend at Iona, Iris, from West Germany, who wanted to go as well. Before we traveled to East Germany, we visited with her parents who were farmers in Bavaria. They welcomed me with gracious hospitality. One night we got into a dialogue about WWII. They spoke little English and I spoke little German. Iris had to translate everything. Before I knew it, I was hearing a discourse on antisemitism and conspiracy theories like I had never heard before. The hatred was almost palpable.

"FDR was a Jew and betrayed us. He stopped the American army before they could take East Germany. The Jews are to blame for our suffering," the mother said.

Iris was not only uncomfortable, but stunned by what her parents were saying. She had to stop.

This animosity toward the racialized other, the monster of European antisemitism, which in the 1940s killed almost of third of all Jews on earth, pierced my heart. My uncle Frank had died fighting fascism in the Battle of the Bulge. I thought about it when I returned to America. Why is there so much projective violence toward the racialized other? Why is it so hard to change the narrative, the road we're on?

Iris and I rented a car in West Germany and we drove across the border. We were soon driving on roads built in the 1930s during Hitler's regime. Then as we entered Wittenberg, a police car with flashing lights suddenly appeared and pulled us over. Iris said, "Be careful." It was the dreaded Stasi. I gave the officer my international license and car registration.

He walked slowly around the car, twirling his staff, looking to me like Colonel Klink from *Hogan's Heroes*.

"Do you have the official papers to drive on this road?"

"What papers?"

"You must have official papers to drive on this road."

"But . . . this is a public road."

"That will be twenty Deutschmarks. And you must leave town immediately!"

I didn't want to give him the money.

Iris said, "You want to go back to America, you give him the money."

I gave him the money.

We drove slowly into Wittenberg. As we parked the car and walked through town, I noticed cheap plastic fruit and vegetables covered with grey dust in the windows of the market. I glanced upward and saw a man looking down at us with binoculars.

After stopping at the locked church, All Saints, where Luther nailed his theses, we decided to have lunch in a medieval pub. As we rounded the corner near the restaurant, we saw two young Russian soldiers walking slowly toward us. They held AK-47s. We moved quickly down the stone road and turned into the open doorway.[4]

After sitting down, an old man and woman began staring at us from across the room; they nodded. We nodded back. They came over and sat down at our table, looking very grey and tired. The woman spoke softly in German. Iris translated.

"We saw what they did to you. You know, they just pocketed the money. They don't have the power they once had. They are toothless tigers now."

"Then why are you whispering," I asked.

The old woman began to cry. She said when she was a girl, the Stasi came and took her little brother away. This was punishment for her parents who were Christians. She had not seen her brother since.

We talked for a while. They were only in their fifties, though they looked so much older. Iris mentioned the nuclear power plant in Chernobyl, a few hundred miles away in Ukraine. There had been a bad accident, and Iris was worried about the radioactive fallout for the farmers. The couple shrugged their shoulders. They seemed resigned, fatalistic.

---

4. Bowlby, "Vladimir Putin's Formative German Years." We did not know it then, but Vladimir Putin was a senior agent overseeing the KGB in East Germany.

I asked, "With the Berlin wall coming down, do you see any hope for the future?"

The woman said, "No, no, there is no hope."

Hope is a dangerous thing. Before leaving Wittenberg, Iris and I went over to the university bookstore. We discovered there was not one book by Martin Luther, no music by Bach, no theological texts anywhere. I sensed how totalitarian ideology and state-based violence can crush hope. Without countervailing communities of disruptive grace and agency, human institutions rot. The salt of courage atrophies. Hope begins to die.

> Work without Hope draws nectar in a sieve,
> And Hope without an object cannot live.[5]

ON CONTRADICTION AND PARADOX

During my period at Iona and afterward, I had time to think through my Christian existentialism and social philosophy in more precise terms. What follows are fragments offered in dialogue with Soren Kierkegaard, Steve Hartshorne, and Coleman Brown.

Contradiction is about living or believing opposites that finally come down to either/or. For example, *either* you affirm all people are created equal with dignity and worth, precious in God's sight, and fight for their life and freedom—as you do your own—*or* you affirm the opposite. In America this is known as white supremacy or double-predestination capitalism with racialized winner-takes-all ethos. There are variations on the theme. A person, community, or nation in contradiction pretends to have certain beliefs about what is right and true, but actually behaves in another way that is the opposite of those beliefs. Contradictory traits can coexist for a time while undermining one another. But then reckoning arrives. C. S. Lewis gets at some of this hard truth,

> William Blake wrote the "Marriage of Heaven and Hell." If I have written of their Great Divorce, this is not because I think myself a fit antagonist for so great a genius, nor even because I feel at all sure that I know what he meant. But in some sense or other the attempt to make that marriage is perennial.
>
> The attempt is based on the belief that reality never presents us with an absolutely unavoidable "either–or"; that, granted skill . . . and (above all) time enough, some way of embracing both alternatives can always be found; that mere adjustment or

---

5. Coleridge, "Work without Hope," lines 13–14.

refinement will somehow turn evil into good without our being called on for a final and total rejection of anything we should like to retain. This belief I take to be a disastrous error.

You cannot take all luggage with you on all journeys; on one journey even your right hand and your right eye may be among the things you have to leave behind. We are not living in a world where all roads are radii of a circle and where all, if followed long enough, will therefore draw gradually nearer and finally meet at the centre: rather in a world where every road, after a few miles, forks into two, and each of those into two again, and at each fork you must make a decision . . . Good, as it ripens, becomes continually more different from evil. I do not think that all who choose wrong roads perish; but their rescue consists in being put back on the right road.[6]

In other words, unless they change their path, "haters gonna keep hating."

Peter Ochs, who taught philosophy and religion at Colgate, gets it right, "The fundamental calling is to respond to cries. God hears. Pharaoh does not. Emulate God, not Pharaoh. You hear cries as God hears cries or you hear cries as Pharaoh hears cries. Those are the only two possibilities."[7]

ON COGNITIVE DISSONANCE AND TRANSFORMATION

Yet thank God for the radical grace which Kierkegaard calls, "help that comes nevertheless." In *The Sickness unto Death*, he writes, "Whether a person has been helped by a miracle depends essentially upon the degree of intellectual passion he has employed to understand that help was impossible, and next upon how honest he is toward the power which helped him nevertheless."[8]

This radical grace can appear first as threat which engenders cognitive dissonance. Cognitive dissonance happens when you get less effective at keeping two contradictory truths together. Life on its own terms begins to engender a deeper truth. When the contradiction is unmasked we are compelled, so to speak, to declare our true loyalties. The more sophisticated may attempt to persist in contradiction through clever self-deception, sometimes religious or ideological self-deception. And yet, this is finally despair, the sickness unto death.

6. Lewis, *The Great Divorce*, 9–11.

7. Peter Ochs, email correspondence, May 18, 2021.

8. Kierkegaard, *The Sickness Unto Death*, 172.

Jesus teaches directly on contradiction: "No one can serve two masters, for either he will hate the one and love the other; or else he will be devoted to one and despise the other" (Matt 6:24). As the New Testament shows, the presence of Jesus engenders cognitive dissonance. Socrates also taught, "The unexamined life is not fit for a human being."[9] Encounters of cognitive dissonance can lead to double-downing on self-deception, but they can also lead to I-Thou breakthrough. That is what I learned in Boston and Iona. Self and community can grow and learn; but it takes both truth and love.

As Coleman Brown said,

> You learn that others may not need or want to be treated exactly the way you want to be treated; sometimes, yes; sometimes no. But, whatever the differences . . . you and the other want to be treated with respect and dignity. To be reminded of that will come like a shock of recognition in your personal conflicts or the conflicts of your group with another group. And much of this shock will call you to give up your self-deception, a very hard thing to give up.[10]

Very hard. Sometimes we fail, try again, and fail better, as Cornel West and Samuel Beckett teach. But perseverance is a gift. The deeper response to cognitive dissonance is a process of mourning and metanoia, what Paul calls "godly grief" (2 Cor 7:10). It involves going from contradiction to awakening and decision, each day dying to the cowardly self—in order to live with courage as the true self in the paradox of beloved community.

ON LIVING WITH PARADOX

As Coleman said, "In order to [live truth] communicate substance, morally and spiritually, we have to think paradoxically. A paradox is a creative tension, tension notice. Paradoxes are made of two matters which seem to contradict each other, but in fact each matter has need of the other to become a valuable truth."[11]

For example, the paradox of self-knowledge and knowledge of the outer world. We need both. Yet they are often set in opposition. "Take away our knowledge of the world and our self-knowledge becomes devoid of meaning, becomes narcissism. Take away our self-knowledge and our capacity to evaluate, to put value on our knowledge of the world, goes out with it."[12]

9. Cf. Plato, *Apology*, 38a.

10. Brown, "Baccalaureate Address."

11. Brown, "Baccalaureate Address."

12. Brown, "Baccalaureate Address."

A second paradox is critical thinking and appreciative thinking. They, too, need each other. Critical thinking demands excellence of analysis, uncovers presuppositions of thought and action, of culture and society. Appreciative thinking affirms truth where it exists and provides hope. Together they bring depth and new approaches to mystery. Appreciative thinking without critical thinking becomes sentimentality and superficiality. Critical thinking without appreciative thinking becomes cynicism. Cynicism at the foundation of our minds corrodes democracy, and, yes, corrodes intelligence. I am glad for the advice, "Know all the cynic knows without being cynical. Hope is at the heart of education . . . Cynicism destroys hope."[13]

A third paradox is living as an individual and in community. Many of us grew up in the American culture of self-reliance. This culture can lead to isolation and an enfeebled self, the precondition for fanaticism and grandiosity. The rise of radical extremist groups and malignant narcissism are connected to this isolated self without communities of character. The healthy self needs community and the community needs healthy selves. As Coleman said,

> America has not much faced the moral paradox that self-reliance and community make each other possible. In order to produce self-reliance that is compassionate and courageous, enduring and wise, there must be a strong sense of community behind it, whether that community be large or small . . . Flourishing self-reliance depends on community in which moral and spiritual integrity are highly valued.[14]

A fourth paradox sorely needed today is prophetic judgment, where we glimpse how all of us fall short of a higher love and justice—and discriminating, pragmatic judgment where we must choose among the lesser of two evils (as seen in recent presidential elections). We need both radical vision that gets to the root and pragmatic wisdom that improvises amidst historical limitations for maximum possibility. America itself has existential limitations rooted in its dirty history of racial, economic, and gender injustice, yet not without new possibilities. This is true for selves, communities, and nations. The flip side of fatalism is fanaticism. Both are expressions of despair.

A fifth paradox is grace understood as mercy and forgiveness—and grace as the power of righteousness and justice. One extreme leads to cheap grace, the other engenders merciless self-righteousness. The Divine paradox of the cross and resurrection, transforms both. As Coleman said, "Each part

13. Brown, "Baccalaureate Address."
14. Brown, "Baccalaureate Address."

of the paradox needs its . . . alternative to avoid becoming merely two op-
posing centers of energy."[15]

ON TRANSFORMATION

The living truth is that ourselves, our communities, our nations are offered
multiple levels of life giving paradox that require living with humility, compassion, and I-Thou courage in real time with limitations. In the blue-jazz
process of integrity and improvisation, we begin to break free from paralyz-
ing contradictions—within and without—that would destroy us.

There is a dynamic of true awakening I learned in the twelve-step tradition connected to this movement of breaking free from contradiction to
the higher ground of wisdom in beloved community. It is known as "Awareness. Acceptance. Action." In my personal experience, I would amend this
to: "Painful Awareness. Reluctant Acceptance. Gracious Action." It takes the
gifts of serenity and courage to change. It takes perseverance and a community of recovery to confront our bird-lime death contradictions and become
more fully alive. It takes holy tears and metanoia to break free from prison
stones of trauma and self-hate. It may eventually take all that we have and
all that we are. When this is being done, so to speak, God is doing for us
what we cannot do for ourselves. It is being done as a whole new way of life.

ON EDUCATION AND TRANSFORMATION

I began to think through my philosophy of education in relation to these
paradoxes in relation to what I learned from my outstanding teachers.

In the Reformed tradition of liberating arts and sciences, education
is for reverence of God and truth, or *Deo ac Veritati*. Education therefore
should liberate and transform our lives and our world. The liberating
knowledge that educates (literally that leads us out) is the knowledge that
yields not only understanding of our complex world and its systems, but
self-knowledge. Both are needed. The former emphasizes learning how our
world works and how to work it. The latter emphasizes "knowing thyself"
and learning how to be a responsible and just person in society.

Good education should include participation and study of our
world—science, geography, politics, history, ethics, culture—along with
practical wisdom in our chosen line of work. But it should also include
insight into our true selves: the purity of our real goals, the ambiguity if

15. Brown, "Baccalaureate Address."

not contradictions of our motives, into our deep need to love and trust. In short, good education enables us to know the truth about ourselves in all our simplicity and duplicity.

Kierkegaard wrote:

> The law for the development of the self with respect to knowledge, in so far as it is the case that the self becomes itself, is that the increase of knowledge corresponds to the increase of self-knowledge, that the more the self knows, the more it knows itself. If this does not happen, the more knowledge increases, the more it becomes a kind of inhuman knowledge, in the obtaining of which the person's self is squandered.[16]

Acquisition of information about our world is mostly a matter of grit, persistence, and skill. And yet for transformation to happen this is not enough. We must come to know ourselves. As Steve Hartshorne wrote, "Yet the hard truth about ourselves, our paradoxical existence as human beings is not something we are eager to encounter, because it will often shatter the pretensions and illusions that bring us status and comfort."[17]

Education that transforms self and world thus happens when the ordinary course of our lives is disrupted by circumstances that we could neither have desired nor foreseen, and yet through such experience we come face to face with ourselves, "in a mirror dimly" (1 Cor 13:12). And by this encounter we are freed. We can then begin to use our education and knowledge of the world and its workings not for deception and self-glory, but for justice and mercy—for God and truth. As Steve Hartshorne wrote, "We know it is not by effort or work alone that we have won it; in a profound sense we have been delivered into the truth. Call it luck or call it grace, it brings to mind the words of the prophet, 'Not by might nor by power, but by my spirit, says the Lord.'"[18]

NIEBUHRIAN FRAGMENTS

Christian existentialism needs a social ethic to ground its theology and depth psychology. After my experience in Boston and Germany, I pulled together fragments from my Harvard thesis. Niebuhr has been critiqued by Stanley Hauerwas, Traci C. West, and James Cone for his flawed doctrine of the church, male bias in anthropology, and lack of existential passion for

16. Kierkegaard, *The Sickness Unto Death*, 31.

17. In other words, "The truth shall set you free, but first it will make you miserable" (John 8:32). Hartshorne, *Hartshorne Speaking*, 7.

18. Hartshorne, *Hartshorne Speaking*, 7–8; see also Zech 4:6.

racial justice. I agree with many of these critiques. Nevertheless, appropriating the critical-appreciative approach to Niebuhr, there are deep fragments of wisdom to receive. His perspective transcends narrow Christian pietism and religiosity—which so many religious institutions historically have fallen into—on the basis of eschatology and ethics.

Niebuhr strongly affirmed a theological emphasis on living out the law of love and justice in a complex and sinful modern world. He understood that sin has an ethical dimension. "The pride which makes itself the source and end of existence subordinates other life to its will and despoils it of its righteous inheritance."[19]

Niebuhr argues that in both personal and social relations, the self and community attempt to overcome anxiety and achieve security and self-glory by subordinating others to one's will. This is done mainly through the unethical use of power, that is, in acts of injustice. Furthermore, the egoism of social groups is always greater that the egoism of individuals because a social group is less reasonable and self-transcending than an individual. In other words, the group is the more elegant and effective channel of arrogance, hypocrisy, and ruthlessness by individuals. Sin can become a structural aspect of social institutions, and therefore injustice is often perpetuated by existing social structures. Niebuhr saw that restraint may be imposed upon these personal and group egoistic tendencies through education, law, and religion, yet mainly through countervailing structures of power. He says, "Man's capacity for justice makes democracy possible; but man's inclination to injustice makes it necessary."[20]

Concerning the interplay of love, justice, and power in modern society, Niebuhr stressed the primacy of the political; that is, how group relations are primarily functions of how much power each group possesses. "It may be taken as axiomatic that great dis-proportions of power lead to injustice, whatever may be the efforts to mitigate it."[21]

A kind of balance of power is then necessary for any proximate attainment of justice. As privileged groups—class, gender, or racial—do not give up power voluntarily, the oppressed must use organization and coercion to gain freedom. Niebuhr believed that the disprivileged have a "higher moral right to challenge their oppressor than these have to maintain their rule by force."[22]

Thus power and conflict are necessary to establish justice. This is asserted over against many ideologies of injustice in which reason and religion are used to justify disproportions of power and privilege. Niebuhr blasts

19. Niebuhr, *The Nature and Destiny*, 223.
20. Niebuhr, *The Children of Light*, xi.
21. Niebuhr, *Nature and Destiny*, 262.
22. Niebuhr, *Moral Man*, 234.

these rationalizations, stating they reveal the immense capacity for self-deception and the power of social groups to manipulate reason and religion. Efforts to deny justice for the oppressed often take the form of blaming the victim and of substituting pietism and charity for justice. This also serves to actively discourage people from organizing for change.

For Niebuhr, agape love is the critical standard by which to judge both personal and social righteousness. History points to agape (for those who will look), but it is revealed fully in the cross of Christ—the suffering love that is directed to all neighbors. "It is the final norm of a human nature which has no final norm in history because it is not completely attained in history."[23]

Agape is then "impossible possibility" in social relationships because while this love is never entirely embodied in any human action, it remains relevant as a standard for true humanity. And if one gives up pretensions to perfection and lives honestly before God, it can be approximated to some degree in personal life and social relations.

Niebuhr maintains that all societies and churches stand under this absolute ethic, therefore none can rest with an easy conscience. Yet because love is not realistically lived out, particularly on a group level, we must search for principles and strategies to approximate it in our sinful world—standing always under the judgment of God. Therefore, though the practical ethical goal in complex modern society is justice, love remains the motive and ultimately the standard by which all proximate structures are chosen and evaluated. In our striving for justice, love is the directive and corrective.

The necessary and often ambiguous striving for justice in history is justified on the basis of that which is in and beyond history, mitigating despair at the tragic violence and self-deception which is part of the human condition.

A final Niebuhr quote presents a broad vision in relation to resisting injustice in church and society:

> Nothing that is worth doing can be achieved in our lifetime; therefore, we must be saved by hope. Nothing which is true or beautiful or good makes complete sense in any immediate context of history; therefore, we must be saved by faith. Nothing we do however virtuous can be accomplished alone. Therefore, we are saved by love. Nothing we do however virtuous looks quite as virtuous from the standpoint of our friend or foe as it does to ourselves, therefore we are saved by the final form of love which is forgiveness.[24]

23. Niebuhr, *Nature and Destiny*, 75.
24. Niebuhr, *Justice and Mercy*, v.

3

Breaking Through the Plate Glass Window

In June 1992, I accepted a call to Second Presbyterian Church in Elizabeth. I started my call exactly six years to the day after I was ordained in Boston.

I felt at first like Jonah being thrown from the belly of the whale onto Nineveh.

What I experienced in New Jersey appeared as an existential wasteland compared to breakthroughs in Boston and Iona. I had underestimated the value of community in strengthening the self. In my arrogance, I had neglected to see how critical friends were to thriving, let alone surviving. In coming to New Jersey there were no long runs along the Charles River, no talking to fellow twelve steppers near Castle Island in Southie, no morning coffee at Frank and Erma's, no sitting around the fireplace at Iona. I grieved the emptiness and isolation.

When I arrived from Boston there was a tea party held in the church parlor to welcome me as the new pastor. After driving four hours from New England, I parked my car and got out. I looked in the window and glimpsed the strange parishioners holding tea cups, eating cookies, and talking loudly in New Jersey accents. I considered getting back in my car and driving back to Boston. It had all been a big mistake.

Instead, I opened the door and walked in.

I moved into to a large English Tudor manse in the wealthier Westminster section of Elizabeth with five bedrooms and four bathrooms. I had never before in my life lived alone. At night when it rained hard, I could hear running water. Where? Was I crazy? In the middle of the night, I went down into the dark basement with a flashlight. There in the far corner was a little trickle running in and out the side of building. It was like the Frank Lloyd Wright house "Fallingwater" in Elizabeth.

NEW CONTEXT AND BEGINNINGS

Elizabeth, New Jersey, is located within ten miles of the Statue of Liberty and has been a port of entry for immigrant populations through most of its history. It is a diverse city of over 120,000 people, similar to many cities experiencing rapidly changing social and economic conditions. During the 1990s, a growing percentage of Elizabeth's population were foreign born. Forty-six nations were represented at the 4,500 member high school, which was the largest in New Jersey, among the largest in the nation. Over thirty languages were spoken, with 67.5 percent speaking a language other than English in their homes. According to the 2000 census, there were 120,568 people residing in the city. The racial makeup of the city was 55.8 percent white (among these 26.8 percent were non-Hispanic/Latinx white), 20 percent Black, 0.5 percent Native American, 2.3 percent Asian, 14.5 percent from other races, and 5.9 percent from two or more races. The city had 55.46 percent of the population listed as Hispanic/Latinx. The per capita income for the city was $15,114. Many urban problems were present in varying degrees. These included homelessness, poverty, unemployment, ecological degradation, high rates of infant mortality and asthma, drugs, crime, youth gangs, organized crime, problems in the schools, and institutional racism.[1]

Amy Shine from Massachusetts, a recent graduate of Yale University, was teaching in the Elizabeth High School. Phyllis from Fourth Church in South Boston knew her and introduced us. Together with elder Virginia Bodden, we started a tutoring program for children in the neighborhood. Virginia said in her memory the church had never done anything for families in the neighborhood. A spark from Southie lit a flame in Elizabeth. Through Amy, I met thirteen-year-old Jerome Dixon and his friend Doug Murray. We started a youth group and then a church basketball league.

I was welcomed by Rev. Jim Reisner at First Presbyterian. We were naturally competitive; he had gone to Williams and Yale, I went to Colgate and Harvard. He was at First, I was at Second. But our edge soon became a dynamic friendship. Together we reentered the world of the academy at Princeton and started a conversation with Dr. Richard Fenn and Rev. Carl Georges. The first president of Princeton University was buried at

1. US Census Viewer, "Elizabeth, New Jersey Population."

First Presbyterian cemetery, along with hundreds of unnamed African Americans—many of whom had been enslaved.[2] I began to host Princeton seminarians for summers in the city. They lived at the manse and worked for forty hours a week at urban field education sites. We'd hold Iona style worship in the mornings, reflections in the evening. Everybody took a turn cooking—Korean, Southern Black, Californian, New England-style food. We hosted Saturday cookouts for the youth group.

When the mostly Black and Hispanic/Latinx teenagers first came over for the Saturday cookouts, they seemed nervous. I asked Jerome, "What's up?"

"Pastor Mike, Black folks aren't supposed to come to this side of town. The police will soon be harassing and beating us up, arresting us. You don't want to mess with them."

There was something here. I was learning the unwritten rule that Black people could not go to certain sections of the city. It reminded me of my experience working as a community organizer in Tulsa, Oklahoma, in 1981. I had heard rumors, folk stories from the Black community about something horrific that had happened in North Tulsa. But it was hidden under the ground, so to speak. It only surfaced years later. In Elizabeth the unwritten code was centuries old, and yet was still present. One neighbor said he almost called the police on us several times. Instead, he unleashed his large boxer dog, which would cross into our yard and growl.

THE FRONT PLATE GLASS WINDOW

Shortly after our conversation, I crossed East Jersey Street one September afternoon. Three young Black teenagers from our new youth group were at my side. The cars on the street in the late afternoon rush hour were temporarily stopped for a red light. Yet as we crossed in front of one large dark car, the vehicle began to move forward, slowly, then faster with deliberate speed—then directly at us. Startled, we jumped for our lives, out of the way, barely escaping injury. I looked over to see four white men inside the car laughing wildly. I realized in astonishment they were police officers in an unmarked car.

Then on Sunday afternoon during my first Lincoln's birthday weekend there in 1993, I noticed a large flag and a United States flag placed together in the front plate glass window. Abraham Lincoln's picture was in the middle. The persons passing by on East Jersey Street could view this display, including myself. Yet as I looked at it—I somehow assumed it was a British flag. Why a British flag was in the church window on Lincoln's birthday I

2. I learned this years later from Dr. Wanda Lundy.

did not then consider. Basically, I was in denial. That evening at the manse I watched a "Sixty Minutes" special on the controversial use of the Confederate flag in Georgia. I then realized, to my horror, this was the flag in the church window! I drove to the church and yanked it out. I tried to tear it in half, like the Nazi flag in *The Sound of Music*. It was too thick. I crumbled it up and stuffed it into a brown bag.

I called several elders to ask why it was placed there. I learned that it had first been put in the front window in 1963 by someone, I never learned exactly whom. It had continued to be placed there on Lincoln's birthday "as a tradition" ever since. When pressed further, another elder professed ignorance and even innocence as to its symbolic meaning. "We're babes with this," one woman said, "you have to educate us."

I asked several Black persons from the community about what this display signified to them. One person, George Taylor said, "I never saw it. But it would have been offensive. For African Americans, the Confederate flag is about death. It just triggers something in me. Putting it in the window, even with an American flag, you are saying—you not only support oppression, you are the oppressor."

I learned the symbol of the two flags together became popular in the United States after Reconstruction, during the era of Jim Crow lynching in the South and white violence against Blacks in the North. It signified a strange bitter fruit of "reconciliation" between whites of the former Confederacy and whites of the North—united in power now under the Jim Crow regime. White brothers from North and South who fought and killed in the Civil War were now "reconciled." And yet at who's expense?

I discovered a passage via Coleman Brown from the autobiography of W. E. B. Du Bois. Martin Luther King Jr. quoted it in his book *Where Do We Go from Here*:

> It is hard for others to see the full psychological meaning of American racism. It is as though one, looking out from a dark cave in a side of an impending mountain, sees the world passing and speaks to it; speaks courteously and persuasively, showing them how these entombed souls are hindered in their natural movement, expression and development; and how their loosening from prison would be a matter not simply of courtesy, sympathy and help to them, but aid to all the world. One talks on evenly and logically in this way but notices that the passing throng does not even turn its head, or if it does, glances curiously and walks on.
>
> It gradually penetrates the minds of the prisoners that the people passing do not hear; that some thick sheet of invisible but

horribly tangible plate glass is between them and the rest ... Then
the people within may become hysterical. They may scream and
hurl themselves against the barriers, hardly realizing in their be-
wilderment that they are screaming in a vacuum unheard and
that their antics may actually seem funny to those outside looking in. They may even here and there, break-through in blood
and disfigurement, and find themselves faced by a horrified,
implacable and quite overwhelming mob of people frightened
for their own existence.[3]

Making use of this metaphor, questions emerged: How do people interpret
and challenge "that thick sheet of invisible but horribly tangible plate glass"
which comes between people(s)? How do they react to the racialized other
who breaks through, sometimes in disfigurement—who disturbs their categories of being human? To go a step further, how do we respond, ultimately,
to the One, human incarnate, bloody and disfigured, who breaks through
for us all—and brings the archetypal Word that we are "to love one another"
(John 13:34)?

Exploring these questions helped me awaken to my own denial
of white racism in self and in church. When Coleman Brown visited, we
went outside on East Jersey and Broad Streets amidst the many people of
color walking by us in Elizabeth. Upon coming inside the church, Coleman
turned and said, "Someone must have worked real hard to keep the Black
people out."

Later that year, my colleague the Rev. Tom Hall at Third-Westminster
Presbyterian Church in Elizabeth and I were talking. He was nearing retirement after serving two very large congregations, over a thousand members,
in the Midwest. Though Third-Westminster was only 250 members or so,
Tom said this was his hardest pastorate. I asked him why. He told me several
church women had recently come into his office.

"Pastor, we have a problem."

"How can I help?"

"Well, you know, it's getting kind of dark in here ..."

"Oh, I understand," Tom said. "Why don't you ladies get together and
make a big sign. And then put that sign up in front of the church so everyone can see, 'Enough dark people here. No more allowed.'"

The ladies were stunned.

"Don't you see how ridiculous that is? If God calls people to this
church, of any color, we're welcoming them in the name of Jesus Christ.
That is the gospel."

3. Du Bois, *Dusk of Dawn*, 130–31.

A year later I was driving one morning on the New Jersey Turnpike near Elizabeth and my cell phone rang. It was the executive presbyter. He told me Tom had just died of a heart attack in his office. Could I go and pray with his wife and daughter?

Tom was only sixty-four years old.

Shortly after this, I was having lunch at a restaurant with a wealthy older church member. He said he wanted to make a donation directly to me, the pastor, for $1,000. He would like to make these $1,000 donations on a regular basis. I told him it was better to send the money directly to the church treasurer. He then changed the subject and declared, "You know, the big problem in Elizabeth are the Blacks and the Puerto Ricans, they're taking over. They want to make America look like Africa."

I told him I saw it very differently. The lunch ended shortly after.

The $1,000 donations to the church never came.

Getting the Confederate flag out of the front window at Second did make a difference. Over time, cognitive dissonance led to dialogue and decision. Some people got off the fence, one way or the other. I began to focus on the youth ministry and working with the community. That was where the energy and excitement were flowing.

Because of Jerome and Doug, the tutoring and youth ministries were growing. We spent most Saturday and Tuesday evenings together. I drove them home to the projects at 10 PM. Then one evening, Doug got into a fight during the game. He said he was done and walked out. This had happened before, but this one time seemed different. I got into my silver Toyota and searched through the city. I found him walking down East Jersey Street, near the drug dealers. I lowered my window, "Doug, get in the car."

"Fuck you!"

I made an illegal U-turn, sped up, and drove onto the sidewalk, directly in front of him. I wanted it to look dramatic. "Doug, get in the fucking car!"

He did.

Word began to spread. Folks from the community, Virginia, Karen, Fausto, Ileanna, Maria, Pedro, Deborah, began volunteering with the tutoring. We partnered with others in the city like Linwood Bagby and Restore Ministries. As in South Boston, their presence changed us.

ON MOURNING AND NEW LIFE

It began to seem that one would have to hold in mind forever two ideas which seemed to be in opposition. The first idea was acceptance, the acceptance, totally without rancor, of life as it is, and

*men as they are: in light of this idea it goes without saying that
injustice is commonplace. But this did not mean that one could be
complacent, for the second idea was of equal power: that one must
never, in one's own life, accept these injustices as commonplace but
one must fight them with all one's strength.*
—James Baldwin[4]

Over time there were breakthroughs, though many resisted. I had learned at
Fourth Church in South Boston to go with the new life, to press into it. There
it was breaking in through the twelve step groups, the ecumenical social witness and desegregation of housing, the new people from different classes and
races coming to the neighborhood Bible study and worshipping community.
The culture of "being church" was transforming. The old was dying, and the
new was birthing. They were breaking bread on the road to Emmaus.

In Elizabeth, new life was breaking in with the youth ministry and
community ministries, but something was blocking the adults on Sunday
morning. It was like Cleophas on the road to Emmaus *before* he broke bread
with Jesus. He was blinded by the light.

One morning, a seminarian from Columbia said the passing of the
peace in Spanish then English; a booby trap exploded in the pew. A woman
began publicly boycotting the worship, sitting outside the door on Sunday
morning. She said we had offended her.

Nevertheless, the church education leadership was graciously handed
over to Deborah, who became the first Black superintendent of Sunday
school. Her love for the children transformed education. It began to include
many Black and Hispanic/Latinx children. Deborah picked children up and
dropped them off in her van. She intuitively knew Paulo Freire's pedagogy,
"What the educator does in teaching is to make it possible for the students
to become themselves."[5] Deborah also knew you have to ask questions with
intensity before you can get answers that have ultimate meaning. She had
her students watch *Terms of Endearment*, in which Debra Winger plays a
single mom who is dying of cancer. The mom puts on her makeup before
they bring her two little boys in for her to tell them goodbye. She sees her
older boy looks sullen. She knows he is upset at her for leaving. She is able to
console him. Where do people get this courage? This is the kind of question
that must be asked. Only then can people begin to experience the grace of
God. We cannot experience the divine from just reading a book or hearing
a sermon unless it causes us to ask intense questions about the meaning of
our lives.

4. Baldwin, *Notes of a Native Son*, 139.
5. Freire, *Pedagogy of the Oppressed*, 74.

DISCOVERING NEW AND OLD FRIENDS

I began to go to Sunday night Al-Anon meetings at Christ the King Church in Hillside. This particular meeting had several women going through menopause. I said during one meeting I was learning more about menopause than I thought I'd ever know. After the meeting, an older woman took me aside. She said, "Michael, you didn't cause your parent's divorce. You aren't to blame."

Getting back into recovery made a huge difference. The bread of healing was there. I had to reach over and claim it, go to meetings, do my running and training, reach out to others in recovery. If I didn't keep working the program—of courage, serenity, and wisdom—then the disease—of fear, insecurity, and doubt—would work me. It was simple. Hope has to do with participation.

I reconnected with an old friend, Roger Badham, in New Jersey. Roger always seemed to go before me. He attended Dorchester Baptist Church in Boston before me. He attended Harvard Divinity School before me. He guest preached at Fourth Presbyterian Church in South Boston before me. And now he was in New Jersey before me—studying at Drew University for a PhD. (I didn't yet know it, but I would follow in a few years.) Just encountering Roger with his intellectual passion and contagious laughter strengthened me. His integration of mysticism and theology connected with my own existential approach. After our conversation talking about Buber, Rosenzweig, and the Beatles, I sensed I was on my path. I had to just keep walking.[6]

It was about this time that I received a phone call one evening from my friend David Clohessy. David had been my first boss working as a community organizer for ACORN (Association of Community Organizations for Reform Now) after I graduated from Colgate. David directed my work organizing in Roxbury before I went to Oklahoma to organize in Tulsa. David was a hard-driving boss, pushing me to the limit. Yet he was fair and kind, and had a wicked sense of humor. He was also a great organizer. David attended my ordination in South Boston. I stayed at his house briefly in Dorchester when I returned to Boston after Oklahoma.

When he called he said he was recently engaged to be married to Laura Barrett, another outstanding organizer. David's voice was shaking. He told me he had watched a Barbara Streisand movie, *Nuts*, and was having flashbacks of being sexually abused during his teenage years. The person who did it was a Catholic priest named John Whiteley. I listened as David wept

6. See Badham, *Introduction to Christian Theology*.

and told his story. I was proud to be his friend. As he spoke, I suddenly remembered something that I had completely forgotten. While visiting David's apartment in Savin Hill in 1981 for a lobster party, I had slept one night on the coach in the living room. There were several people visiting that weekend from out of town. I remember waking up in the middle of the night and screaming. Someone had been inches from or touched my face. It was very dark, I could see no one. I yelled out, "Who's there?" There was no answer. I thought it was a bad dream and I went back to sleep. In the morning while getting coffee in the kitchen, I looked over at the person who had been sleeping on the other side of the living room. He looked away. I remember thinking, something's off here. I almost confronted him, yet he was a Catholic priest. The man was John Whiteley. He was visiting David and his roommates from Missouri for the weekend.[7]

I had forgotten all about this experience until David called. I told David on the phone about my flashback. I wanted him to know I stood with him; his trauma was real. David listened. As he courageously worked through his trauma in the months that followed, with the help of Laura and other survivors, I sensed David was rightly named. He became national director and spokesman for the Survivor's Network of those Abused by Priests (SNAP). His courageous speaking truth to power and organizational brilliance helped bring to light the sex abuse scandal in the Catholic Church and other religious organizations. He broke through the denial and abuse of power in the institutional church. David has been quoted in the *Boston Globe*, the *New York Times*, *Good Morning America*, *The Oprah Winfrey Show*, *The Phil Donahue Show*, and *60 Minutes*.[8] His tremendous example of moral courage and perseverance on behalf survivors of sexual abuse are a profile of breaking through the plate glass window for us all.

The next summer, I met Karen Hernandez. She was the dynamic and beautiful new pastor of Westminster Presbyterian Church in Trenton. We were introduced to each other at a Church Redevelopment Conference by the Rev. Bob Washington. We dated for a year and were engaged to be married the following September.

Shortly before our wedding, on a hot August night in 1996, Karen and I went to see the Kyiv Symphonic Choir and Orchestra play to a packed church of six hundred Ukrainian-Americans at Second Presbyterian Church in Elizabeth. They sang and played in multicolored folk costume, including, "Prayer for Ukraine." Members of Second Church hosted the

7. See Acuff and Hardison, "Update." Bishop Shawn McKnight named John White-ley as "credibly accused of sexual abuse" and removed him from ministry.

8. See Bruni, "Am I My Brother's Keeper?"

seventy-five or so performers from Kyiv overnight in their homes. I had seven musicians stay in the manse. Several became friends. They gave me a large Orthodox cross and invited Karen and me to visit their homes in Ukraine. We could see how deeply they cherished their self-determination and self-development as a free people.[9]

Karen and I were married at Westminster Presbyterian Church, Trenton, on September 29, the Feast of Michael the Archangel and all Angels.

Later I told a friend, "This day, because I need all the help I can get."

Without hesitation, she replied, "No, this day because your wife needs all the help she can get!"

Coleman Brown offered up these words of invitation:

> There is no audience today—not really. And, finally, no performance is being offered here. We are a congregation, a community called together today as people of God. We are the community in which—and before whom—Karen and Michael know themselves—and know themselves now called into marriage.
>
> We are the community of their unity and encouragement. This community includes both the living and the dead. We are here not only as individuals, not only as ourselves; we are here on behalf of all those in Karen's and Michael's past—living and dead—who have loved them and strengthened them, taught them and called them to account. And we are here on behalf of all those who in the future enter into the lives of Michael and Karen, and into whose lives they enter.
>
> So, we are not simply an audience but part of a celebration and a service of worship. And this wedding service asks something of us all. Karen and Michael are counting on us. They count on pledging themselves and listening with our support and strength—both now and in the days to come.
>
> It takes a lifetime to say and hear, and learn, the important things—and even then we miss and falter (as those of us who are older know best of all). So let us not say, "They shouldn't have" or "They should have," or judge at all. Judge not that you be not judged. As the Scriptures have it, "See to it that . . . no 'root of bitterness' spring up." Instead, let us receive the mystery and wonder of it all.
>
> Learn again even to forgive. For as we forgive, so we experience forgiveness.

---

9. Later our hearts were broken by the demonic violence inflicted by a murderous tyrant upon vulnerable people. We remembered the anthem the choir sang. May God have mercy on the people of Ukraine.

Renew your own vows, your own best commitments; renew your hope, your joy, your courage, and your love.

This marriage is not just a private good but for the common
good.

Be of good cheer. Be amused. Fear neither your laughter
nor your tears.

Begin to see again that the Lord our God is good; has given
us food and drink, and life itself. Even one another—God has
given us. Even the presence of God among us we have been given.

O God, Creator of all that is,
Savior of the lost and Spirit of eternal life,
we would enter in and celebrate
and worship in your name.

In 1997, our daughter Mikaella was born, and then in 1999, our daughter
Olivia. Later we would get our dog, Charlie. I was learning to build a home
with the Spirit, to be irreverent and real in my reverence. I am still learning.

LIVING THE INTERSECTIONS OF THE CROSS

During the 1990s, I was introduced to multiple faith activists in the region,
Sister Jacinta and Sister Edie, Salaam Ismael, Newton Burkett Jr., Rev. Anthony Wilcots, Rev. Bob Buffalo, Rev. Joe Garlic, Rev. Amy Ruemann, Larry
Hamm, Rev. Brooks Smith, Hazel Garlic, Rev. Howard Bryant, and Rev. Joe
Parish. I met attorneys like Delores Mann, Jim Keefe, Bob Ungvary, and
later Jim Vigliotti. Some of these folks became friends and partners, a feisty
team, gifts of God. One could receive them in gratitude and freedom, or not.

A few of us worked with the Industrial Areas Foundation and participated in Ten Day Training. Others worked with People Improving Communities through Organizing (now Faith in Action) and did their trainings. The
bottom line is we learned better how to do one-on-one meetings, identify
issues in the community, conduct power analysis, and lead public actions
with clear objectives and goals.

Along with Faith Temple, a Black Pentecostal congregation, and their
pastor, Overseer Bernice Jackson, Second Church hosted the city's Martin
Luther King Jr. service several times. Over six hundred people attended
these events. Some white members complained to me. They said the balconies couldn't hold this amount of people.

We began doing stations of the cross outside in the city on Good Fri-
days. We started with the Catholic stations of the cross and readings from
the New Testament. But then conversations with people in the city changed

them. We connected with youth who were directly affected by drugs and violence. We talked to survivors of domestic abuse. We partnered with persons who were formerly incarcerated. Together we would write meditations and prayers and choose songs for each station. The themes were criminal justice and incarceration (court house, county jail), ecological justice (held facing the Bayway Refinery), policing (Elizabeth police station), domestic violence (the site where a woman was murdered), urban education (in front of the Elizabeth high school), structural racism (by the site where three leaders of a slave revolt were burned at the stake in 1741), and violence against immigrants (facing the Elizabeth Detention Center).

Edie recalls,

> We always included mimes. They did a powerful performance. People took turns carrying the Cross. A key Station was at the County Jail. In earlier years, the prisoners would watch and wave to us. Later years, they weren't allowed. When a few tried, they were punished. There too a famous Black musician, Milton Entzminger, played "Amazing Grace" on the trumpet. During Lent we'd gather every Wednesday to imagine, pray, and discern the Stations. I'm still immersing myself in those Graced Kairos moments.[10]

One young Black woman who participated in the walk was Charlene Walker. She was going to high school in Hillside near Elizabeth. She was president of her youth group at the Hillside Lutheran Church. Charlene spoke at one of the stations of the cross.

"Why do all the Black kids sit separately in the cafeteria," she asked? "Because our town is redlined and segregated. This plays itself out in our schools and neighborhoods. And in policing. When the Black kids go to the white side of town the police stop us. Black kids walking down the street are stopped and questioned by the police all the time."

Later, Charlene told me that while home for the holidays from Syracuse University she was visiting her boyfriend who was Black and lived with his family in the Westminster (white) section of town. They were sitting in front of his house talking in the evening. A police car drove up and stopped. The police told them to stand up and put both their hands on the car. Charlene said this was such a common occurrence, they complied automatically. She realized then that growing up in Hillside they had been conditioned. The police ran her boyfriend's license through their system. They confirmed this was his home. As the police were leaving, they turned and said, "You have a nice backyard. You should be talking back there."

10. Edie Cheney, email correspondence, May 15, 2021.

Charlene is now the director of "Faith in New Jersey." She's been to the Slave Museum in Montgomery, Alabama, and says it was a transformative experience. She supports the Lost Souls Project in New Brunswick, which is a community-centered memorial dedicated to the free Blacks who were kidnapped and sold to slavers in the South by the Van Wickle Slave Ring in the nineteenth century.[11] She says there should be a community memorial in Elizabeth where the three leaders of a slave insurrection were burned at the stake in 1741. Charlene talks about harm reduction and building systems of care in the community, of dismantling policing paradigms based on white supremacy, "which dehumanizes us all." She says we should be not just allies, but co-conspirators in solidarity and liberation. "Justice begins at our intersections, and is rooted in our relationships."[12]

With Charlene and other young people from the community, our early morning Good Friday walk grew in visibility and numbers over nine years. Then our community of walking and praying stumbled again upon a bulldozer in the city: policing, violence, and white supremacy.

> One cannot level one's moral lance at every evil in the universe. There are just too many of them. But you can do something; and the difference between doing something and doing nothing is everything.
>
> —Daniel Berrigan[13]

One afternoon in the late nineties, two teenagers from the church youth group were crossing the intersection of Broad Street and East Jersey Street, just a block from the church's front glass window. According to the youth, they were crossing with the walk sign. Suddenly a police car turned and nearly struck them. As they jumped out of the way, one teenager yelled, "Hey!" The car screeched to a stop, and two beefy white policemen got out. One officer grabbed the young man and pulled him down into the back seat of the car. He punched him in the head. When they arrived at the police station, he was taken inside where he was thrown into a jail cell without medical attention. When several hours later his grandfather arrived to bring him home, he was told his grandson had fallen while getting out of the police car. No charges were ever filed against the teenager.

This teenager was a leader in our church youth group and never missed a cookout at the manse. He showed up at church the next morning with a

11. See https://lostsoulsmemorialnj.org/.

12. Charlene Walker, interview, May 15, 2021.

13. Berrigan, quoted in Safi, "The Saint I Never Met," para. 7. Daniel Berrigan spoke a few years later in Elizabeth at St. Mary's Church.

bloodied purple head and side, and huge swollen eyes. He looked to me like Jesus after they tortured him.

I was so angry I wanted to go down to the police department and bang my fists in rage against their bulletproof glass window. A Black church woman in Elizabeth took me aside, "Michael this is not checkers; it's more like a chess game. You have to think strategically."

I had heard rumors of a white supremacist group in the Elizabeth police department. My friends Jim, Jacinta, and Edie had also heard about them. There seemed to be an extraordinary amount of police violence in the city. Jim had encountered it directly at the train station and elsewhere. He had spoken out publicly with Jacinta, Edie, and Rev. Joe Garlic. At this time, I met a New Jersey State policeman, somewhat randomly, who directly confirmed there was a white supremacist group in the Elizabeth Police Department. It was called "The Family." He said they were now almost a fifth of the department, "a leaven of evil." He told me to be careful.

Jacinta and Edie were leaders at St. Joseph's Social Service Center which worked with the poor. Edie said sometimes people came into their center with broken arms from the police. They started a group which gathered testimony on police brutality. They heard about multiple events of violence. At one meeting with the police director, Sister Jacinta said, "When you are right, we will support you. When you are wrong, we will confront you." After that, Edie says the police became more hostile in their interaction with them. The police would sometimes drive near the property, park and stare at them, then drive away. When Jacinta and Edie would come up to greet them, the police would look away. Sometimes they would drive onto the property and arrest someone from the neighborhood. The police would order Edie and Jacinta to move far away, but they would stay nearby to witness everything that happened. This was before phone cameras.

With Jim and other city activists, we decided to have a large public forum on policing at the parish house of First Presbyterian Church. We invited public officials, community leaders, and journalists to hear direct testimony from the community. Edie moderated the event. There were many people that night who lifted up horrific experiences of police brutality.

Yet despite promises of change, police violence continued in the city.

A group of interfaith leaders met with several public officials. We called the prosecutor's office and the state attorney general. We even called the federal attorney. People didn't return our calls or gave us the run around. They didn't seem to care.

I decided to call Coleman. We talked at length. He suggested I call Chris Hedges. Chris was just back from the Middle East working for the *New York Times* out of Manhattan. I had last seen Chris in Jerusalem when he was the Middle East bureau chief for the *Times*. We had gone to a B. B. King concert together and he dropped me off near my hotel by the old Wall.

Chris checked with his editor and agreed to come and investigate. He worked out of my office. He used to sit in a blue reclining chair working on his laptop. Sometimes late in the evening he'd nap there while waiting to interview a police officer getting off his night shift. The chair had been given to me by a feisty older member, Dot Benn. I promised him Dot's chair one day for his hard work.

The article came out on a Saturday in May 2000. It was on the front page, "Blue Shadows in Elizabeth."[14] That morning, I searched through the city but couldn't find a single *New York Times* anywhere. They had all disappeared. The following Sunday morning, all the cars in front of Second Church on East Jersey Street were ticketed.

In the weeks afterwards, many people called my church phone to tell of incidents with the police. I heard of people being beaten, harassed, run over, and worse. I heard so many stories that I felt overwhelmed. I referred many people to civil rights lawyers and to the FBI. I suggested to the Presbytery they establish a fund to help pay for attorneys for poor people brutalized by the police. This went nowhere. I contacted regional law firms for *pro bono* work. Some helped.

Shortly after the article was published, the leader of the "Family" was forced to retire, others were demoted or reassigned. The federal prosecutor and the FBI began to return our calls. They said they were actively monitoring the situation. Later they met with us. Police violence began to visibly lessen. The best disinfectant indeed is sunlight, visibility. The article and its aftermath exposed patterns of white supremacy in the police department. Salaam Ismael recalled,

> The police in Elizabeth like in many other urban cities were bent on shake downs, intimidation, corruption, and abuse. The "Family" clique inside the Elizabeth Police Department didn't like me and my name was on a "hit list." My work on exposing police brutality around New Jersey got me many death threats and attempts at intimidation . . . Of course, decades later I am never going to leave the fight against institutionalized police racism.[15]

After the article came out, one Elizabeth police officer, Lt. Bill Dugan, called the church to ask if the police could play basketball two afternoons a week in our new gym. He went to St. Mary's Church and knew Fr. Bill Crum.

14. Hedges, "Blue Shadows in Elizabeth."
15. Salaam Ismael, email correspondence, May 16, 2021.

At first I was suspicious, but then I realized he was one of the good police officers. We wanted to work with them. Sister Jacinta recalls her experience:

> During my years in the Elizabeth community, I saw the best and the worst of the Elizabeth Police Department. Certainly, Eddie Gray tops the list of the best, one who truly loved the community he served. There were other good cops too, who truly lived their motto of protecting and serving the community. The worst were those who were part of a sick, secret group called "The Family" who used their power to abuse, ridicule and harass people in the community, especially minorities. They were racists, sexist, and used physical force to "control" the community. Their superiors were complicit by condoning or overlooking this behavior. Other police officers obeyed the blue wall of silence out of fear and a false sense of loyalty.
>
> At St. Joseph Social Service Center, we formed a committee called "Community on the Beat." We interviewed dozens of people from the community who were victims of police brutality. Their stories were similar. Police stopped them or entered their homes illegally, often with minor or false charges. They roughed them up, threatened, and intimidated them. Those who filed complaints found no recourse. Their complaints were reviewed internally by a so-called police review board and subsequently dismissed.
>
> We made many attempts to improve relations between police and community, through meetings with the mayor, the police leadership and representatives of the police force. We held prayer vigils outside of city hall and police headquarters. We supported the victims and their families. Only when a front-page article by Chris Hedges appeared in the *New York Times* did "The Family" finally come under investigation . . .
>
> From my experience and seeing what is happening all over the country, it is evident that there is, and has been for a long time, a "police culture" which allows and even encourages these negative attitudes and behavior. It is the police against the community, not for and with the community. We need more Eddie Grays, more good police.[16]

It took sunlight and salt, "courageous people in many places," to keep the meat from rotting. Young adults and teenagers like James Carey, Charlene Walker, Kason Little, and Archainge Antoine were inspired by these "good

16. Jacinta Fernandes, email correspondence, May 17, 2021.

troublemakers." James Carey, a Black Lives Matter activist, wrote on social media during the summer of 2020,

> While purchasing something to eat for my daughters, I was asked what inspired me in becoming an activist. I informed the postal worker that activism was lying dormant in my DNA, because both of my grandmothers were advocates. However, what ignited my passion was Salaam Ismael and Rev. Michael Granzen [and others] in the 90s when they courageously/defiantly exposed the "Family," a once fringe sect of the Elizabeth Police Department. After reading their respective quotes [in the *New York Times*] my mind was made up, I knew advocating for the marginalized and disenfranchised is my calling.[17]

New groups were formed in the city and state like the "New Jersey Clergy Network for Justice," "First Friends," and "Make the Road New Jersey." They became countervailing institutions for accountability on policing, racial justice, and ICE abuses.

Young clergy began to rise up and claim their voices, like Rev. Barry Wise, Rev. Carmine Pernini, Rev. Kathyrn Irwin, Rev. Ramon Collazo, Rev. Erich Kussman, and Rev. JerQuentin Sutton. Along with veterans of hope like Rev. David Ford, Rev. John Howard, Elder Skip Winter, Dr. Michael Christopher Jones, Dr. Ronald Owens, Elder Madelynne Lindsey, Rev. Sharon Culley, Rev. George Britt, Rev. Steffie Bartley, Rev. Raul Burgos, Rev. Joseph Adair, Rev. Jupiaci Carneiro, Rev. Carlos Cedano, Rev. Leonard Grayson, later Rev. Daniel Mendez, and Dr. Wanda Lundy, among others . . . They became salt not saccharine in the city, changing the whole for justice.

At one protest, two dozen people stood outside a church in four degrees in late January when the governor came to speak for the Martin Luther King Jr. service. Lobbied by the police unions, he had resisted signing legislation mandating that the state attorney general's office investigate when a police officer killed an unarmed person. Charlene Walker, the former high school student at our Stations, spoke as a leader that day and posted this on social media,

> I stood outside on one of the coldest Martin Luther King Days in Elizabeth in protest to urge Governor Murphy to sign the Independent Prosecutor bill. Why? Because I am angry! I am fed up with seeing Black bodies slaughtered on TV by those that are charged with the task to protect and serve with no recourse. I am angry that today could be the day I become the next hashtag . . .

17. James Carey, Facebook post, July 23, 2020.

I am angry that I live in a state where 100,000 people can't vote due to criminal convictions as part of a criminal justice system riddled with systemic racism simply to limit the impact of the Black vote . . . I am angry that we have an opioid crisis being addressed with treatment when our white brothers and sisters became impacted but could not do the same when Black families were crying out for help after the government fed drugs into our community. Instead, those suffering from addiction were criminalized and our children were separated from their families . . . I am angry that our government commits torture by placing inmates in solitary confinement, causing mental illness, then releasing them into society. I am angry that the school to prison pipeline in NJ is a literal manifestation . . .[18]

The governor signed the bill into law three days later.

The Stations became a paradigm for prophetic ministries in the city, a signal to join together with the poor in the work for justice.

Monsignor Bob Harrington invited me to preach at St. Mary's. I was nervous that morning as I had not spoken before at a large Sunday Catholic Mass. As I walked forward to deliver the homily, Bob handed me a little folded note. I opened it as the opening hymn concluded, "Michael, it's great to have you here this morning. Please give a good message. But not too good!"

I spoke to the packed church about the many faces of Jesus with the poor in Elizabeth. The sermon seemed to go well. As I returned to my seat, Bob quietly slipped me another note: "You didn't listen to me!"

Rev. Harrington, along with Charlie and Geri Mulligan, invited several of us together to respond to the needs of incarcerated immigrants and refugees at the Elizabeth Detention Center. Rev. Harrington, Rev. Bill Crum, and Rev. Jack Martin at St. Mary's reminded me of Rev. Al Puccini and Rev. Tom Clark in South Boston. They were priests who talked the talk and walked the walk.

First Friends was organized with donations from St. Mary's Church, including free office space, and a $10,000 grant from the PCUSA. It was formed in the aftermath of 9/11 to uphold the dignity and humanity of detained immigrants and asylum seekers through visitation, resettlement assistance, and advocacy. First Friends now serves thousands of people in the Elizabeth Detention Center, the Essex County Correctional Facility, the Bergen County Jail, and the Hudson County Correction and Rehabilitation Center.

A few years later, hundreds of people gathered at a vigil organized by Make the Road New Jersey and First Friends outside the Elizabeth Detention

---

18. Charlene Walker, email correspondence, May 15, 2021.

Center. They were resisting the policy of separating children from their families at the border. Because a United States senator was speaking that day there was a large cluster of media from the metropolitan area. Clergy are often asked to wear their collars and stand silently in the background at such protests. This has symbolic value. Yet sometimes we are asked to speak. I learned to write it out, especially if it is short, go slow—and improvise from the heart.

> I'm with the New Jersey Clergy for Justice and a Presbyterian pastor in Elizabeth.
>
> Jesus said, "Do unto others as you would have them do unto you."
>
> Who would have their child separated from them and not know if they will be reunited? Who would have that happen in their family, or in their community, or in their nation?
>
> Jesus also said, "As you do it unto the least of these you do it unto me."
>
> People are outraged by what is happening. It is the highest level of anger in this whole eighteen-month nightmare. People can identify with what it is like to have children ripped from their families. And it comes from a very deep level. I know in my own extended family, through death, where a two-year-old lost her mother, and she never fully recovered.
>
> Down this path lies dehumanization.
>
> Down this path lies genocide.
>
> There is a reason that one of the key moments in the Biblical story of Pharaoh is when he orders the babies killed. And in the New Testament when Herod orders the children killed.
>
> This is a moment when a tyrant becomes a monster.
>
> We must stand up with all people of good conscience and good will and seek the common good—to defend the vulnerable, the widow, and the orphan.
>
> And for the sake of the traumatized children, who we know actually have their brain structures damaged by this early trauma, it is urgent to act.
>
> And have a zero-tolerance policy—every single child must be united with their parent.
>
> And never, never, never give up on this!

Some undocumented persons and their advocates resisted ICE abuses by forming "Committees for the Defense of the Community." These groups held meetings to teach people how to protect themselves, filmed ICE raids with phones, raised funds for legal services, performed skits to prepare people for encounters with ICE and the police, appealed to churches and communities to join the sanctuary movement, and used social media to send out alerts about raids, arrests, and deportations.

Sara Cullinane, co-founder of Make the Road New Jersey and an outstanding organizer, spoke about the ICE abuses in the region:

> People are being picked up in front of their homes when they leave for work. When ICE has administrative warrants, not judicial warrants, they know they cannot go inside. They use subterfuge. They wear plain clothes and drive in unmarked cars and carry a picture of the person they want. ICE agents can arrest people if they are only suspected of having engaged in criminal activity, no matter how minor. I have never seen this level of fear.[19]

GOING THROUGH THE FIRE

What is the nature of this light that shines in the darkness? It is a divine light in the mortal light . . . It is a light that reveals to us the glory of God in Jesus's face and shines in our own lives.[20]

I was visiting with an Indian-American family in Elizabeth who had just lost their father, when several texts came on my phone. They were from Karen. The ultrasound for our fourteen-year-old daughter Mikaella had revealed a large mass in her abdomen. The doctor said we needed to take her immediately to the emergency room of Children's Hospital of Philadelphia (CHOP). I drove home in a blur. We gathered our things and drove to CHOP in Philadelphia.

A series of tests and consultations through the next forty-eight hours with doctors, nurses, specialists were mind-numbing and scary. The medical phraseology was confusing. I tried to research online using my cell phone, I called friends who might know more than me. Time was pressing. They held out hope for a benign tumor. The percentages were in our favor.

It's hard to convey how much your life can change in the blink of an eye. The world is turned upside down at high speed in slow motion. Along with this goes the illusion that you or your loved ones are exempt from life's unfairness. The most important thing I learned was to do the next right action, and then the next right action. This required making right decisions as best as one could.

19. See Hedges, "Terrorizing the Vulnerable."
20. Moltmann, *Resurrected to Eternal Life*, 76.

The doctors scheduled my daughter for surgery the next morning. I wanted the best surgeon, I wanted a surgical oncologist in case it was not benign. They said that was not possible, this was the only surgeon available, and it was probably benign. I researched the surgeon, but could find little. We went ahead.

The surgeon removed the mass the next morning. When he greeted us he couldn't hide his body language. He said we'd have to wait for the lab results.

Two days later, on February 1, the pediatric oncologist assigned to us came in our daughter's hospital room with the surgeon; they said it was malignant, a germ cell tumor. My daughter wept. It seemed unreal. The oncologist said it was only stage one and she didn't need chemotherapy. We would actively monitor her through blood tests. This was the best approach.

We were relieved. We wanted to trust him. We wanted to believe his expertise concerning this optimistic diagnosis and treatment plan. We knew little. I googled his name and found out he was doing a major research project on children with stage one germ cell tumors, to learn whether or not eschewing chemo was as effective as using chemo, which had a 90 percent cure rate.

My father, who had died in 2005, always told me to get a second opinion with major medical decisions, sometimes a third. I wanted badly to talk with him. A friend gave us the name of her adult oncologist at UPenn. The doctor had an opening in two weeks. We made the phone calls and filled out the paperwork to transfer the medical and pathology reports.

Two weeks later, the three of us were sitting in her office. She was visibly upset. The pediatric oncologist had missed one sentence on the pathologist report. It was stage two, not stage one. There was still cancer in her body. While we were sitting there, she called the pediatric oncologist directly, but he wouldn't or couldn't come to the phone. Later he said that germ cell cancer was different with children, that active vigilance was still the best approach. He said pediatric oncology was different than adult oncology. She seemed to yield to his authority. I googled and found that both doctors were professors at University of Pennsylvania Medical School. She was an assistant professor, he was an associate professor.

Shortly after this, I dropped the girls off at school and was stopped at a traffic light. I felt overwhelmed with dread and uncertainty. I prayed the serenity prayer. When I opened my eyes, I saw the words "conquer cancer" on the license plate in front of me. I called Karen on my cell phone. We agreed we needed a third opinion.

When I got home, the phone rang, it was the Black oncology nurse from the adult oncologist at UPenn. She was checking in with us—and recommending that we get a third opinion from a pediatric oncologist. I asked if Sloan-Kettering was good. She said, the best. That was Monday. Time was racing. The nurse helped us get all the reports and pathology specimens from CHOP and UPenn in record time to get the appointment at Sloan-Kettering by Friday.

This nurse was God's angel for us.

On Friday morning, Mikaella, Karen, and I sat together waiting in the consulting room on the ninth floor of Sloan-Kettering. The multiracial team of doctors were returning from two hours examining the medical and pathology reports. The head doctor stepped forward and spoke solemnly. He said our daughter was being subject to a dangerous research protocol. She needed chemotherapy immediately.

As he spoke, the church bells started ringing.

Karen and I wept.

When we returned home that evening, the pediatric oncologist from CHOP had left a message on our home phone. He had changed his mind, our daughter did need chemotherapy.

Early the next Tuesday morning, I dropped Karen and Mikaella off at Sloan-Kettering for her ear and lung tests. She would begin chemo the next day, March 1. I parked the car, then walked quickly down First Avenue to join them. I walked into the waiting room and saw my former teacher, Ada Maria Isazi-Diaz, talking with Karen. Why was she there? She had just been diagnosed with stage four ovarian cancer. She was starting chemotherapy. I told her about Mikaella. Ada Maria and I held each other and wept. Mika came out and the two talked together. Then it was time for Ada Maria to go in for her tests. She hugged Karen and Mikaella.

She then she turned and looked at me with great intensity. I saw the light in her eye.

"Michael, we will pray for each other. *And I will pray for your daughter.*"

She said these last words very firmly.

That was the last time I saw her.

The protocol for Mikaella's chemotherapy required that we stay in the Ronald MacDonald House (RMC) several blocks north during her four days of treatment, then it was three weeks at home recovering and monitoring white blood cell counts, before the next round. The chemo would be infused each day from 8 AM to 6 PM. Mika had to sit in a little stall with a white curtain for eight to ten hours. Sometimes she could walk around the floor with a pole holding the chemo bags. She was surrounded by dozens of children and teenagers in other stalls getting infusions. You could hear the children crying and moaning. Their parents would comfort and soothe, sometimes sing to them. I heard a rabbi chanting in Hebrew. These parents and children and friends were profiles in courage. Where did they get this beautiful courage?

Sometimes I spoke with other parents while getting a coffee. We strengthened one another. Get through the hour, the day; this is a marathon, not a sprint; stay strong; don't get upset at the small stuff; focus on the present moment; sometimes we would just look each other in the eye and gently nod; sometimes we couldn't hold back the tears.

It was the community of children and parents on the ninth floor of Sloan Kettering.

Mikaella had a port put in her chest. She lost her hair. She struggled with fatigue each day. Sometimes she wore a backpack with water infused into her body through the night at RMH. Karen would lie next to her and hold her through these long painful nights. I slept on the coach. Mikaella couldn't go to school, she had to be tutored. The teachers and community at Princeton Friends School rallied. They bought her an iPad and other gifts. Mikaella did her homework and studied for her part in the school play, "Once on This Island." It was scheduled for late May. We had to find her a wig. She was supposed to graduate that June.

Olivia, our younger daughter, stayed with friends and family during these intense cycles of chemotherapy. It was especially hard on her in these times of separation from her sister and parents. She was brave beyond words through these difficult months.

The nurses and doctors were extraordinary, especially Dr. Chris and the multiracial pediatric oncology team. They had both excellent minds and good hearts. The leader of the pediatric oncology unit at Sloan-Kettering told me he made regular time for them to express their emotions together. This was important. Our social worker, Kristy, was tremendous. She had been taught by a teacher at Hunter College connected to St. Joseph's in Elizabeth. There were many friends, including both our congregations and the students at NBTS, who rallied in radical love for Mikaella. They gave us not only food, but heart prayers and themselves. Some people could not deal with what was happening and pulled away. Others like Peter Campbell called every single day. Peter would alert me if someone like the president was visiting Manhattan that morning and suggest the best driving route. Some people called to just listen. This made a huge difference. We were freed to focus on doing the next right action in a marathon race, telephone pole by telephone pole. That's all we could do. Yet to do this one thing well over the long haul, we needed the tender mercies of our brothers and sisters.

I prayed the serenity prayer several times each day.

One cold windy morning in late March, Karen, Mikaella, and I were waiting for a cab in front of RMH to go to Sloan-Kettering for another long day of chemotherapy. The cab never came. We decided to walk to York Avenue and hail one. It was colder than we anticipated. The cabs and limos were rushing by. We could walk, but it was several long blocks against the wind. Mikaella began trembling. I gave her my coat. We huddled together. The three of us began to walk slowly in the direction of Sloan-Kettering.

Just then a school bus pulled up directly in front of us. The bus stopped and the doors opened. The driver looked down.

"What are you waiting for? Get in."

Karen fell down in shock. It was the sister of Karen's good friend in Brooklyn who had just died. Karen thought it was her good friend who had just died.

I lifted Karen up and we got in the school bus and sat down speechless. The friend's sister, Mildred, had just dropped off her school children in upper Manhattan and was on her way back to Brooklyn when she somehow saw us walking on the street. Mildred drove us down the several blocks to the front entrance of Sloan-Kettering. We stepped off.

This was a glimpse for us of the mystery of God's light that shines in the darkness. We were not walking alone.

Three weeks after finishing her last cycle of chemo, Mikaella performed in her school play as Erzulie, the goddess of love. It involved singing some demanding parts. Those who saw the play will not forget.

Mikaella entered freshmen year at Princeton High School that fall wearing a wig. It was not an easy freshman year. Boys sometimes can be cruel. The next year we got a therapy dog, Charlie, who helped us mend as a family.

The hardest part for me in the months and years that followed was waiting for test results of blood work and scans. We would get up very early, drive to Sloan-Kettering that morning for the tests, have lunch, then drive back to New Jersey. Dr. Chris would call in the evening on my cell phone with the results. Every time it was nerve wrecking. Every time you didn't know. It's hard for people to fully understand who have not gone through this kind of experience themselves or with loved ones. I highly recommend Kate Bowler's book *Everything Happens for a Reason (and Other Lies I've Loved)*. She gets it right on many levels.

Things happen—and God loves us.

These tests continued for four years until Mikaella was declared cancer free in 2016. She gave the keynote speech that year at Sloan-Kettering for the young people treated for cancer as children or teenagers who were graduating high school. In 2021, in the midst of COVID-19 Mikaella graduated from Wesleyan University at the top of her class. We are thankful for every day we have together. We are thankful for the community of encouragement and character that holds us all in the infinite light of God.

BLUES/JAZZ ORDINATION

During this season of walking through fire, I reconnected with Chris Hedges and his wife, Eunice Wong. They were very supportive of Mikaella and our family.

In 2014, Chris circled back to Elizabeth. Cornel West and James Cone came to speak for his ordination as a PCUSA minister. The Michael Packer Blues Band sang the blues and spirituals. Chris had started the ordination process in Albany Presbytery in the mid-1980s. He picked it up again thirty years later. I think this set the record in the PCUSA for years under care. Clergy and lay leaders from New Jersey, New York, New England, seminarians from Union, Princeton, Drew, New Brunswick, returning citizens, assorted activists, friends, and family participated. It was a great day. A highlight was seeing Chris and his wife Eunice come forward and dance with abandon as the Michael Packer Blues Band played, "Swing Low Sweet Chariot."

> I looked over Jordan, and what did I see
> Coming for to carry me home
> A band of angels coming after me
> Coming for to carry me home
>
> If I get there before you do
> Coming for to carry me home
> I'll cut a hole and pull you through
> Coming for to carry me home . . .

Chris became Associate Pastor for Prison Ministry at Second Church. He taught in state prisons and helped returning citizens find housing, education, and employment. Mike Gecan with the Industrial Areas Foundation helped Chris find full-time jobs for eleven returning citizens as associate and lead organizers. I never heard of anything like this before. At one class Chris taught at Eastern State Prison in Rahway, he helped his students write the play *Caged*. Part of it was performed in the prison with James Cone and Cornel West attending.[21] It was later performed at the Passage Theatre in Trenton. Boris Franklin, who helped write the play in Rahway, was brilliant as an actor. Karen Hernandez-Granzen helped organize the Trenton community to participate. Almost every performance was sold out. Many people came down from Elizabeth and Newark to see it, some more than once. It is now published in book form. One reviewer wrote,

> While the play's characters ring with authenticity, *Caged* never
> neglects its serious political messaging. The play illustrates

21. Hedges, "The Play's the Thing."

Black lives in dialogue with a racist system, in which state power reinforces cycles of violence while moments of extraordinary integrity and bravery break through the cracks. Fifteen minutes before the play begins, a dimly lit stage reveals a barred cell. Inside, Shaky Brown, "a gifted blues musician serving a life sentence," plays the blues. Throughout the play, his cell haunts the stage. Yet, his music—at once marginal and persistent, beautiful and full of grief—remains as well.[22]

I learned in Boston, Iona, and Elizabeth that change is possible, though hard and incomplete. It is a process, unfinished here on earth. We keep trying to run and hide from God—through hubris, idolatry, self-hate—but God's grace keeps bringing us back.

As Steve Hartshorne said in his last sermon at Colgate University,

We try to flee, but God (blessed be God's name forever!) won't let us go. For when we try, the world turns against us, becomes empty of meaning, crushes our illusions, and we seek the solace of a comforting god only to discover that god isn't there.

We don't seek God; God seeks us. God is always with us, seeking us. Escape God we cannot. Nor will God forsake us. "If I descend into hell, behold though art there." As to Ezekiel of old, God says to us in our hurt and loneliness, "Stand upon your feet and I will speak to you." Hear that word and you will find the Peace that God has given you. You will find the One who long since has sought you and found you.[23]

Sometimes the living boundary between the seeking agnostic and the perplexed Christian can be very thin. There are many lives that have tragically fallen into the abyss—of what eye has not seen, nor ear heard, nor the heart conceived. There are many questions of theodicy that cannot be answered—on this side of the veil of death. There is mystery and jagged incompletion, yet there are fragments of hope. It is by trusting the "void beyond the void" that eschatological love springs forth.

There is a final judgment and hope for us all.

Thomas Merton writes in *Conjectures of a Guilty Bystander*:

One of Julian of Norwich's most telling and central convictions is her orientation to what one might call an eschatological secret, the hidden dynamism which is at work already and by which "all manner of things shall be well" . . . Her life was lived

22. Adler, "A Review of New Jersey Prison Theater Cooperative's Caged," para. 4.
23. Hartshorne, *Words of Hope and Meaning*, 135–36; adapted.

believing in this "secret" . . . when all partial expectations will be exploded . . . It is the "great deed" of the eschaton which is still hidden, but already at work in the world, in spite of its sorrow.

This is, for her, the heart of theology: not solving the contradiction, but [courageously] living in the midst of it . . . To have a "wise heart," it seems to me, is to live centered on this dynamism and this secret hope—this hoped for secret.

It is the key to our life, but as long as we are alive we must see that we do not have this key: it is not at our disposal. Christ has it, in us, for us. We have the key insofar as we believe in Him, and are one with Him. So this is it: the "wise heart" remains in hope and in contradiction, in sorrow and in joy, [actively] fixed on the secret and the "great deed" which alone gives Christian life its true scope and dimensions!

The wise heart lives in Christ.[24]

What began with a Confederate flag in the front glass window became a fragment of prophetic witness by organic activists, and the likes of James Cone and Cornel West. The title of Dr. Cone's sermon was "Do not think that I have come to bring peace to the earth, I have not come to bring peace but a sword." A sword of truth-love and agency indeed is needed to "cut a hole and pull you through" (Matt 10:34).

What is hidden in the hard defenses, the invisible but tangibly real plate glass window(s) that separate us from ourselves, each other, and finally God? There are deep insecurities, dread, and wounds that must be faced and owned. If they are not, then the separation only gets thicker and more destructive.

William Stringfellow addresses this in his conclusion to *My People Is the Enemy*,

> What it means to be human is to be free from idolatry in any form, including, but not alone, idolatry of race. What it means to be human is to know that all idolatries are tributes to death, and then to live in freedom from all idolatries. To be human means to be freed from the worship of death by God's own affirmation of human life in Jesus Christ.
>
> Reconciliation one to another first requires that we be reconciled to ourselves; to love one another means first the freedom to love yourself in the way that God has shown that God loves every person . . . In that freedom, from time to time, men and women are born into the society of all humankind wrought by God . . . In that freedom is the way and witness of the Cross

24. Merton, *Conjectures*, 210–11; adapted.

. . . In that freedom is the love and unity among human beings which can endure death for the sake of all, even unto a person's own enemy, even unto my own enemy, even unto myself.[25]

May it be so.

25. Stringfellow, *My People Is the Enemy*, 166.

SECTION II

Historical Fragments

INTRODUCTION

Writing is like pulling together puzzle pieces, fragments. Living at the intersections of church, society, and now academy, I began to develop a more critical understanding of race, class, and religion in America. This involved confronting my own denial of white racism more severely. This process occurred in ongoing conversation with friends, colleagues, and teachers, especially Traci C. West, Ada Maria Isasi-Diaz, Richard Fenn, Laurel Kearns, Otto Maduro, and Ken Rowe. It included intense dialogue with the outstanding students in the classes I taught at New Brunswick Theological Seminary and Drew University. It also included conversations with my wife, Karen, and daughters, Mikaella and Olivia. These are nevertheless my own limited thoughts. I am thankful for such a community of intellectual passion and integrity.

This section moves from the perspective of biography to that of history. I am not an academic historian, but this is a form of "disruptive remembering." It is a fragment of scholarship for those who want to dive deeper in exploring the question of how the Confederate flag got in the front window of the Presbyterian church in 1993. And how it gets into the front window of American democracy in 2021 and into police departments today. These questions are connected to the original bulldozer, so to speak, of white supremacy and exploitation of the poor in America. This is my own attempt to face that history, to dive deep and surface. I did not learn this in high school or college history classes. Why not?

The first section on biography draws from fragments which were lived mostly during the years in which Martin Luther King Jr.'s vision of multiracial democracy had the upper hand, at least where I was located, culminating in the election of Barack Obama as president. This section narrates historical fragments of forces of white supremacy and violence which raised their ugly heads anew in the years after his election. In 2017, I knelt down to pray in solidarity with Black Lives Matter activists during Sunday worship and two white members walked out.

They were always there, of course. As Spencer Crew observed, "Before democracy, chattel slavery was born in the United States."[1] What are the specific sources of post, post racial America? And how is the white church implicated in this narrative? As pastor in Elizabeth, I observed meaningful interracial worship and personal exchanges across racial-ethnic lines. Yet I have overheard church members stubbornly say, "Black is for sin," and examined old photographs of church minstrel shows from the 1930s and '40s. I discovered with a seminarian an ugly anti-Semitic and racist tract in a church bookshelf, complete with a "how to" for organizing against desegregation of neighborhoods.

Derrick Bell, in a prophetic editorial written in the late 1990s for the *New York Times*, critiqued President Clinton's intentions in creating yet another national commission on race. He suggested that the national debate should be redirected:

> The Rev. Dr. Martin Luther King Jr. once observed that plenty of studies had detailed the damage racism has done to blacks. What is needed, Dr. King said, is a study of racism's corrosive effect on whites . . . We should not waste any more effort on what amounts to studies of the worthiness of blacks. Nor do we need another study to see how welfare and housing policies affect us. The board should ask some other questions: what does it really mean to be white, not as a matter of pride in cultural heritage, but as social and economic facts of life in the United States? And are whites willing to build a stable society, one that does not denigrate blacks in order to bind together whites across vast chasms of income and social class?[2]

These are painful questions to ask and harder to live. Yet the hard questions and judgments, according to the Bible, should begin with the church. Racial estrangement is an excellent lens through which to better understand what is happening in human hearts and polities, to discern both the traces of sin

---

1. Crew, *Black Life in Secondary Cities*, 3.
2. Bell, "A Commission on Race?," paras. 8, 9–10.

and, one hopes, God's grace. As William James noted, "There is no doubt that healthy-mindedness is inadequate as a philosophical doctrine, because the evil facts which it positively refuses to account for are a genuine portion of reality; and they may after all be the best key to life's significance, and possibly the only openers of our eyes to the deepest levels of truth."[3] Or more succinctly, as Thomas Hardy put it, "If a way to the better be, it lies in taking a full look at the worst."[4]

This section traces the historical seeds of destruction, of contradiction, and of social death in Elizabeth and New Jersey, into the post-civil rights era of "violent innocence." Then it asks the question, from the perspective of Christian social witness: How can we break through the false peace, the multiple plate glass windows, with the agency of truth-love today? How can we critically respond, change the path we're on?

3. James, *The Varieties of Religious Experience*, 137–38.
4. Quoted in Becker, *Escape From Evil*, iv.

4

Seeds of Destruction

Human beings are historical selves located in social groups shaped profoundly by the past. To break through the plate glass window of denial on racism in our communities and in ourselves it is necessary to re-center marginalized testimonies and texts from the past. The lacuna of social memory regarding the extraordinary racial violence in American history participates in what sustains it today. Historical amnesia lays the groundwork for present injustice. Paul Connerton writes, "Mental enslavement of subjects begins . . . when their memories are taken away."[1] The presentation of the self and community in everyday life without historical context leads to distortions of freedom and agency. In order to hope, we must remember.

FORMATION OF CHATTEL SLAVERY, C. 1600–1700

America's contours of white terror against non-white populations started early. In Elizabeth and New Jersey, the trajectory of violence against non-whites goes back to its very founding in 1664, which coincided with the establishment of slavery and white Christianity.

In the early seventeenth century, the Dutch West India Company participated in the Atlantic slave trade and through extraordinary violence brought African peoples in bondage onto lands occupied by the indigenous Lenape tribes. The planters colonized the region they called the "New Netherlands," which includes present day New Jersey. This was sanctioned by

1. Connerton, *How Societies Remember*, 14.

the Dutch Reformed Church. As early as 1628, the leader of the First Dutch Reformed Church of New Amsterdam, the Rev. Jonas Michaelius, referred uncritically to "the Angola slaves."[2]

While occupying by force the lands of indigenous peoples, the Dutch created a social structure known as the "Patroon System," where they placed in bondage non-white peoples along with poor whites.[3] For the first several decades, Dutch laws governing the treatment of enslaved Africans and indentured servants were similar to those for Europeans. Certain laws protected both groups, with some rights given to hold property, legally marry, receive an education, and in some cases obtain freedom. During this early period, the bondage of both poor whites and Blacks was the central method of obtaining cheap labor for agriculture. Both groups struggled to survive what one historian called "the big planter apparatus and social system that legalized terror against black and white bondsmen."[4]

The potential for revolt against this radically violent social order was demonstrated by protests such as Bacon's rebellion, which occurred within a decade of Elizabeth's founding. Nathaniel Bacon was a property owner in Virginia who led a group of poor whites and Blacks in an effort to overthrow domination by the planter elite. The planters were given land grants from British royalty and occupied lands from Native Americans, so as to control all economic options for freed whites and Blacks. Bacon developed plans in 1675 to take some of these "uncultivated lands" for himself and others. He condemned the planter elite for their harsh treatment of indentured servants and organized to overthrow the prevailing order. The rebellion was defeated by military force and promises of amnesty. Many of those who participated in the revolt were tortured and executed.[5]

As word of the rebellion spread, there were additional uprisings. These early revolts directly challenged the white planter elite who were already apprehensive that coalitions of indentured servants and enslaved Africans could displace their social order. In a cunning move to sustain domination, the planters shifted their strategy of obtaining cheap labor to the exclusive enslavement of African peoples, dividing poor Europeans from enslaved Africans. The rising ideology of white supremacy was used to justify Black enslavement and undermine resistance. The seeds of the white "racial bribe"

2. Cohen, *The Ramapo Mountain People*, 25.

3. Wright, *Afro-Americans in New Jersey*, 18–19; Cunningham, *Colonial New Jersey*, 1–18.

4. Bennett, *Shaping of Black America*, 62; Crew, *Black Life in Secondary Cities*, 3–5.

5. Alexander, *The New Jim Crow*, 24–25; L. Carr, *Color-Blind Racism*, 14–16; Morgan, *American Slavery, American Freedom*.

with its violence against non-whites were planted.[6] As Spencer Crew summarized, "Before democracy, chattel slavery in the United States was born."[7]

These seeds sowed division between descendants of poor Europeans and enslaved Africans. The former were given access to indigenous lands, economic incentives, and social privileges in an expanding slave-based order policed by the state. Poor whites were given a direct stake in the development of chattel slavery.[8]

This original sin of white racism took root in the soil of hubris, power, and greed and grew over time, adapting to changing social conditions. The capture by Great Britain in 1664 of New Amsterdam and its surrounding territories—including Elizabeth—brought rapidly declining conditions for non-whites. During this early period, East and West Jersey laws regarded Africans in similar ways to white apprentices and bondsmen. Yet after Bacon's rebellion in 1682, laws were passed which forbid the purchase of goods from enslaved Africans without their masters' permission in contrast to laws for white indentured servants. Shortly after this, laws forbidding Blacks and Native Americans from carrying guns, buying rum, and practicing certain acts were passed by the legislature.[9] These laws included monetary fines for white violators, yet violent whipping, castration, and burning at the stake for Blacks and Native Americans who violated the same strictures.[10]

During this period of expanding slavery, the town of Elizabeth was organized in 1664. As part of land colonized by English settlers from Connecticut, it was named for Elizabeth Carteret, the wife of the colony's first governor. One of Elizabeth's early leaders, Cornelius Hatfield, made his living as a slave dealer. Many early settlers owned several enslaved Africans.[11]

Slavery in New Jersey was encouraged by legal directives from England. One mandate, "The Concession and Agreement of the Lords Proprietors of the Province of New Caesaria, or New Jersey," ordered that any Europeans settling in New Jersey would receive sixty acres for each enslaved person they imported from Africa in 1665, forty-five acres for each enslaved person imported in 1666, and thirty acres for each enslaved person imported in 1667.[12]

6. See Matthew 13.

7. Crew, *Black Life in Secondary Cities*, 3.

8. Carr, *Racism*, 14–16; O'Rourke, *How America's First Settlers Invented Chattel Slavery*.

9. Wright, *Afro-Americans*, 18–23; Crew, *Black Life*, 3–8.

10. Alexander, *The New Jim Crow*, 25–26.

11. Crew, *Black Life*, 8; Washington, *Union County Black Americans*, 11–29.

12. Wright, *Afro-Americans*, 19.

In 1702, when the provinces of East Jersey and West Jersey were united as one colony, Queen Anne ordered the first Royal governor of New Jersey to strengthen the institution of slavery with new laws strictly policing Black life, violent punishment for those who resisted, and more importation of enslaved persons from Africa. These state directives worked to the direct profit of the Royal African Company of England, in which Queen Anne and her royal government had financial interests. They insured that the economic interests of whites in New Jersey would be interwoven with the enslavement of African peoples.[13]

How did the system of chattel slavery coexist with Christianity? Torturing and enslaving "savages" was less of a moral problem for the planters than doing so to human beings, so ideological justification rose along with state sanctioned violence. Legalized terror and cruelty were cloaked with claims of religious innocence.

The sanction of slavery as the "will of God" became the religious basis for justifying these practices. This involved a distorted reading of a text in the Old Testament (Gen 9:18–27) and its later interpretation in Talmudic writings. In Genesis chapter 9, the story is told that after the flood, Ham looked upon his father's nakedness as Noah lay drunk, but the other two sons did not. When Noah awoke, he cursed Canaan the son of Ham, saying he would be the "servant of servants." The extreme distortion is clear in that the story says nothing about skin color. In subsequent parts of the Talmud, this story is told in a way that changes the original text and makes black skin a curse. This interpretation of the curse of Ham was expounded in the doctrine of white supremacy for over 350 years. In a tape-recorded sermon in 1958, Jerry Falwell is heard espousing this doctrine.[14]

Spencer Crew argues that in practice the application of slave laws in New Jersey varied by the stance taken by the religious community in the region. Religious attitudes on slavery profoundly differed in East Jersey versus West Jersey. East Jersey consisted of lands granted to George Carteret by the Duke of York, while West Jersey was on lands granted to John Berkeley. While Carteret maintained control over his lands, Berkeley sold his property to John Fenwick, a Quaker convert. This region became a refuge for Quakers who fled to New Jersey and Pennsylvania to escape religious persecution in England. Quaker theology opposed the institution of slavery. In 1696, Quakers living in West Jersey directed that all members refrain, on penalty of exclusion from the community, from importing or owning

13. Crew, *Black Life*, 9.

14. Smith, *Racism in the Post-Civil Rights Era*, 6–12; Hood, *Begrimed and Black*, 133–55; Davis, *Inhuman Bondage*, 48–75, 124–40.

enslaved persons. A report from a monthly meeting of Friends in 1738 states that for many years none of their members imported or purchased enslaved persons.

Throughout the colonial period there were significantly fewer enslaved persons living in West Jersey than East Jersey. In the second half of the eighteenth century, the Quakers sought to abolish the institution in the state. John Woolman was a leader in this campaign. He organized, spoke, and wrote tracts against slavery. In 1744, the Quakers helped persuade the New Jersey Assembly to pass legislation banning importation of enslaved persons. Though the governor vetoed the bill, they continued to work to change the law. In 1769, legislation was passed and signed by the governor which restricted importation of enslaved persons into New Jersey. This was the final action limiting slavery in New Jersey for several decades.[15]

Because New York and Pennsylvania imposed economic duties on the importation of enslaved persons, New Jersey had become the major importer of enslaved persons to the region. In 1726, there were 2,581 enslaved Africans in New Jersey. By 1790, there were 14,185: 8 percent of New Jersey's population. This was the highest per capita number in any Northern colony.

In Elizabeth, growing concern developed among whites over the expanding numbers and resistance from the Black population. These fears of rebellion were used to justify more white terror. Of all the Northern colonies, New Jersey and New York had the most violent slave codes. Beginning in 1704, laws were passed that mandated forty lashes and the branding of a "T" on the left cheek for any Black, Indian, or "mulatoo" caught stealing between five to forty shillings. Punishment for those caught stealing more than forty shillings was burning at the stake. The penalty for any Black male who attempted or had sexual relations with a white woman was castration. These laws forbid more than five Blacks to meet together at one time, with the punishment of twenty lashes for doing so.[16]

The slave laws could not eliminate the threat of Black resistance. The *Pennsylvania Gazette* carried an article in 1737 about white fears in New Jersey concerning free Blacks caught selling potions to enslaved persons so they could poison their owners. Throughout this period there were notices in newspapers publicizing rewards for catching runaway enslaved persons and severe penalties for assisting them. In 1734, a revolt by thirty enslaved Black persons in Somerville, New Jersey, was used to justify mutilation and execution of several dozen Blacks. Whites arrested at least thirty Blacks, hanged one enslaved leader, and whipped and chopped off the ears of others.

15. Crew, *Black Life*, 5–8.
16. Wright, *Afro-Americans in New Jersey*, 19–22.

In 1735, an enslaved Black person in Hackensack was burned at the stake for burning down a barn. In 1741, a revolt of enslaved persons broke out in New York City. More than two hundred Blacks in New York were violently punished; some were burned at the stake. Hoping to escape capture, three leaders sought refuge in Elizabeth. They were caught and charged with murder. The court convicted all three and sentenced them to execution. They were tied to stakes in front of the courthouse and burned alive. City records indicate local whites received reimbursement from the town treasury for wood they supplied for the event. A subsequent law directed white masters to severely punish Blacks accused of disorderly conduct with hard labor and thirty lashes of whipping. The severity of the sentence was left to the discretion of Elizabeth's mayor.[17]

GRADUAL ABOLITION, C. 1770–1800

In the late eighteenth century, increased Black resistance, new affirmations of freedom based on natural rights, and evangelical beliefs regarding the liberating effects of baptism combined to bring about a "First Emancipation" from slavery. Though emancipation was gradual and not immediate. Pennsylvania led the way in 1780. New Jersey was among the last of the Northern states to enact gradual abolition in 1804.

During the Revolutionary War, Elizabeth had at least one slave insurrection. In June 1779, whites in the city learned of a plot among enslaved persons to revolt for their freedom. Several Blacks were arrested. Although they were caught before the rebellion took place, this caused great anxiety among whites. According to local newspapers, whites at the time framed their bondage of Blacks into the narrative of liberty. Black leaders seeking liberation from slavery were viewed as treasonous to white liberation from British rule. Whites thus built their freedom on the enslavement of Blacks.

Robert C. Smith and others argue that without the presence of this discourse of freedom in the Revolutionary War, racial injustice in the United States may have developed with less attention doctrinally to Black degradation. The Declaration of Independence explicitly affirmed, "We hold these truths to be self-evident, that all men are created equal, that they are endowed by their creator with certain inalienable rights and that among these are life, liberty and the pursuit of happiness." Given such a strong affirmation of the value of liberty, it was then necessary to overcome

---

17. Crew, *Black Life*, 9–11; see also Ottley and Weatherby, *The Negro in New York*, 2–9, 27–30; Hatfield, *History of Elizabeth*, 364; Cooley, *A Study of Slavery in New Jersey*, 11.

cognitive dissonance and justify the bondage of millions of Blacks by undermining their humanity. Thus, along with the doctrine of equality came the ideology of black sub-humanity as articulated in the Constitution's three-fifths clause, Article I, Section 2.[18]

Slavery survived and even grew as an institution in New Jersey in the decades after the Revolutionary War. James Gigantino argues in *The Ragged Road to Abolition* that the economic devastation wrought by the many battles fought in New Jersey contributed to this development. As the economy began to recover, the numbers of enslaved persons in New Jersey actually grew.[19] Gigantino asserts that Governor Livingston "identified the state's decision to sell the remaining confiscated loyalist slaves at auction at the end of the war as the 'fatal error' that doomed abolition in 1785. Their sale gave a 'greater sanction to legitimate the abominable practice.'"[20] As the trajectory of the new nation was launched, the crucial either/or decision regarding Black freedom was decided by the state in favor of slavery. Gigantino concludes, "The decision to sell loyalist slaves therefore opened lawmakers to charges of hypocrisy if they forced abolition after profiting from the state's own slaves, resulting in few working to advance black freedom. After abolition's 1785 failure, slavery grew increasingly pervasive in both New Jersey and New York."[21]

Some whites dissented as individuals from owning enslaved persons. Governor Livingston of Elizabeth freed his two enslaved persons, because of "the national liberties of mankind, and in order to set an example."[22] A woman named Lucie was given her freedom in 1795 from Cavalier Jouet, who admitted slavery was in contradiction "with the Precepts of Humanity and of the Christian Religion."[23] Yet these were rare acts. Slavery remained a huge profit-making institution policed by the state. An advertisement in 1802 for an Elizabeth runaway named "Phillis" warned that any person helping her "may rely upon being dealt with according to the law."[24]

The Gradual Abolition Act of New Jersey was finally passed in 1804. It stated that as of July 4, 1804, every child born from an enslaved person in the state would be free. However, the child remained the "servant" of its mother's master until that person became twenty-five years old if male,

18. Smith, *Racism in the Post-Civil Rights Era*, 8–9.

19. Gigantino, *The Ragged Road to Abolition*, 65–66.

20. Gigantino, *The Ragged Road to Abolition*, 67.

21. Gigantino, *The Ragged Road to Abolition*, 67.

22. Crew, *Black Life*, 11.

23. Crew, *Black Life*, 11; Thayer, *As We Were*, 169–70.

24. See Herbst, *New Jersey: The Afro-American Experience*, 10.

and twenty-one if female. *Prior to this age, the white master could sell or trade the labor of a Black child to whomever they wished, including to the deep South.* This allowed whites in New Jersey to sell Black children for profit to Southern plantations.

Congress voted to end the international slave trade in 1808, but the domestic slave trade and institution of slavery subsequently grew. The enslaved Black population in the nation was about one million in 1808. It increased to four million by 1860. Many children were sold from New Jersey to the South, especially to New Orleans, where there was growing demand for slave labor in cotton cultivation. Participation by New Jersey whites in the interstate slave trade continued well into the 1850s. This was the "other underground railway" in which white gangs "legally" and illegally abducted Blacks in New Jersey and sold them as enslaved persons in the South.

Other ties between New Jersey and slavery included the highly profitable market to provide goods for slave plantations by the state's manufacturing industries. Newark was called a "Southern workshop." Among products sold were shoes, carriages, saddles, harnesses, and clothing to Southern plantations by New Jersey businesses. This continued into the 1860s.[25]

With these strong investments in slavery in New Jersey, the next major legislation against it did not come until 1846. The law that year replaced the word "slavery" with "apprenticeship for life." It stated that children born to apprentices for life were now formally free and no longer bound in service to the mother's "master." It removed the enslaver's right to sell the services of apprentices to others without the signed consent of the apprentice. The law gave Black apprentices access to limited education and the right to seek legal redress against their enslavers for grievances. Two hundred twenty-five years after the Dutch first brought Africans in bondage to New Jersey, laws regulating their violent enslavement had come back to apprenticeship.[26]

Yet this law again stopped short of abolition. It allowed Blacks to continue in bondage in New Jersey until 1865, later than any other Northern state. During the Civil War, the New Jersey legislature sought to sustain the state's economic profits from slavery by passing the notorious "Peace Resolutions," which disputed Abraham Lincoln's authority to free enslaved Blacks in the Confederacy.

New Jersey was the only Northern state to vote against Abraham Lincoln for president both in 1860 and 1864. In 1865, the legislature refused to ratify the Thirteenth Amendment which abolished slavery. In 1868, the legislature rescinded its ratification of the Fourteenth Amendment, which

25. Wright, *Afro-Americans in New Jersey*, 14–16, 25–28; Farrow, *Complicity*, 139–55.
26. Wright, *Afro-Americans in New Jersey*, 28; Farrow, *Complicity*, 139–55.

guaranteed citizenship rights for everyone born in the United States. It also voted against the Fifteenth Amendment in 1870, which extended the vote to men of all races. *New Jersey was the only Northern state to vote against all three constitutional amendments.* When these amendments were finally passed by the majority of states, New Jersey was forced by federal intervention to abolish slavery and grant citizenship to Blacks.[27]

PRESBYTERIAN STANCES ON SLAVERY, C. 1700–1860

During the first one hundred years of New Jersey's history, Presbyterians largely endorsed slavery as sanctioned by the "providence of God." This was done in spite of earlier evangelical affirmations regarding the liberating effects of baptism for all humanity. It wasn't until the late eighteenth century that some Presbyterians openly opposed the institution of slavery. One Elizabeth Presbyterian who did so was William Livingston, governor of New Jersey during the Revolution. He tried in 1778 to pass legislation to abolish slavery in the state. Another Elizabeth Presbyterian who fought to eliminate the institution was Elias Boudinot, who urged Congress to abolish the slave trade and defend the rights of free Blacks. In 1807, he helped an ex-enslaved person put his narrative into a book which exposed some of the evils of the institution. The Rev. Jacob Green, a Presbyterian pastor in Hanover, New Jersey, preached a public sermon in 1779, "An Acceptable Fast," in which he strongly opposed slavery. He made slaveholding a barrier to Christian fellowship in the church of which he was pastor, though his church was later attacked and ransacked by whites for this public stance.[28]

The Rev. Samuel Miller opposed slavery in the early years after the American Revolution. He rejected the idea of colonization of Blacks to Africa as impractical. In a 1793 Fourth of July sermon, he declared, "Nor is it political slavery alone, that yields to the mild and benign Spirit of Christianity. Experience has shewn, that domestic slavery also flies before her, unable to stand the test of her pure and holy tribunal."[29]

In 1797, Miller delivered an address to the New York Society for Promoting the Manumission of Slaves. He appealed to the universal principles of human liberty, in which the law of God was seen to be in harmony with the Declaration of Independence: "It teaches us, in a word, that

27. Wright, *Afro-Americans in New Jersey*, 28–29; Zilversmit, *The First Emancipation*.

28. Murray, *Presbyterians and the Negro*, 12–15.

29. Murray, *Presbyterians and the Negro*, 14–15; Pingeon, "Slavery in New Jersey on the Eve of the Revolution."

love to man, and a constant pursuit of human happiness, is the sum of all social duty—Principles these, which wage eternal war both with political and domestic slavery—Principles which forbid every species of domination, excepting that which is founded on consent, or which the welfare of society requires."[30]

A crucial question for Presbyterian churches regarding slavery was the action of its judicatories. Judicatories could act either by issuing pronouncements which had teaching authority or through disciplinary action. Disciplinary action was crucial as a method for change as it enforced accountability. Tragically on the issue of slavery, the judicatories consistently refused to use disciplinary action, claiming it would threaten the unity of the church. Instead, the Presbyterian Church largely relied on pronouncement.

The issue of slavery was first raised at a meeting of the Synod of New York and Philadelphia in 1774. The Synod received a letter from New England ministers asking for funds to educate two Black students to go as missionaries to Africa. After vigorous debate, the synod voted to support the missionary project as "the will of God," but refused to take a stand on slavery. This reveals the tepid anti-slavery stance in the church's highest governing body on the threshold of the American Revolution.[31]

After the war, the Synod's Committee on Overtures met in 1787 to bring a resolution affirming liberty for whole the human race and to urge the synod to resolve that its churches and member "do everything in their power consistent with the rights of civil society, to promote the abolition of slavery, and the instruction of negroes, whether bond or freed." Yet the resolution was defeated by the larger synod, which endorsed universal human liberty, yet with the caution that freedom without preparation would be disastrous for Blacks. It urged members to give enslaved persons "such good education as to prepare them for the better enjoyment of freedom; and they moreover recommend that masters, wherever they find servants disposed to make a just improvement of the privilege, would . . . grant them sufficient time and sufficient means of procuring their own liberty at a moderate rate." Thus only gradual abolition was affirmed. Church members were urged to "use the most prudent measures, consistent with the interest and the state of civil society, in the counties where they live, to procure the final abolition of slavery in America."[32]

In 1793, a petition was presented to the new General Assembly of the Presbyterian Church by Warren Mifflin, a Quaker, calling for immediate

30. Murray, *Presbyterians and the Negro*, 14–15.
31. Murray, *Presbyterians and the Negro*, 17.
32. Murray, *Presbyterians and the Negro*, 17.

abolition of slavery. The assembly tabled his petition and adopted a reaffirmation of the weaker synod action of 1787. In 1795, it was asked to rule on the morality of slaveholders maintaining communion with non-slaveholders in the church. The assembly recommended that both groups join together in unity.[33]

By the end of the eighteenth century, the General Assembly had condemned slavery in the abstract while leaving it to local judicatories to apply these principles in practice. The result was that presbyteries followed the dominant stance toward slavery in the geography where they were located. Presbyterian churches in New Jersey endorsed gradual abolition and did not resist the expansion of slavery in the South. Presbyterian churches in the South tolerated and endorsed slavery. This was done in spite of notorious practices, such as one Southern Presbyterian congregation paying 1,410 pounds to purchase eight enslaved persons in order for them to labor in bondage to pay for their pastor's salary. New Jersey Presbyterians did not challenge the pronouncement of the Synod of the Carolinas who declared it illegal in 1796 "to admit baptized slaves as witnesses in ecclesiastical judicatories."[34] In other words, the unsupported testimony of non-white members concerning any matter, including violence done to them or their loved ones, would not be admitted into ecclesiastical courts.[35]

GENERAL ASSEMBLY OF 1818

Some historians claim that Presbyterian opposition to slavery reached a high point with the General Assembly of 1818, then there was a decline in the church's antislavery stance, until division at the time of the Civil War. The Assembly of 1818 did adopt an anti-slavery resolution, yet it endorsed colonization of free Blacks to Africa and supported the exclusion from ordained ministry of a key Presbyterian opponent to slavery, the Rev. George Bourne.[36]

The 1818 resolution stated that slavery was a violation of the law of God and the Golden Rule, and that it was the duty of all Christians to eliminate it. Yet the resolution sympathized not with the enslaved persons, but with the difficulties of white slaveholders. White slaveholders, it stated, genuinely wanted to eliminate slavery. But, "where the number of slaves, their ignorance, and their vicious habits generally, render an immediate and universal emancipation inconsistent alike with the safety and happiness

33. Murray, *Presbyterians and the Negro*, 16–18.
34. Gillett, *History of the Presbyterian Church*, 285.
35. Murray, *Presbyterians and the Negro*, 18.
36. Murray, *Presbyterians and the Negro*, 20.

of the master and the slave," this was necessarily a slow process.[37] Though
slavery might be a curse, abolition was the greater curse. "We cannot indeed
urge that we should add a second injury to the first, by emancipating them
in such a manner that they will be likely to destroy themselves or others."[38]

The anti-slavery resolution concluded with a call for Christians not to
censure slaveholders. It urged support of the American Colonization Society
to solve the problem of slavery through the exportation of Blacks to Africa.
Regarding accountability in practice for whites who inflicted terror and violence on non-whites, such as owning, torturing, or selling fellow Christians
and their children as enslaved persons, it left this to the discretion of local
sessions and presbyteries. By leaving enforcement to Southern polities and
leadership, Northern Presbyterians betrayed Blacks into the extraordinary
cruelty of chattel slavery.[39]

THE AMERICAN COLONIZATION SOCIETY

The existence of slavery in America always carried with it the possibility
that free Blacks might unite with others to seek liberation and justice. The
colonization movement was in part the fruit of white anxieties toward the
growing free Black population cloaked in religious discourse. With gradual
abolition accelerating, this movement sought to crush the growing agency
of free Blacks. Rather than repenting of America's original sin of slavery and
white supremacy, colonization sought to avoid the consequences by excluding Blacks to Africa.

The American Society for Colonizing the Free People of Color in
the United States (ACS) was established in Washington on December 21,
1816. The organization was co-founded by a Presbyterian minister, the Rev.
Robert Finley of Basking Ridge, New Jersey. It sought to unite whites of
diverse denominations, ethnicities, and creeds against the growing presence
of free Blacks. William Lloyd Garrison's *Liberator* commented, "in its ranks
have stood, hand in hand, the Presbyterian and the Quaker, the Episcopa-
lian and the Baptist, the Methodist and the Unitarian, the Universalist and
Infidel—the freeholder and slaveholder."[40] Many white churches passed
resolutions to support its work, including the General Assembly of 1818.

37. PCUSA, *Extracts from the Minutes of the General Assembly*, 5; Murray, *Presbyterians and the Negro*, 27.

38. Murray, *Presbyterians and the Negro*, 27.

39. Murray, *Presbyterians and the Negro*, 26–28.

40. Murray, *Presbyterians and the Negro*, 76.

Many churches began the tradition of taking collections for the ACS on the Sunday nearest the Fourth of July.

The ACS wanted to deny accusations of forced deportation, so they obtained land in Africa. The colony called Liberia was established on the west coast of Africa in 1818 and was promoted for colonization. By 1820, Liberia had a population of 12,000 free Blacks from the United States. The leaders of the ACS hoped for massive federal aid from the sale of Western lands to fund their movement. Colonization appealed to evangelical Presbyterians who affirmed white supremacy and exclusion of Blacks under the veil of spreading "Christian Civilization" through the providence of God. As one missionary put it, "We must save the Negro, or the Negro will ruin us."[41]

In 1833, the Presbyterian president of Centre College, John Young, expressed the hope that slaveholders would join with the colonization movement in sending Blacks to Liberia. Young said colonization would unite the North and South and stop the drift toward civil war. He envisioned a world divided into two spheres of influence for Britain and America, and believed that "Asia, in this great partition of benevolence, will fall to Great Britain; and Africa will be ours. By this holy alliance we can girdle the earth with a zone of light." In a future age, Young envisioned Blacks in Africa telling their children of the kindness of white Americans in restoring them to their native land: "I see those little ones raising their eyes glittering in tears, and asking with eager voice the name of that generous people. His answer is 'the Americans.'"[42] The export of free Blacks to Africa would overcome divisions between Northern and Southern whites in a new united venture of white supremacy.

Colonization appealed to whites in New Jersey. From 1852 to 1859 the New Jersey legislature appropriated $1,000 annually to transport free Blacks from New Jersey to Liberia.[43] In the South, colonization was viewed either as a support for the institution of slavery in removing free Blacks or it was attacked as a conspiracy to end slavery. One of the first ACS societies was organized in Princeton, New Jersey. Professor Archibald Alexander of Princeton Seminary was an ardent supporter who wrote a history of the movement. Presbyterian minister Rev. Robert Baird traveled to Great Britain and sought to defend white Christianity against criticism of its "toleration" of slavery. Baird argued that colonization of Blacks to Africa was the final solution to slavery. Some Presbyterians who were first attracted to colonization in the 1820s left in the 1830s. These included Albert Barnes,

41. Davis, *Inhuman Bondage*, 256.

42. Murray, *Presbyterians and the Negro*, 78–79.

43. Wright, *Afro-Americans in New Jersey*, 14.

Lyman Beecher, and William E. Dodge. Others, like A. T. McGill of Princeton Seminary, supported colonization even after the Civil War.[44]

Another Presbyterian, Rev. Brechinridge of Kentucky, proposed that free Blacks should be forcibly moved to Africa. Breckinridge preferred that Blacks emigrate voluntarily but said, "If it is our deliberate judgment that they ought to be removed, let us remove them. Let us so do it as for the common good of all—not sordidly and wickedly—but with a compassion and a conviction, as earnest as the force which necessity may oblige us to employ."[45]

The most effective resistance to colonization came from Black leaders in the North. This became visible immediately after the colonization movement began. In the 1819 memoirs of co-founder Robert Finley, a conversation in the afterlife is imagined which sought to answer free Black objections to colonization. This dialogue in heaven takes place between William Penn, Paul Cuffee, and Absalom Jones. In the exchange, Penn admits that some people are opposed to the idea of colonizing Blacks back to Africa, while Cuffee says that Blacks themselves are divided on the subject. Absalom Jones is introduced and he opposes the plan. Penn then consults with George Washington, who lends his weighty support to the movement. When Jones points out that Blacks have lived for generations in the United States, he is assured that no coercion will be used and that only those who volunteer will be sent. Penn argues that prejudice is very strong in America, and so Blacks will have little choice but to emigrate. Cuffee concludes by affirming that the great value in colonization is the evangelization of Africa.[46]

This dialogue reveal that as early as 1819, Black opposition to colonization was strong. Two Northern Black Presbyterian ministers, the Rev. Samuel Cornish and the Rev. Theodore Wright, wrote scathing critiques of colonization. They pointed out that free Blacks organized many meetings in opposition. At one in Philadelphia, it was voted "that all projects which contemplate our removal from the land of our birth and affections will be looked upon as SPECULATIVE, DETESTABLE, and TRAITOROUS."[47] Cornish and Wright argued that colonization was notoriously supported by slaveholders who wanted to get rid of free Blacks who were organizing against slavery. They ridiculed the idea that freed enslaved persons would bring Christianity to Africa. The authors said the real problem was the

44. Murray, *Presbyterians and the Negro*, 78–80.

45. Murray, *Presbyterians and the Negro*, 81–83.

46. Murray, *Presbyterians and the Negro*, 84–85.

47. Murray, *Presbyterians and the Negro*, 85.

demonic institution of slavery which must be fully and immediately abolished, without compensation for slave owners.[48]

Black abolitionists like Cornish of New York, Wright of Philadelphia, and the Rev. Henry Highland Garnet of New Jersey exposed the underlying racism of the ACS and demonstrated how it supported the slave system. They showed how their alleged "concern" for Blacks actually served to legitimate the "bedrock" assumption of white racism that Black sub-humanity was irrevocable. They pointed out that without free Blacks to subvert slavery and sustain the Underground Railroad, the slave system would be strengthened. They persuaded white abolitionists like William Lloyd Garrison to strongly denounce colonization and affirm that any effective anti-slavery movement "must accept the equal coexistence in America of Blacks and whites and combat racism in the North as well as bondage in the South."[49]

The growing abolitionism movement in the 1830s and 1840s was indebted to this resistance in the 1820s by Northern Blacks to Colonization, which culminated in David Walker's influential *Appeal to the Colored Citizens of the World* in 1829.[50]

With opposition growing in the North, the ACS could obtain only minimal governmental funds and had to depend largely upon private financing. The ACS was unable to achieve its goal of mass deportation of Blacks to Africa. Underlying the ACS approach was a pattern of contradiction and doublemindedness. The discourse of colonization denigrated the underlying worth of Blacks while claiming to help them as human beings. It denied the violent trauma of slavery and white supremacy, the contribution of Blacks to building America, and the fundamental hypocrisy of the movement.[51]

Andrew Murray writes that the "tendency to blame the sin of racial pride on the providence of God, was perhaps the most deadly legacy of the colonization movement. It encouraged a kind of respectable racism under the cloak of benevolence and was shocked when those it tried to help rejected their efforts for them." Murray continues, "It was a movement which enabled men to hold . . . mutually contradictory ideas at the same time, and to see them as the work of God's inscrutable providence."[52] Stanley Elkins writes that the Colonization Society's failure included its inability to satisfy white contradictions of guilt and moral cowardice: "The Society's ultimate

48. Murray, *Presbyterians and the Negro*, 85–86.

49. Davis, *Inhuman Bondage*, 258.

50. Davis, *Inhuman Bondage*, 257–58.

51. Staudenraus, *The African Colonization Movement*.

52. Murray, *Presbyterians and the Negro*, 82.

vulnerability lay in the fact that its program was designed for men who felt guilty about slavery but did not want to do anything drastic about altering the institution."[53]

THE RISE OF FREE BLACK CHURCHES, C. 1800–1850

As Blacks in New Jersey were gradually freed from slavery after 1804, their participation in Sunday worship grew. Segregation in white churches included separate pews, balconies, tables, and even Communion cups.[54] At Second Presbyterian Church, trustee minutes record that Blacks were moved in worship from standing in the aisles to sitting by the back wall, to sitting in the balcony. Why they were moved so frequently is not stated. For example, the trustee minutes of March 28, 1826, note: "Resolved, that the Committee of Repairs cause a bench of seats to be made and placed in the Gallery, along the northern wall for the use of the Colored persons attending this church instead of those seats now occupied by them."[55]

Many free Black churches were organized during this period. The move to separate congregations and ecclesial organizations occurred first in urban centers like Philadelphia and New York where free Blacks were settling in growing numbers. The movement unfolded gradually—racially separate congregations emerged, new publications appeared, then racially separate denominations and organizations were formed. Black church and political leaders in the New York region helped form the nation's first Black newspaper, *Freedom's Journal*, in 1827, which operated out of Mother Zion African Methodist Episcopal Church in New York City. The paper was dedicated to the cause of extending human freedom to all people. Black church and political leaders in the region united in 1830 to form the American Society of Free Persons of Color, which was designed to coordinate the Black abolitionist movements. During this period in the South, major slave revolts occurred, one led by Denmark Vasey in South Carolina in 1822 and another led by Nat Turner in Virginia in 1831.

The Rev. William Pennington was licensed in 1823 by the Presbytery of New Jersey to preach the gospel to Blacks in Elizabeth and Newark. In 1824, he was reassigned for reasons unknown to the island of Haiti.[56] It wasn't until the 1840s that free Black churches were legally instituted in Elizabeth. These

---

53. Elkins, *Slavery*, 180.
54. Banks, *The Black Church in the U.S.*, 12.
55. Second Presbyterian Church, *Trustee Records*, March 28, 1826.
56. Wright, *The Education of Negros in New Jersey*, 86–88.

included a Presbyterian church led by the Rev. Daniel Vandeveer and an African Methodist Episcopal church under the pastorate of the Rev. Alfred Lawrence. In September 1859, the First Colored Presbyterian Church purchased its own building in Elizabeth and was publicly dedicated. The Rev. Henry Highland Garnet from Shiloh Presbyterian Church in New York gave the keynote sermon. The African Methodist Episcopal Church in Elizabeth emerged during the late 1840s and was formally established in 1861 as Mt. Teaman A.M.E. Church (which was later a focal point of civil rights organizing in the 1960s). Siloam Hope Presbyterian Church began during the early 1840s as a missionary school of the First Presbyterian Church of Elizabeth. Formal ties were severed with First when the mission incorporated separately in 1866. The Rev. John J. Jackson served as their first pastor.[57]

ANTI-SLAVERY AND PRO-SLAVERY PARTIES EMERGE, C. 1830–1860

After the 1830s, Southern religious leaders increasingly sought to defend slavery based on biblical texts that condoned slavery during the Roman Empire, such as Col 3:22–25, Eph 6:5–8, 1 Tim 6:1, and 1 Cor 7:21–24. Southern apologists affirmed a white supremacist ideology that claimed slavery was not just a "necessary" evil, but a good thing for the enslaved persons as well as the "owners."[58] Southern white supremacists expelled and lynched abolitionists and censored anti-slavery literature. In the North, Black and white abolitionists organized to expose the radical evils of slavery along with renewed opposition to colonization. This led to a growing abolition movement which called for immediate, unconditional, and uncompensated emancipation of enslaved persons. The American Anti-Slavery Society was founded by Black and white abolitionists in 1833. Leaders such as Frederic Douglass and Harriet Beacher Stowe publicized the horrors and cruelty of slavery.[59]

EMANCIPATION, RECONSTRUCTION, AND JIM CROW SEGREGATION, C. 1860–1890

President Lincoln's Emancipation Proclamation in 1863 declared enslaved persons "forever free." After the war ended, civil rights legislation was passed

57. Crew, *Black Life*, 16–18.
58. Davis, *Inhuman Bondage*, 186–92.
59. Davis, *Inhuman Bondage*, 260–67.

in Congress in 1865. Federal troops were dispatched to the South to protect the voting rights of former enslaved persons and dismantle the Ku Klux
Klan. Blacks were able to participate in electoral politics for a brief period.
Yet the national battle against white supremacy and Jim Crow was just beginning. The federal government's reconstruction initiatives were deeply flawed,
and a rage of white terror ensued. In 1877, white allies in the North and
South betrayed the newly freed Blacks. In exchange for Southern electoral
votes in a deadlocked presidential election, the Republican party agreed to
withdraw federal troops from the South, ending reconstruction. President
Hayes's compromise of 1877 revoked the rights promised to Blacks at the
end of the Civil War.

Whites in the South sought to "redeem" their military defeat in the
Civil War by imposing a brutal tyranny on Blacks. Segregation laws, called
"Jim Crow" laws after a nineteenth-century minstrel song, were enacted,
setting up the South's elaborate system of white supremacy and segregation.
Northern whites segregated Blacks in many public accommodations. This
including schools, public transportation, restaurants, hotels, restrooms,
drinking fountains, playgrounds, and swimming pools. In 1883, the Supreme Court nullified the Civil Rights Bill of 1875. This set up the infamous
Plessy v. Ferguson decision of 1896 which approved the "separate but equal"
doctrine affirming the constitutionality of segregation and making it official
public policy. The court decision remained in force until the 1950s.[60]

POST-RECONSTRUCTION LYNCHING

A new wave of white killings of Blacks by hanging and burning started after
the end of Reconstruction. In just the years between 1884 and 1900 alone,
scholars estimate more than 2,500 lynchings of Blacks occurred, often to
cheers of white citizens, including religious and community leaders. These
public murders were carried out with the purpose of scapegoating and terrorizing Blacks to stay "in their place" in the white supremacist social order.
Southern mania for purity enabled the South to become both the nation's
"Bible belt" and the lynching capital of the United States.

Although most lynching occurred in the South, forty-six states reported lynching, including New Jersey where the KKK was strong through
the 1930s. A *New York Times* article in 1922 describes the procession during a Sunday worship service by five members of the KKK in white hoods
down the central aisle of Third Presbyterian Church of Elizabeth. The ritual
included the presentation of the American flag, a gift of money, and a note,
which the pastor received. He read the note publicly to the congregation.

60. See Litwack, *Been in the Storm*; Litwack, *How Free Is Free?*

It proclaimed, "white supremacy," "protection of white women," and "pure Americanism."[61]

IMMIGRATION AND EXPANDING BOUNDARIES OF WHITENESS

European immigrants coming to America sought to be included in the white supremacist social order, which included the "wages of whiteness." These wages included legal rights, such as the right to marry other whites, the right to testify against other whites and serve on juries, the right to equal public accommodations, the right to become naturalized citizens, and the right to vote and hold political office. David Roediger and others have shown how these nineteenth-century European immigrants, who initially defined themselves as Irish, German, Polish, or Italian, came over time to view themselves as "white." This entrance into the boundaries of whiteness in America allowed for the dissipation of European cultural diversity while denigrating the non-white as subordinate.[62]

Roediger and others argue that white elites responded to labor unrest among European immigrants in the mid-nineteenth century with an increased emphasis on solidarity for whites. Whiteness was expanded to include new immigrants to encourage their alliance with white business owners who had economic interests in the exploitation of free Blacks and working-class whites. Particularly striking was the way in which many Irish immigrants who had themselves been victims of racialized oppression became anti-Black in their attitudes and practices. Among the Irish and other European ethnic groups, this movement into the solidarity of whiteness and exclusion toward Blacks was fostered by political and economic organizations, newspapers, government, and cultural and religious institutions.[63]

In Elizabeth, practices of Black exclusion expanded during this period of nineteenth-century industrialization. Large influxes of Irish and German immigrants entered the city with an accompanying per capita decline in the free Black population. This decline occurred in spite of huge increases in employment in the city. During the decade of the 1830s, the construction of two major railroad lines in Elizabeth caused the city's infrastructure

61. See "Ku Klux Klan Takes $25 Gift To Church"; see McVeigh, *The Rise of the Ku Klux Klan*; Dray, *At the Hands of Persons Unknown*.

62. Roediger, *The Wages of Whiteness*.

63. Roediger, *How Race Survived U.S. History*, 64–98; Du Bois, *Black Reconstruction*. Roedigar draws from Du Bois's earlier description of the white "public and psychological" wage.

to rapidly develop. In 1835, Edward Kellog and other business elites from New York brought a tract of land in Elizabeth which they named the New Manufacturing Town of Elizabeth Port. Within two years, industrial development was accompanied by a massive influx of Irish immigrants. During the 1840s, the census shows large increases of Irish immigrants living in several city wards.[64]

Spencer Crew's research on Elizabeth confirms that as Irish immigrants moved to the city, they embraced anti-Black violence. Blacks in the city were further segregated into substandard housing and discriminated against in employment and education. Many Blacks chose to leave the city. Some went to the British colonies of Guiana and Trinidad. Representatives from these colonies advertised in Elizabeth newspapers and offered to pay emigration costs for Black workers. The influx into the city of German and Eastern European immigrants in later decades further heightened anti-Black violence. Many Blacks continued to leave the city.[65]

The First Presbyterian Church in Elizabeth started a literacy program in 1815 for the newly freed Black population. Rev. John McDowell and leaders of the church were hoping to "raise the tone of public virtue" and to "extend the means of knowledge" by establishing the Elizabeth Free School Association in November 1815.[66]

The first programs held by the group were in segregated classes, with both adults and children studying the Bible, spelling, and reading. To accommodate the growing interest of students, the group recruited volunteers and increased the frequency of classes from weekly to daily. The academic progress of the Black students was praised in annual reports of the Association. One report stated:

> These scholars have given a practical refutation of that slander which prejudice and selfishness have often cast upon the descendants of Africa, that they are destitute of talents and incapable of much mental improvement, and indeed this whole school presents practical refutation of this slander. It is doubted whether the same number of whites placed in similar circumstances of depression, ignorance and of the same age, could be selected in this or any country, who in the same time and with the same opportunities for study would make greater improvements.[67]

---

64. Roediger, *How Race Survived*, 12–15; Roediger, *Wages*, 15–20.

65. Crew, *Black Life*, 13–14.

66. Crew *Black Life*, 18; Thayer, *As We Were*, 218.

67. Crew, *Black Life*, 18–19.

Yet the school increasingly suffered from a lack of white support. The school's directors struggled to obtain funds to keep operating. In 1859, the integrated Free School Association at First Church closed.

NORTHERN SEGREGATION, C. 1860–1900

During the decades following the Civil War, Elizabeth experienced a growth in overall population and employment, yet a decline in the percentage of free Black residents. In 1860, there were 11,567 total residents in Elizabeth. In 1920, the population reached 95,783. Despite the rapid increase in employment, the Black population went from 301 residents in 1860 (2.6 percent of total) to 1,970 residents in 1920 (2.1 percent of total).[68]

This decline in the Black population occurred in spite of the fact that the city lay along the Southern-Northern route of the Pennsylvania, Erie, and B&O Railroads. Along this path thousands of Blacks traveled north for employment to Baltimore, Philadelphia, and New York. Yet as Southern Blacks arrived in Elizabeth, they were not welcomed. Housing in the city became even more segregated. Census figures show that after 1900 for the first time in its history several city wards had no Blacks residing in them. This trend of segregation continued throughout the twentieth century into the 1990s.[69]

In the economic sphere, similar patterns prevailed. Almost all manufacturing jobs went to whites in the city. In 1915, figures show that 82.9 percent of Black men were listed as common laborers, unskilled workers, or in service jobs. Among Black female workers more than 80 percent held service jobs.[70]

This was done in spite of Black resistance. Excluded from white-led organizations, Blacks formed religious, educational, and political institutions of their own. Soon after they received the vote, Blacks in Elizabeth started their own Republican organization. The first major organizational push came in November 1872 at a rally in Elizabeth's opera house. Several prominent Black speakers from around the state spoke, as did white leaders from the Republican Party. Blacks also organized to desegregate the schools and attain public appointments in the police department. In 1906, Black residents attempted to get Mahlon Gibbs appointed to Elizabeth's police force. They sent two petitions to the city council but were denied. Spencer Crew asserts that there was a pattern of "disregarding by city council

68. Crew, *Black Life*, 37–74.
69. Crew, *Black Life*, 69–70.
70. Crew, *Black Life*, 101–2.

members of the repeated requests by black residents for the appointment of an African American to the city police force."[71]

In 1910, the city made its first political concession to the Black community when the Board of Education appointed Mary Malson as the first Black teacher in Elizabeth's public schools. She taught first grade at School Number 7. Malson's grandfather came to the city in 1804 and worked for one of Elizabeth's prominent white families, the slave-owning Hatfields. The Malson family was one of the founders of the Siloam Presbyterian Church. Mary Malson was the first Black person appointed to a public position after two hundred and fifty years of Black existence in Elizabeth.[72]

BLACK RESISTANCE, C. 1900–1950

Black resistance to white supremacy in the twentieth century predated by four decades the civil rights breakthroughs of the 1950s. Blacks relentlessly battled Jim Crow by founding such organizations as the NAACP (1909), National Urban League (1911), Commission for Interracial Cooperation (1919), and the Association of Southern Women for the Prevention of Lynching (1930). The virulence of white supremacy and lynching during World War I transformed Black political consciousness and stimulated a new generation of activists. As Leon Litwack chronicles in his book, *How Free Is Free? The Long Death of Jim Crow*, resistance to Jim Crow was an odyssey of defiance and resiliency defined by everyday acts of courage.[73]

In 1942, the Congress of Racial Equality (CORE) was founded by two University of Chicago students who believed in nonviolent resistance. James Farmer was Black and George Houser was white. CORE conducted the first sit-ins by both Black and white students protesting discrimination in Chicago restaurants. The national organization was established a year later. In 1946, President Harry Truman agreed to create the President's Committee on Civil Rights by Executive Order. The following year Truman integrated the US military, yet the army delayed implementation until the middle of the Korean War in 1951.

Gradually more young people began to participate in political resistance. In 1947, the first Freedom Riders rode public interstate transportation in the South to test the 1946 Supreme Court decision that declared segregation in interstate travel unconstitutional. The two leaders of the Congress on Racial Equality, George Houser and Bayard Rustin, organized eight

71. Crew, *Black Life*, 184.
72. Crew, *Black Life*, 170.
73. Litwick, *How Free Is Free?*, 51–94.

Black men and eight white men to go together into the Upper South. This interracial team of freedom riders exchanged seats on interstate buses over two weeks, Blacks in front, whites in back, from Washington, DC, through the Upper South. Sometimes they were ignored and even supported. Other times they were arrested and attacked. CORE gained national recognition when four of the riders were arrested in Chapel Hill, North Carolina, for violating Jim Crow laws. Three riders were forced to work on a chain gang for twenty-two days. This later inspired a second major wave of Freedom Riders which challenged segregation in 1961.[74]

In the 1950s and early 1960s, several breakthroughs occurred in dismantling public segregation. In the midst of the Cold War, more nations began criticizing America for its treatment of Blacks. In 1951, fourth-grader Linda Brown wanted to go to the local school in Topeka, Kansas. But the nearest school was only for white children. When she was forced to go to the segregated black school a distance away, her father, the Rev. Oliver Brown, an African Methodist Episcopal pastor, sued Topeka Kansas school board on behalf of his daughter. In 1954, the US Supreme Court decision, *Brown v. Board of Education*, ruled for school desegregation nationwide, "with all deliberate speed." "Separate educational facilities," the high court declared, "are inherently unequal and unconstitutional."

In 1955, Rosa Parks, African Methodist Episcopal deaconess and NAACP branch secretary, refused to give up her seat to a white bus rider in Montgomery, Alabama. The Montgomery bus boycott led to a new civil rights organization in 1957, the Southern Christian Leadership Conference (SCLC). SCLC chose twenty-six-year-old pastor, Martin Luther King Jr., as its president, launching him as a national civil rights leader. That year, President Eisenhower signed into law the Civil Rights Act of 1957, reinforcing voting rights guaranteed by the Fifteenth Amendment. It was the first civil rights bill passed by Congress since 1875. In 1957, Congress also established an independent Civil Rights Commission. The commission conducted public hearings, prepared reports, and recommended new protections that would later be passed in the Civil Rights Act of 1964 and the Voting Rights Act of 1965. Through the courageous actions of those who organized, boycotted, spoke out, went to jail, and even died, these laws broke the back of legal segregation in the nation.

74. Litwick, *How Free Is Free?*, 95–100.

CIVIL RIGHTS MOVEMENT AND
WHITE BACKLASH, C. 1960–1990

After World War II, as Southerners journeyed north seeking jobs in the growing manufacturing sectors in the region, Blacks in Elizabeth grew to over one tenth of the population. Their visibility in conjunction with the civil rights movement began to threaten white hegemony in Elizabeth. As the civil rights movement grew in momentum during the late 1950s and early 1960s, public protests for equality in employment, housing, and education began in Elizabeth. Several white Presbyterian members recall that the NAACP demanded that white churches cease hosting minstrel shows. Some members claimed in the 1990s that these shows were mere fundraisers. "We were just having fun and raising good money for charity," one man who dressed in blackface lamented. "We tried to continue with the shows dressed as hobos, but it just wasn't the same."[75]

The year 1963 was a critical one in the struggle to overturn the three-hundred-year-old white supremacist regime in Elizabeth. Black-led protests against discrimination were conducted on unprecedented scale. They were organized by the Union County Civil Rights Coalition (UCC). The largest demonstrations took place at the intersection of the Union County Courthouse and First Presbyterian Church. This was the precise location where three Black leaders of a slave insurrection had been burned at the stake in 1741. At this intersection, the UCC confronted the white governor, mayor, county freeholders, and labor unions with nonviolent demands for racial equity in employment.

The campaign began in June 1963 with hundreds of protestors demonstrating at the construction site behind First Presbyterian Church. The protests were over the complete lack of Black employment in the seven major electrical, plumbing, and construction unions. These unions were contracted by the government with public money to build a $5.5 million courthouse annex. After a month of daily protests, in July 1963, construction on the courthouse was halted. Negotiations began between the Union Trades Council and the UCC. The Trades Council rejected demands for two Black apprentices to be hired by each union. Shortly after, both the annex construction and the protests begin again.

By early August, hundreds of protestors were walking to the Courthouse from the nearby African Methodist Episcopal Church and began to use civil disobedience to block the movement of trucks to the construction

---

75. Interview by author, Elizabeth, NJ, May 10, 1997. See Lott, *Love and Theft*. Lott interprets black-face minstrelsy as gendered cross-racial immersion which dramatized white working class hostilities, envy, and dread toward Blacks.

site. Many protestors were arrested. With the city in upheaval, Mayor Bercik asked New Jersey Governor Hughes to intervene and negotiate a settlement. Union County Freeholder Thomas Dunn publicly criticized Bercik and stated there was no racial discrimination against Blacks by the unions.[76]

Soon after, dozens of Black youth and adults chained themselves to the courthouse annex, halting construction. At this point, the unions agreed to negotiate, yet construction began again. Hundreds of demonstrators then practiced civil disobedience daily for the next two weeks in August. The Elizabeth police were criticized by civil rights leaders for using unnecessary violence while arresting protestors. On August 20, formal negotiations between the UCC, the unions, the mayor, and governor began, and the protests were halted. At this time, over 130 demonstrators had been arrested. Later that week, five thousand people from New Jersey, including Elizabeth, participated in the "I Have a Dream" march on Washington led by Martin Luther King Jr.[77]

Two days later, Governor Hughes and Mayor Bercik publicly called on the unions to hire a limited number of Blacks. In response, Dunn accused the UCC of conspiring with communists to undermine law and order. This was refuted by Black leadership. When the unions refused to make any concessions, civil disobedience at the site began again on September 9.

The UCC strategy was broadened to include white economic interests in the city. Hundreds of Black protestors begin marching peacefully on shopping nights on Broad Street, every Monday and Thursday night. Protests were expanded to include demonstrating against unions at private construction sites. These tactics made an impact, as in mid-September the seven unions agreed to conduct entry level tests for two Black persons per union. Yet the unions wanted sole control of the testing and scoring for the candidates. The coalition demanded that the tests be independently conducted. On the following day, September 20, hundreds of white youths attacked six hundred Blacks peacefully demonstrating on shopping night in Elizabeth. The whites used cherry bombs, rocks, and bottles to attack the nonviolent demonstrators. Two hundred police intervened, with many Blacks injured. No whites were arrested. This stands in sharp contrast to the public orders to "shoot to kill" used by Mayor Dunn a few years later against Blacks.[78]

The white moderate religious community began to publicly weigh in on the situation. In late September, a white Catholic priest called on civil

76. See "Police Haul Away Pickets."
77. See "New Jersey Puts 5000 in Washington DC March."
78. See "Police Bar Violence as Youth Rush Bias Marchers."

rights protestors to end the marches for the sake of law and order. *It was during this year that the Confederate flag was first placed in the Second Presbyterian Church front glass window.*[79]

One month later, the unions conceded on the issue of who would evaluate tests for new Black apprentices. The UCC officially ended protests on October 16. Over the six month campaign, they accomplished several objectives, including new jobs for Blacks in unions and an empowered Black community.

Actions of police and the white political backlash in November of 1963 revealed the deep investment in white supremacy and anti-Black violence in the city and state. After the elections, Union County Freeholder and City Councilor Thomas Dunn emerged as the spokesperson for the forces of white backlash in Elizabeth. Republicans had won new majorities in the state legislature and the Union County Freeholders. Dunn claimed that supporting Blacks and the New Jersey Fair Housing Bill was a mistake for Democrats. In a post-election interview with the *Daily Journal*, Dunn claimed that alliances with Blacks caused the defeat of Democratic State Assembly Majority leader James McGowan. Dunn criticized Democratic leaders on local and national levels for "molly coddling" Black civil rights leaders.[80]

The white political backlash continued the next year with the campaign and election of Dunn as "strongman" mayor of the city.[81] He held on to power for twenty-eight years, from 1964 to 1992. In 1967, Dunn proclaimed shoot to kill orders toward "Black rioters."[82] As Hispanic/Latinx grew in numbers in the city, Dunn declared that speaking Spanish at City Hall was forbidden.[83]

During Dunn's long reign as mayor there was a growing presence of organized crime in the city. Dunn was investigated several times by the federal attorney, yet always escaped indictment. Dunn hosted known leaders of organized crime in his backyard for a barbecue.[84] A white Presbyterian church member active in politics during this period said that during a meeting discussing a public works project, he heard the mayor say, "If this helps

79. See "Father Carter Urges Bias Foes to End Midtown Marches."

80. See "Republicans Win State Legislature and Union County Freeholders"; "JFK at Lowest Level Since Inauguration: Reason Civil Rights Factor."

81. See "Club Formed to Back Dunn, Mayoralty Race Hinted."

82. See Haggerty, "Elizabeth Police Top in Civil Control"; Ryan, "Jacinta Fernandes."

83. Smothers, "Thomas Dunn, 76, Longtime Elizabeth Mayor."

84. See Grutner, "Mafia Secrets Revealed in Federal Court by Transcript of FBI Bugging," 1; "Organized Crime in Elizabeth"; "Mob in Elizabeth Union"; Sullivan, "Gallagher Pleads Guilty to Tax Evasion," 1.

the n*****s, I don't want it!"[85] It is significant how this statement reveals not just a pro-white position, but a militantly anti-Black one.[86]

Not surprisingly, the KKK recruited in Elizabeth with the state Klan leader living in the city. Nor was it hidden knowledge, as the local newspaper declared, "Klan Leader Living in Elizabeth" in 1965.[87]

One Black man who grew up in the Elizabeth area said in an interview:

> Yes. You knew the Klan was around then. You knew the John Birchers were in positions of authority—in law enforcement, heavy into politics, even in the educational hierarchy. In eighth grade, I scored second in my whole grade level in Math and second in English. But nobody scored better than me in both. I had always wanted to be an attorney. I told my guidance counselor this. But he placed me in the vocational direction, into business curriculum. He put lies down about me on my record, like I did things that I didn't do. There were many like that in the schools. And we were pulled off the street often by the police, just for walking down the street and looking in a window. You don't understand what it is like until a policeman puts a gun to your head and you hear, "N****r, do you want me to shoot your fucking head off!" When we were marching, you'd see police lining up down the street ready to go, ready to come get you.[88]

85. George Taylor, interview by author, Elizabeth, NJ, May, 15 1998.

86. Carter, *The Politics of Rage.*

87. See "Klan Leader Living in Elizabeth"; "Elizabeth Drive Begun by Klan"; see also, Smothers, "Thomas Dunn, 76, Longtime Elizabeth Mayor."

88. George Taylor, interview by author, May 21, 1998.

5

Violent Innocence in the Post-Civil Rights Context

During 350 years of slavery and segregation, whites used the ideology of white supremacy and state-based violence—terrorism, police patrols, and lynching—to maintain a racialized social order. Free Blacks were profiled by whites with the burden of proof on Blacks to identify and prove they were not enslaved persons or criminals. As early as 1793, this practice was encoded in law through the passage of the Fugitive Slave Act. When slavery was abolished in 1865, whites developed written and unwritten codes of racial domination that were enforced by state violence and vigilante gangs for a hundred years. Practices of violence included rioting, torture, and public lynching. As these public practices were powerfully resisted in the civil rights movement, new forms of white supremacy took shape.

In *The First R: How Children Learn Race and Racism*, Joe Feagin and Debra Van Ausdale show how young people learn their first "R" not so much because "they are carefully taught," but by growing up in a particular social context:

> Racism surrounds us, permeates our ideas and conversations, focuses our relationships with one another, shapes our practices, and drives much in our personal, social and political lives. There are few social forces so strong. Children are neither immune to it nor unaware of its power. A social reality this mighty is bound to become an integral part of their lives, and thus it endures

from generation to generation, perhaps changing somewhat in
form but still strong in impact.[1]

Institutional racism endures in part because it is made up of socially accepted ways of "not seeing" oppression against non-whites. Institutions
reproduce social inequity which make underlying ideologies of whiteness
functional. This interplay of cultural meaning, structural injustice, and
mediating institutions is intentionally elusive. Normative forces of white
supremacy must deploy practices of exclusion toward socially constructed
"others" more covertly in the post-civil rights era.

   This historical narrative of New Jersey shows that the reproduction
of injustice is a historically mediated process, with each period having an
impact on the next. Seeds for post-civil rights racism in the present were
planted in the early 1600s with the enslavement and stigmatization of African populations. This became a central part of a racialized social order.
Dehumanization against non-whites was sustained by a religiously sanctioned system that claimed normative innocence reaching across societal
institutions. White supremacy revealed its expanding character by adapting
to include new European populations with the exclusion of the non-white
as a central point of reference.[2] When slavery was gradually abolished in
New Jersey beginning in 1804, and then by federal mandate in 1865, the
forces of white supremacy adapted with written and unwritten codes which
were enforced by state violence and vigilante gangs. White supremacy used
culturally and legally sanctioned methods of violence to maintain domination after slavery.[3]

   As these practices of Jim Crow violence were openly resisted, different
forms of more "covert" profiling against the non-whites took shape in the
criminal justice system. As Manning Marable summarizes:

> The informal, vigilante-inspired techniques to suppress Blacks
> were no longer practical. Therefore beginning with the Great
> Depression, and especially after 1945, white racists began to rely
> almost exclusively on the state apparatus to carry out the battle
> for white supremacy. Blacks charged with crimes would receive
> longer sentences than whites convicted of similar crimes. The
> police forces of municipal and metropolitan areas received a
> carte blanche in their daily acts of brutality against Blacks. The
> Federal and State government carefully monitored Blacks who
> advocated any kind of social change. Most important, capital

1. Van Ausdale and Feagin, *The First R*, 198.
2. See Roediger, *The Wages of Whiteness*; Rothenberg, *White Privilege*, 35–54.
3. Wright, *Afro-Americans in New Jersey*, 25–45; Davis, *Inhuman Bondage*, 327–31.

punishment was used as a weapon against Blacks charged and convicted of major crimes. The criminal justice system, in short, became a modern instrument to perpetuate white hegemony. Extralegal lynchings were replaced by "legal lynchings" and "capital punishment."[4]

After civil rights laws were passed in the 1960s, the patterns of scapegoating toward the racialized other began to play themselves out through forms that were more difficult to unmask. These post-civil rights forces of structural racism were expressed through white political backlash, neoliberal economics, environmental racism, housing segregation, policing, and mass incarceration. They converged to create a social ecology of *violence innocence* against the racialized other. We are still living with the consequences.[5]

ECONOMIC DEINDUSTRIALIZATION IN ELIZABETH, C. 1980–1990

By the mid-1980s in Elizabeth the white working class was grieving the loss and protections of manufacturing jobs, white ethnic neighborhoods, and networks of the past. They were living increasingly precariously to maintain their economic situation. They were filled with inner conflict as they measured their diminished value against those lives to which society seemed to give a higher premium. The white working class has been shown in studies by Sennet and Cobb and others to have a low sense of self-worth as measured against society's standards of ability and status. Many see themselves as lacking in economic and educational tools to combat the vicissitudes of life in an unfettered free market economy. At their work, they endure lack of agency and limited mobility in contrast to jobs associated with the middle and upper-middle classes, even though in some cases their incomes are "middle class."[6]

In predominantly white neighborhoods in Elizabeth, whites were clinging to whiteness as a defense against perceived marginalization. Many families were trying to hold together two and sometimes more paychecks to meet the widening income, healthcare, and pension gaps that were spurring the "disintegration" of their way of life. In this context of economic dislocation, the crisis of whiteness took the form of cynicism and despair so

4. Marable, *How Capitalism Underdeveloped*, 120–21.

5. Perkinson, *White Theology: Outing Supremacy*, 166: "To the degree white identity covertly mediates life chances, it simultaneously rations death encounters."

6. Sennet and Cobb, *The Hidden Injuries of Class*; Weis, *Class Reunion*; McDermott, *Working-Class White*; Newman, *Falling from Grace*.

pervasive that efforts at racial solidarity were openly rejected. Many whites gave up struggling with the cognitive dissonance of either "justice for all" or "white racism" and embraced the harmony of racial-ethnic scapegoating under the guise of victimization.[7]

Katherine S. Newman, in her book *Falling from Grace: The Experience of Downward Mobility in the American Middle Class*, studied Elizabeth and the 1982 closure of the Singer industrial plant as an example of "mass, community-based downward mobility—the ways in which plant closures affect the identity of workers and the communities they live in."[8] She observed, "Workers reflect warmly on 'the good old days.'" And yet she saw a collective sense of loss and grief—"that the best is behind us." Remarking that "the haunting shells of once-bustling factories . . . provoke the unemployed survivors and their neighbors to wonder whether the world they live in hasn't changed in fundamental ways—for the worse."[9]

The worst jobs in the Singer plant had long been held by Blacks. They had worked in the foundry which made cast iron parts for the sewing machines and employed up to a thousand people. The work had low pay and was dangerous, and it was the only part of the plant where Blacks could get jobs. They were segregated there from the rest of the workforce—until the early 1960s. Only with the political breakthroughs of the civil rights movement were Blacks allowed onto the factory floor with better paid and less dangerous jobs. Beginning in the 1960s, immigrants from Cuba, Haiti, and Central America also began to work on the factory floor. The integration of these non-whites into the Singer workforce coincided with federal equal employment laws barring discrimination in hiring, the civil rights demonstrations in Elizabeth, and, in 1967, race riots in Newark.[10] In the midst of their longing for the past and coping with consequences of economic dislocation, Newman observed much anxiety about their future:

> Blue collar workers . . . face the question of where (or whether) they belong in postindustrial America. Their dilemma is fundamentally different from that facing managerial workers or even air traffic controllers [whom she also studied]. The latter groups knew that, whatever their personal troubles in finding employment, the modern America needs people like them. But blue-collar men and women cannot respond with equal

7. Newman, *Falling from Grace*, 170–75; Reich, *The Work of Nations*.

8. These are Newman's descriptions of what people experienced confirmed by my own observations and interviews. Newman, *Falling from Grace*, 170–75.

9. Newman, *Falling from Grace*, 175.

10. Newman, *Falling from Grace*, 193.

certainty: they face replacement by robots or by low-paid workers in runaway shops around the globe and absorption into a service economy that promises them less money and less job security.[11]

The painful changes in the structure of the global economy—under historical and cultural conditions of structural racism—led many blue-collar whites in Elizabeth to blame Blacks and Hispanic/Latinx for their plight. As Newman observes, "Most of the old-timers owed their Singer jobs to family reputation and ethnic solidarity. Nepotism benefited the workers in that it offered them a degree of influence over the economic fate of their family members. Recruitment into the plant was strictly an ethnic affair."[12]

Now that this was ending—who was to blame?

Interviews confirmed the narrative of violent innocence, with racial-ethnic scapegoating becoming pervasive after the plant's closure. Here is how one former white worker interpreted the situation, "We more or less had to hire a certain amount of [Blacks] and for a time, Singer would cater to them more and they would get away with more. If they did bad work, instead of letting them know about it, they would cover up. But if you [a white] had done bad work, they'd lower the boom on you."[13] For white workers, the plant closing was a drama interpreted through white victimization. As Newman confirms, "When analyzing the demise of the Singer plant, ethnic antagonism became fertile ground for scenarios of blame that laid responsibility for the closure at the feet of 'undesirable' nonwhite workers." As one interviewee told her, "The new element in there. . . they weren't doing the work properly. Puerto Rican people and coloreds too, they have a different conception of working."[14] This was confirmed in my own interviews, "Blacks and Puerto Ricans ruined Singer," said one woman, "They made me lose my job and my apartment."[15]

The attribution of Singer's demise to the non-white workforce was reinforced by the declining social and economic conditions where the plant was located after it closed. One white man advised Newman, "The area that is our ghetto used to have a lot of hard working people in it, a lot of whom worked at Singer's . . . Have you taken a ride to the [plant]? Keep your doors

11. Newman, *Falling from Grace*, 175.

12. Newman, *Falling from Grace*, 182, 192.

13. Newman, *Falling from Grace*, 195.

14. Newman, *Falling from Grace*, 194.

15. Interview with author, Elizabeth, NJ, May 1998. Evidence from several studies confirms white racism among blue-collar whites. See Patterson, *Ethnic Chauvinism*; Halle, *American's Working Man*.

locked; if you hear a little bump on your fender, don't get out. If someone steps in front of you, run him over."[16] This was reminiscent of my experience crossing East Jersey Street with three Black teenagers and almost being run over by an unmarked police car.

Newman's analysis shows that decisions by executives to diversify Singer and move the industry to locations with cheaper labor costs, coupled with structural changes in the economy, were responsible for the closure of the plant. After World War II, Singer's female clientele increasingly went into the workplace, with less demand for domestic sewing. "This coupled with increased availability of inexpensive, ready-to-wear clothing, diminished the market for the machine. These losses spurred Singer to diversify to sectors such as military contracting and move its American manufacturing operation overseas."[17] These trends signaled larger changes in globalization in the United States which began in the late 1970s and accelerated in later years—of plants closings, massive layoffs of workers, and the shrinking of manufacturing industries such as machine tools, electrical appliances, steel, rubber, automobiles, and auto parts. In the year of Singer's closure in Elizabeth, there were 2,696 plant shutdowns, causing over 1,287,000 job losses in the United States.[18]

Although corporate profits soared as elites pursued global investments in technology, health, financial services, and elsewhere, the decline of the industrial sector in cities like Elizabeth with decent jobs, pension, and health benefits for the working class spiraled downward. Some commentators at the time, including President Reagan, defended the plant closures as the "creative destruction" of the free market.[19] These defenders of the oligarchy claimed that workers displaced by plant shutdowns could find better jobs in new sectors. Yet there is little evidence that displaced workers from these industrial centers found equivalent opportunities. On the contrary, in Bluestone and Harrison's study, *The Deindustrialization of America*, they show that only 3 percent of displaced workers from New England manufacturing industries found jobs in the region's new economic sectors. Their study concluded, "Losing one's job as a result of deindustrialization tends to propel one downward in the industry hierarchy toward lower productivity jobs—not upward."[20]

16. Newman, *Falling from Grace*, 196, 290.

17. Newman, *Falling from Grace*, 177.

18. Newman, *Falling from Grace*, 175–95; Bensman and Lynch, *Rusted Dreams*, 3.

19. Rothschild, "Reagan and the Real America," 12–18.

20. Bluestone and Harrison, *The Deindustrialization of America*, 97.

When the Singer plant closed, workers under age fifty-five lost all retirement benefits, even if they had worked for the company for thirty plus years. In looking for work, they faced an employment market in New Jersey which had lost thousands of jobs in manufacturing. What happened to the dimension of social misery for these people which was omitted from the calculus of the oligarchy and its defenders?

Studies of Ohio, Michigan, and Southeast Chicago show that as industrial plants close, their working-class communities unravel. Many small businesses dependent on the major industries went bankrupt. Generations from the same family who worked for these industrial plants and related businesses suffered not only material loss, but a diminishment of the "good" and "virtuous" as they perceived it. As unemployed persons, they were stripped of their daily work routines, social bonds, and generational goals that shaped social expectations and identity. They could no longer count on a steady income, health coverage, and a secure retirement for themselves and their families. Marriages and neighborhoods were torn apart with increasing domestic violence, drug use, alcoholism, and crime.[21]

Immersed in this dislocating existential anxiety, many white people chose the underlying option of whiteness to blame the racialized other. Most studies of deindustrialization in the United States do not look through the lens of structural racism to examine forces that direct economically dislocated whites into racial scapegoating.[22] Yet in Elizabeth the option of violence—under the guise of white victimization—was very present. It provided a "common sense" (sense of the community) interpretation of their suffering and economic alienation. This epistemological clinging to anti-Black violence under post-industrial conditions of inequity played itself out especially with the more vulnerable members of the non-white community.

ENVIRONMENTAL RACISM

> *They have a problem out there in the suburbs, and that is that they have no landfill space. So, they're going to build an incinerator, and 127 trucks a day will drive through this neighborhood bringing the trash of the county in to be burned amongst us. The people went away and sent us back their rubbish; they sent us back their trash and their sewerage and . . . anything they didn't want. And*

21. Bensman, *Rusted Dreams*, 5–10.

22. Bluestone and Harrison's *The Deindustrialization of America* is one example. Other studies that look at the social costs of plant closures without including the dynamics of white racism include Gordus et al., *Plant Closing*; Buss and Redburn, *Mass Unemployment*.

then they say to us, "Well, how come you're not coming back?"
Well, I want to say, "You got your foot on my neck; that's why I
can't stand up."
—Fr. Michael Doyle[23]

Amidst economic deindustrialization, white flight, and growing racial diversity in Elizabeth, forces of environmental racism increased after Singer closed in 1982. As with other cities experiencing industrial decline in New Jersey—such as Camden, Newark, Trenton, and Patterson—white elites turned to dumping hazardous wastes in poor neighborhoods. The ground breaking study of toxic waste by the United Church of Christ revealed these rising patterns of racial and class disparity in the distribution of hazardous wastes were even greater than reported.[24] The realities of environmental racism were confirmed by several other studies.[25]

These practices assaulted the more vulnerable—young mothers, pregnant women, children. This was undergirded by a rising national policy of "welfare reform," with declining public assistance that curtailed resources available for survival. The value of public assistance and minimum wage fell radically in real monetary terms during this period, depriving many families of minimal means of life. Corporate media launched assaults against the premise that the poor were even deserving of public support.[26] Media caricatures of the "welfare queen" and "Willie Horton" were lifted up as tropes of non-white criminality. The term "underclass" was used more often by conservative scholars, suggesting a permanence to poverty that defied social intervention.[27] Elites claimed they were morally justified in expanding their privileges. One sociologist, Norman Fainstein, wrote in 1995, "For whites, the physical ghettoization of nearly all blacks, along with the media focus on the 'worst' black neighborhoods and the most socially deviant elements in them has reinforced a stereotyped image of black people . . . equating blacks with criminals and welfare mothers, whites are freed from guilt or even sympathy."[28]

It is helpful to specify the "atmosphere" of life and death in Elizabeth. There was an elevated fourteen-lane highway running through the city—the

23. Quoted in Gillette, *Camden after the Fall*, 95.

24. Bullard et al., *Toxic Wastes and Race at Twenty*, 10.

25. Bell, *An Invitation to Environmental*, 119–20.

26. Gillette, *Camden after the Fall*, 3–4. See also Jargowsky, *Poverty and Place*, 48, 144.

27. Examples of these include Gilder, *Wealth and Poverty*; Murray, *Losing Ground*; Herrnstein and Murray, *The Bell Curve*.

28. Fainstein, "Black Ghettoization and Social Mobility," in Smith and Feagin, *The Bubbling Cauldron*, 137.

New Jersey Turnpike built in the 1950s—which contributed deadly exhaust fumes to poor neighborhoods and effectively divided the city in two. There were three runways from Newark Airport in Elizabeth adjacent to these neighborhoods—built in the 1970s—which contributed an estimated seven times the pollution of the Turnpike. There was the nearby Bayway Refinery which had expanded in size since the late nineteenth century. Glimpses of the refinery at night resembled scenes from Dante's *Inferno*—huge flames, belching wisps of smoke, acidic odors (at least three distinct smells), and, during the month of December, bizarre holiday lights draped over the multi-sized smokestacks.

Regarding the air quality in Elizabeth, one cleric with a PhD in bio-chemistry from Harvard, the Rev. Joe Parish, said, "You can buy bottled water, but you can't buy bottled air. The air quality in Elizabeth is simply unacceptable for human health."[29] According to Parish, truck, car, and plane traffic in the Elizabeth area engendered some of the highest concentrations of ground level ozone east of the Mississippi River, among the highest in the United States.

The multiple refuse incinerators in the region also contributed to this problem. Over two billion pounds of garbage, medical, and industrial waste were incinerated over Elizabeth releasing a variety of compounds burned into the air. For example, the dioxins produced by these incinerators ex-acerbated the already critically polluted air, inflamed human lung tissue, reduced immune function, contributed to the onset of asthma, emphysema, and cancer, and interrupted the gestation process of infants.[30] Several stud-ies on similar areas concluded that air pollution is especially harmful to pregnant women and children. They found that air pollution is so danger-ous that it can kill.[31] According to the Elizabeth Gazette and Joe Parish, the rate of childhood asthma in the city increased annually in the 1990s. The general population in Elizabeth had an estimated incidence of respiratory disease of over 35 percent and a cancer rate double the national average.[32]

29. Joseph Parish, interview by author, Elizabeth, NJ, June 9, 1997. See Hwang et al., "Childhood Asthma Hospitalizations."

30. Joseph Parish, interview by author, Elizabeth, NJ, June 9, 1997.

31. See Mortimer et al, "The Effect of Air Pollution"; Kim et al., "Ambient Air Pollution."

32. Parish, "Environmental Update"; and email correspondence, May 30, 2010; see State of New Jersey, "Air Toxics."

HOUSING SEGREGATION

The decline of the city's ecology occurred while state wide patterns of "white flight" and housing segregation were rising. The segregation of the poor into urban areas excluded them from resources in the more affluent suburbs. In an assessment of housing trends in the nation, Massey and Denton, in *American Apartheid*, agreed with the Kerner Commission, "No group in the history of the United States has ever experienced the sustained high level of residential segregation that has been imposed on Blacks in large American cities for the past fifty years."[33]

According to the University of Minnesota's Myron Orfield, segregation by class and race in urban geographies like Elizabeth "destroys the lives of children in poor schools by depriving them of opportunity, intensifies health risks and crime, and destroys the urban fabric and the fiscal base of cities."[34] Although the migration of middle and upper-middle income Blacks and Hispanic/Latinx from urban areas to suburban areas in the nation increased to about one-third of these populations by 2000, this failed to overcome larger structural forces of segregation for the other two-thirds of Blacks and Hispanic/Latinx.

During this period, New Jersey became one of the most segregated states in the nation by class and race.[35] Residential segregation in New Jersey was shaped in part by white backlash to Supreme Court decisions in 1975 and 1983, known as *Mount Laurel I* and *Mount Laurel II*. These landmark decisions led to state laws that prohibited local zoning practices which excluded low-income housing and required suburbs to provide their "fair share" of affordable housing. Yet white suburban political influence created two critical loopholes. First, responsibility for overseeing the affordable housing process shifted from court-appointed judicial monitors to a state administrative agency, the Council on Affordable Housing (COAH). This agency was more vulnerable to political pressures through its selection by the sitting governor. Second, the legislature approved a device known as Regional Contribution Agreement by which any town could be relieved of up to half its affordable housing obligations by paying money to a city or other town. What followed was a process of power politics and cunning litigation used to sabotage fair housing laws. Affluent white suburban towns

33. Gillette, *Camden after the Fall*, 5. The Kerner Report was released in February 1968. It said, "Our nation is moving toward two societies, one black, one white—separate and unequal."

34. Gillette, *Camden after the Fall*, 6.

35. Gillette, *Camden after the Fall*, 185; see Cohen, *A Consumer's Republic*, 228–40.

across New Jersey successfully evaded their affordable housing obligations and the court ordered mandate to achieve desegregation.

An analysis of this process published in the *Seton Hall Law Review* in 1997 showed that the landmark court decisions had done almost nothing to achieve desegregation of the state's poor non-white populations. In its implementation, the affordable housing program was overwhelmingly used by young white suburbanites seeking starter homes and by elderly whites seeking affordable housing to meet new limits set by retirement.[36] Arnold Cohen, coordinator of the state's Affordable Housing Network summarized, "It's not that there isn't a need to provide housing for such groups. But when it began, one of the main ideas of the program was to provide lower income people with an opportunity to live where there were more jobs."[37] Another housing analyst wrote that New Jersey fair share housing laws "failed to integrate neighborhoods and, indeed, has perpetuated segregation."[38]

In his study *Poverty and Place*, Paul Jargowsky concludes that patterns of residential segregation in suburbs are the institutional context that supports other racially discriminatory processes—such as racial profiling, incarceration, environmental racism, and economic discrimination—and binds them together into a system of white supremacy. Until segregation in suburban housing is changed, dismantling racial inequality in other areas will be limited.[39]

RACIAL PROFILING IN ELIZABETH POLICING

New Jersey's failure to desegregate its suburbs and provide affordable housing is also the context for practices of racialized policing in cities like Elizabeth. A glimpse of these patterns in Elizabeth can be seen through documentation that surfaced in court records and sworn testimony regarding police profiling against Black and Hispanic/Latinx persons.

In 1982, the year in which the Singer Manufacturing Plant shut down, a secret white group called "The Family" was formed by police officers in Elizabeth, supposedly as a white study group preparing officers for police exams. The group surfaced in 1994 when a dozen officers staged a "sick out" over the growing influence of the Family within the department and their intimidation

36. Wish and Eisdorfer, "The Impact of Mount Laurel," 1303; Gillettte, *Camden after the Fall*, 169–80.

37. Gillette, *Camden after the Fall*, 175–76.

38. Gillette, *Camden after the Fall*, 175–76.

39. Gillette, *Camden after the Fall*, 5–6.

of other police.[40] The officers were particularly upset about the group's grow-ing control over the allotment of overtime and other police practices. These protesting officers complained that leaders of the group had harassed police who resisted their influence and practices. The protesting police distributed fliers in the station with about seventy names of the people they said belonged to the Family. This dispute prompted a departmental investigation, yet the official inquiry focused not on investigating the Family—but on the coura-geous police who had protested! Retired police lieutenant Daniel Wood later acknowledged this bias of police leadership toward the Family and the ac-companying conspiracy of silence regarding racist practices: "The department had no interest in investigating the Family or its activities."[41]

While the actions of the Family received favorable treatment by the department hierarchy, this was effectively hidden from the larger public. Throughout the decade, the Elizabeth police had gained a reputation among Black and Hispanic/Latinx activists and public defenders for practices of ra-cial profiling, brutality, planting of drugs, and making false arrests of young Black and Hispanic/Latinx men. During this period, the department had only four Hispanic/Latinx and no Blacks among its sixty superior officers. It was an overwhelmingly white force policing a mostly Hispanic/Latinx and Black city.[42]

When community activists learned of the group's existence in 1998, it was seen as an organized expression of the larger police culture and prac-tices of white racism in the city. Black and Hispanic/Latinx residents had told horror stories about Elizabeth police brutality, excessive and arbitrary use of weapons, planting drugs, and selective enforcement of drug deal-ing. Because of public protests, press conferences, and subsequent lawsuits, there were further investigations into the Family conducted by the police department, Union County prosecutors, and in 2000 for the *New York Times*. A secret grand jury report in 1998 said that nearly *one-fifth of the 370-member Elizabeth force* belonged to the Family. Officers on the police force testified under oath that the group led by the day shift commander Lieutenant Szpond conducted bizarre initiations and rites of entrance—and held threatening excommunication rituals for those who resisted racist codes of behavior. In several criminal prosecutions and internal depart-mental inquiries, members of the Family were accused of threatening Black and Hispanic/Latinx officers, controlling promotions and overtime, perva-sive racial profiling, brutality, and planting drugs on Blacks and Hispanic/

40. Hedges, "Blue Shadows in Elizabeth."
41. Hedges, "Blue Shadows in Elizabeth."
42. Hedges, "Blue Shadows in Elizabeth."

Latinx men. One apparent member of the Family, Mary Rabadeau, served as Elizabeth police director and was later promoted to chief of the New Jersey Transit Police Department. She acknowledged in an interview with the *New York Times* in 2000 that she had belonged to the Family, but characterized it as a study group.[43]

The existence of the Family had also become visible in 1998 during the criminal trial of an Elizabeth policeman, William Burdge, who was indicted on an assault case of an unprovoked attack on a sixty-seven-year-old woman and her brother. At his trial, Burdge claimed that he had attacked the woman and her brother after drugs were slipped into his drink at a local bar. He claimed that the Family had been behind the action. Officer Burdge was convicted, but his allegations prompted the grand jury report—which publicly confirmed the existence of the Family. It said that the group tried to run much of the department's business. The cautious report said that the activities of the group were "most disturbing," and that they did not "further the legitimate goals of law enforcement."[44]

Daniel John Sargent, an Elizabeth police sergeant, said, "There was a subversion of standard police practices. There was escape from punishment if there was wrongdoing because they were members. There was a numbers game, trying to make narcotics arrests for promotion."[45] It was also uncovered that after the 1994 police protest against the Family, Elizabeth's newly elected mayor Chris Bollwage (who defeated Mayor Dunn) had ordered that Szpond be removed from his position as day shift director. One policeman Maloney said, "When Eddie was moved to the basement, it didn't solve the problem, but it made it much more difficult for him to recruit people."[46]

An examination of the sworn testimony given by police during the internal investigations reveals the extreme culture of racial violence by Elizabeth police. Szpond and other police leaders continually referred to Blacks in ugly racist ways; they called the department's patrol cars "panzer columns," and they declared in meetings that if Hitler were alive he would have rewarded them with an Iron Cross. Glimpses of the white solidarity and codes of behavior in the police are found in the sworn testimony given by William Capraun during the 1998 internal police investigation. According to the transcript, Capraun said he met Szpond at the house of Mary Rabadeau, the interim director of the Elizabeth Police Department and later

43. Hedges, "Blue Shadows in Elizabeth."

44. Hedges, "Blue Shadows in Elizabeth." Burdge claimed that he attacked the elderly people because he had become disoriented by the drugs and thought he was breaking into his own home that night.

45. Hedges, "Blue Shadows in Elizabeth."

46. Hedges, "Blue Shadows in Elizabeth."

chief of the New Jersey State Transit Police. There Capraun was asked to join the Family. Szpond told him with whom he could speak and even associate with on the police. Years later, Capraun was "excommunicated." "I want to go on the record," Capraun testified, "saying I'm a victim of extreme, bizarre behavior that went unchecked for twelve, thirteen and God knows how many years, that . . . completely, ultimately destroyed this department."[47]

In October 1998, a Black Elizabeth police officer Leon Thomas, allegedly shot himself in the head in his apartment. The bullet was fired under suspicious circumstances. Thomas had been arrested the day before by Elizabeth police at a drug store. He had been working off duty as a security guard, and was leaving his shift when police arrested him for stealing items they said he put on the ground under his car. Thomas left behind a nine-page detailed letter naming numerous instances of police planting drugs on suspects, obviously worried that something might happen to him. According to his mother and sister, he kept a journal of extreme racist practices by Elizabeth police and said he was going to give it to prosecutors.

After his death, local prosecutors investigated. Thomas Manahan, the county prosecutor, said in a statement that his office had checked into Thomas's claims, but the investigation was closed because there was insufficient evidence to warrant prosecution. But Thomas's family, as well as other Black police in whom Thomas confided, remained unconvinced. Three officers, Tracy Finch, Michael Brown Sr., and Lateef Banks, said Thomas told them before his death that he kept books full of detailed notes describing false arrests and violence used against Black and Hispanic/Latinx persons in Elizabeth. Officer Thomas's sister, Tawana, said the books had been taken by the Elizabeth police from her brother's apartment after his death, and that only one page had been left. That page of notes described a September 1996 arrest in which a Black suspect was brutally beaten by three Family members. The officers then planted drugs on the suspect to justify the violent arrest.

Tawana Thomas said, "The notebooks had logs detailing police wrongdoing and discriminatory treatment by the Family since the day of Leon's hiring." Community activists and public defenders said the same names of certain police officers kept coming up when they heard complaints of police brutality and false arrests. "There are a number of Elizabeth police officers who usually work in teams who account for an excessive amount of very suspect drug busts," said James Kervick, who headed the public defender's office in Elizabeth during the 1990s. Kervick said there was a pattern of inconsistencies in

47. Hedges, "Blue Shadows in Elizabeth."

the police reports over the years, revealed by the consistent statements made by his clients disputing certain officers accounts of drug arrests in Elizabeth.[48]

Sergeant John Guslavage, a veteran of thirty-one years on the Elizabeth police force, contended that the Family protected racist behavior—*and distributed drugs in the community.* In 1995, Guslavage sued the Elizabeth police department under the state's whistle-blower statute, claiming that they shut down a drug investigation to protect members of the police. The City of Elizabeth and the Police Department denied the allegations in court filings. But according to the suit, Guslavage, then a member of the police narcotics unit, was investigating drug sales in Elizabeth in 1994. During the investigation, evidence surfaced that narcotics officers, all members of the Family, were present during the drug deals. But when Guslavage reported that information to his superiors, the investigation was ended. Guslavage took his evidence to the United States Attorney in Newark. But federal prosecutors turned the information over to local prosecutors, who then gave it back to the Elizabeth police. Guslavage wound up being accused by his own department of having gone "out of the chain of command." The sergeant was removed from the department's narcotics unit and suspended. Guslavage would not expand on his lawsuit's accusations, saying he feared retaliation.[49]

The *New York Times* story on the situation showed how broad the problem was in Elizabeth. "What amazes me," said retired police lieutenant Daniel Wood, "is that they have gotten away with this for so many years." Hassen Abdellah, a Black lawyer, agreed, "I hear frequent reports that the police use excessive force . . . use the derogatory N-word while on duty and plant drugs on suspects. This has produced widespread feelings of fear and apprehension."

Richard Mixson, a twenty-seven-year-old father of three, said he was falsely arrested in February 1997 by two police—both identified as members of the Family—who planted drugs on him. Mixson, who worked nights as a janitor for Merck, in Rahway, New Jersey, said he was outraged. At the trial, he was acquitted. He then sued the police department, hoping to force the courts to examine the conduct of the police. "I have many friends who can't get jobs, can't serve on juries and who have reached a dead end because they have records they do not deserve. It is criminal what is going on here, and even with the risk of a three-year jail term if I lost, I decided it was time someone in our community stood up to them."[50]

48. Hedges, "Blue Shadows in Elizabeth."
49. Hedges, "Blue Shadows in Elizabeth."
50. Hedges, "Blue Shadows in Elizabeth."

MASS INCARCERATION

Racial profiling in policing contributes to mass incarceration among target-ed populations. Because police consistently search for criminal contraband primarily among the Black population, they will arrest a disproportionate number of Blacks with contraband. The reverse picture of incarceration would emerge if police arbitrarily targeted another group. According to a federal study in 2000, whites were 71.3 percent of crack cocaine users in America, yet comprised only 5.7 percent of those arrested for crack pos-session. Blacks, on the other hand, were only 17.7 percent of crack cocaine users, but comprised 84.2 percent of those arrested![51]

It is important to note that racial profiling first surfaced as a public is-sue in relation to the rapid increase in the rates of unemployment and mar-ginalization among young urban Black males in the late 1980s. This group became increasingly racially profiled and incarcerated during this period. This in turn contributed to new levels of stigmatization in the media.

Martin Free observes that in the twentieth-century trajectory of incar-ceration by race in state and federal prisons, it was not until 1989 that Blacks became the majority. The racial composition of those in American prisons went from 79 percent white and 21 percent Black in 1926, to 57 percent white and 42 percent Black in 1981, to 27 percent white and 55 percent Black in 1993.[52] This trend has been accompanied by the criminalization of the urban Black male in mainstream culture by the media and conser-vative politicians. At the heart of this new type of politics was a political trope: crime meant urban, urban meant Black, and the war on crime meant a bulwark against the increasingly political and vocal racial other by the predominately white state.[53]

A study of prime-time television in 1996 revealed that Blacks were shown more frequently in the menacing "offender" role than in the sympa-thetic role of "victim." The opposite was true for whites. Overall, the image of offender-to-victim ratio in national news was two times higher for Blacks than for whites. In national news, this ratio was four to one. These findings are consistent with other studies of the media.[54]

By the late 1990s, the patterns of policing were such that incarceration rates of Blacks increased even more rapidly during the Clinton years than they did under the Reagan and first Bush administrations. Incarceration

51. Harris, *Profiles in Injustice*, 23.

52. Free, *Racial Issues in Criminal Justice*, 45.

53. Free, *Racial Issues in Criminal Justice*, 46–47.

54. Escholz, "The Color of Prime-Time Justice," 71.

continued to rise under the second Bush administration. Martin Free argues the purpose of policing in America is devoted not primarily to criminal "justice," but to maintaining white solidarity and legitimacy as the social group in power. By identifying Black males as "social enemies," largely deserving of criminal punishment, social policies are developed to contain the threat from these enemies. Such policies are inherently inadequate to the task of affecting real social change. This lack of effectiveness and misallocation of social resources perpetuates derogatory racial attitudes and punitive actions against a constant supply of racially coded offenders. It regenerates "moral" outrage and fear from the "victimized" white community, that is, violent innocence. As a result, states spend far more on incarceration than on education, jobs, and employment training. The department of corrections has become the single largest state expenditure across the nation.[55]

The dominant but unspoken context of these regressive criminal justice policies and practices is race. As Michael Hallet observes,

> To deliver up bodies destined for profitable punishment, the political economy of prisons relies on racialized assumptions of criminality such as images of black welfare mothers reproducing criminal children and on racist practices in arrest, conviction, and sentencing patterns. Colored bodies constitute the main human raw material in this vast experiment to disappear the major social problems of our time. The prison industrial system materially and morally impoverishes its inhabitants and devours the social wealth needed to address the very problems that have led to spiraling numbers of prisoners.[56]

These patterns suggest that certain segments of society benefit from the vicious cycle of racializing crime. Insofar as the highest priority of the criminal justice system becomes the arrest, conviction, and punishment of crimes by non-whites (as opposed to white corporate or political elites), this shapes cultural meaning of normality and deviancy. As public perceptions and interpretations of crime by race shape American culture, they trigger an increased probability that non-whites will be racially profiled. This increases the likelihood that more non-white persons will be detained and incarcerated, which increases social marginality, and further limits employment and political organizing possibilities. This in turn increases cycles of re-offending which further shapes public perceptions of deviancy and stigma.[57]

55. Free, *Racial Issues in Criminal Justice*, 70–71.
56. Free, *Racial Issues in Criminal Justice*, 50–51.
57. Free, *Racial Issues in Criminal Justice*, 52.

Racial profiling can thus be viewed as a social expression of a vicious pattern of institutional white violence against non-whites manifest in the post civil rights era. It is a concrete expression of an American cultural-political trope which, as Free summarizes, is a bulwark "against the increasingly political and vocal racial other by the predominately white state."[58]

58. Free, *Racial Issues in Criminal Justice*, 47.

6

Portraits of White Racism

People who shut their eyes to reality simply invite their own destruction,
and anyone who insists on remaining in a state of innocence long after that
innocence is dead turns himself into a monster.
—James Baldwin[1]

In *Portraits of White Racism*, David Wellman addresses the normative question of what is at stake culturally for the white community in the post-civil rights era. He explores the meaning of whiteness in relation to resistance to racism by non-whites. He acknowledges that whiteness is about maintaining social power and privilege but asserts, as many do, that it is also a component in the construction of cultural identity and meaning. In particular, he asks what it means to be white when the other is symbolically marginalized. How are the white self and community socially constructed when the other is culturally scapegoated? Based on his research in California and Brooklyn, Wellman argues that white identity as whiteness has always been constructed on a largely negative basis. It is more an identity of what one is not, rather than what one is. He summarizes, "Racism is a structure of

1. Baldwin, *The Price of the Ticket*, 89.

134

discourse and representation that tries to expel the Other symbolically—
blot it out, put it over there in the Third World, at the margin."[2]

This structure of whiteness and violence takes different forms in different contexts. These contexts are shaped by economic, social, and cultural forces. It is different, for example, in Berkeley, California, than in Bensonhurst, New York. Yet both highly educated white students in Berkeley and working-class whites in places like Bensonhurst express the underlying identity and pattern of excluding the racialized other. According to Wellman, in the early 1990s in Berkeley, being "American" meant not being for affirmative action; in Bensonhurst, it meant not having Blacks visible in one's neighborhood. In both places, being "American" means not being Black. These constructions of whiteness by definition exclude and marginalize the racialized other. Yet the category of being white as normal is taken for granted. The life world of white "Americans" is normality rather than their whiteness. The privileges of being white are not seen as collective advantages, but as "the way it is."[3]

Yet since the civil rights movement, this normative sense of being white and "American" has been more directly contested by people of color who through social, political, and moral visibility directly confront these assumptions. As a result, whites have begun to feel white, which can be a deeply unnerving and dizzying experience for many. According to Wellman, students at Berkeley and working-class whites in Bensonhurst both feel victimized as whiteness is no longer taken for granted in the United States. Their identity as besieged victims in fact has grown as the conflict over the meaning of "America" and "whiteness" has intensified.[4]

Thomas Merton, in *Conjectures of a Guilty Bystander*, prophetically affirmed what is at stake for the white community under conditions of resistance by people of color to normative white identity:

> Blaming the Negro: this is not just a matter of rationalizing and verbalizing. It has become a strong emotional need for the white man. Blaming the Negro gives the white a stronger sense of identity, or rather it protects an identity which is seriously threatened with pathological dissolution. It is by blaming the Negro that the white man tries to hold himself together. The Negro is in the unenviable position of being used for everything, even for the white

2. Wellman, *Portraits of White Racism*, 243.

3. Wellman, *Portraits of White Racism*, 245.

4. Wellman, *Portraits of White Racism*, 246; Thandeka, *Learning to Be White*, 137. Thandeka examines the class dimensions of white shame. "My approach begins elsewhere . . . in [how] the Euro-American child learns to think of itself as white as a self–protection against racial abuse from its own community."

man's psychological security. Unfortunately, a mere outburst of
violence will only give the white man the justification he desires.
It will convince him that he is for real because he is right.[5]

In other words, the endangered white self and community have an increasing moral stake in provoking and blaming the non-white to mask their own
tribal violence and privilege. Such stigmatization is used to hold together
the insecure life-world of whiteness which is at serious risk of dissolution
through confrontation with people of color as equals in a more just multiracial society. The need for justifying anti-Black violence with stigmatization
is a long-standing objective of ideological white supremacy. As Joe Feagin
writes, "Whites need to constantly legitimate the mistreatment of people
of color and defend their self-construction as actors and observers in anti-
black dramas."[6]

THE UNDERLYING RACIAL COVENANT

I agree with Charles W. Mills who argues that with the advent of European
colonialism over the last five hundred years, European peoples developed
an underlying "racial contract" to justify white exploitation of "nonwhite"
populations and lands. He argues that this racial contract, which included
the hierarchical classification of human races, emerged as an ethos of domination and subordination over indigenous peoples. This racialized covenant
and social order is to be distinguished from earlier fragments of xenophobia
and ethnocentrism.[7]

Mills's notion of the racial contract incorporates the normative dimension of whiteness and "innocence" which accompanied the underlying violence of subordinating indigenous peoples. In moral terms, it points
to the truth of the Black folk aphorism: "When white people say, 'justice,'
they mean 'just us.'" This overarching covenant by which white supremacy
was defined as "normal" infected categories of religion and justice. Western
conceptions of ethics and spirituality were distorted by this ideology and
underlying racial contract. Because this racial contract was present at its
conception, assumptions of the modern social contract contain internal
contradictions and flaws which serve to sustain racial hierarchy and subordination of non-whites. According to Mills, these violent contradictions
between theory and practice obfuscate the struggle for racial justice and

5. Merton, *Conjectures of a Guilty Bystander*, 33.
6. Feagin, *Systematic Racism*, 228–29.
7. See Mills, *The Racial Contract*.

human flourishing. As Mills puts it, "Apparent racist violations of the terms of the social contract in fact uphold the terms of the Racial Contract." The latter words are put in capital letters in order to emphasize their dominance in everyday life.[8]

VIOLENT INNOCENCE AS INTERSUBJECTIVE DECEIT

If white racism is about maintaining group position, it is also about the defense of a conception of being human that defines the self largely by what it is not. James Baldwin first noted that being white in America means never having to think about it. Toni Morrison also wrote, "It seems both poignant and striking how avoided and unanalyzed is the effect of racist inflection on the subject."[9]

Joel Kovel argues that whites in the United States unconsciously reject "Blackness" because they project their own repressed hostilities rooted in childhood processes onto the otherness of the Black community. In this socialization process, whites are taught consciously and unconsciously that Blackness symbolizes dirt, danger, laziness, and violence. Anti-Black impulses, he claims, are profoundly shaped by these forces of the psyche. White racism in thought and practice weakens the empathy that people need for healthy intersubjective relationships. The "others" are no longer regarded as "us." Blacks become less than human, as inscribed in the three-fifths clause of the United States Constitution. White privilege is thus rooted in deceit about the white self and community that dehumanizes the other. This breakdown of empathy creates the social conditions for racial profiling and institutional racism.[10]

Christopher Bollas, an American-born psychoanalyst based in England, also explores these dynamics of intersubjective violence with emphasis on the mask of innocence. He suggests that the desire for innocence is a particular characteristic of the American psyche. Bollas recounts Arthur Miller's play *The Crucible*, when Miller used the Salem witchcraft trials to express his outrage over what was occurring in the McCarthy era:

> In the third act of the play, to my mind the most harrowing moment in American drama, Abigail [the accuser] is confronted by Mary Warren, one of her girlfriends. Mary reveals the girls'

8. Mills, *The Racial Contract*, 4.

9. Morrison, *Playing in the Dark*, 11.

10. Kovel, *White Racism*, xl–xlii; Feagan, *The White Racial Frame*, 109–10.

culpability [in falsely accusing others of being witches], and an infuriated Abigail assumes the position of innocent witness to the presence of evil, as stricken, she says, "A wind, a cold wind, has come." In the seventeenth century this signified the presence of the devil, and everyone looks at Mary, who—"terrified, pleading"—yells, "Abby!"—knowing now that Abby is setting her up to embody evil. Eventually Mary joins the now hysterical group of young girls who mime the devil's somatic influence.[11]

Bollas elaborates on the dynamics of violent innocence between subject and other. "By provoking the other, the violent innocent stirs up distress, ideational density, and emotional turbulence in the other, a simple self sponsored by the sadistically cool and 'objective' complex self, detached from the other's anguish."[12]

He gives the example of a patient who consistently denied her conflicted emotions and deeper complex self. Bollas struggled with this patient's evident self-disclosures yet unwillingness to own them. Unsuccessful in liberating her repressed emotions through interpretation, he began to focus on the transference in the relationship as he experienced it. Bollas gradually understood the complex dynamics of violent innocence:

> The (innocent self) sponsors affective and ideational confusion in the other, which he or she then disavows any knowledge of—this being the true violation. The recipient is invited to sink into an intense lonesomeness, where feelings, thoughts, and potential verbalizations have no reception. Here the recipient sits at a doorway, between . . . intersubjective existence, where a fundamental question is posed: "Am I alive to the other to whom I speak, or am I dead to be there—in intermediate space—to live only in my carefully managed land dehydrated internal world?"[13]

These are the intersubjective dynamics of what I call post-civil rights "violent innocence." The experience of the recipient can be likened to having wasp eggs implanted in one's intestines—and experiencing them hatch over time—while the other disavows any responsibility. W. E. B. Du Bois's description of being entombed behind the invisible but horribly tangible plate glass window of whiteness comes to mind. The recipient is further betrayed by the denial of culpability. "He [or she] has been disturbed by the actions

---

11. Bollas, *Being a Character*, 166.
12. Bollas, *Being a Character*, 169.
13. Bollas, *Being a Character*, 181.

of the other who projects something into him or her, or who evokes an unprocessed mental content."[14]

The mask of the innocent self so fiercely denies ant-Black violence that this intersubjective trope could be called "people of the lie." That is, the greater collective evils in society are accomplished by those people who are not publicly labeled "criminal," but who hide behind the big lie which masks underlying dynamics that direct others toward such label. When whites claim they are "just like babes," completely ignorant in regards to the history and dynamics of white racism and its consequences—is this not the trope of violent innocence? That is, the wearing of an innocent "simple" self that hides the more sadistic self and community, "detached from the other's anguish."

As the young teenager in Elizabeth learned during the ritual of violence on Broad Street: those coming up against the plate glass window "may scream and hurl themselves against the barriers . . . in a vacuum unheard and their antics may actually seem funny to those outside looking in."[15] Accompanying the big "lie" is negation, cynicism toward the other, an absence of hope. "Beneath the structure of the projective identifications . . . there is a profound despair and an insidious cynicism."[16]

VIOLENT INNOCENCE AS IDOLATRY OF WHITENESS

This thesis of violent innocence in post-civil rights whiteness can be grounded theologically by appropriating the thought of H. Richard Niebuhr on value and social sin. Throughout his writings, Niebuhr affirmed that human persons and communities are historically conditioned agents oriented by social interpretations and practices of faith in relation to centers of value. Niebuhr defines faith in terms of embodied trust in relationship, quoting Martin Luther, "Whatever then thy heart clings to and relies upon that is properly thy God."[17] Drawing on Jonathan Edwards, Niebuhr affirms that human persons and communities inescapably make some value *supreme*, even if it is the narcissistic value of one's self or social group. In Niebuhr's typology, henotheistic faith focuses the supreme *center* of value on its own social group, which then profoundly shapes practical reasoning and moral behavior.

14. Bollas, *Being a Character*, 181–82.

15. Du Bois, *Dusk to Dawn*, 131.

16. Bollas, *Being a Character*, 185.

17. Niebuhr, *The Meaning of Revelation*, 17.

Niebuhr asserts that institutional religion must be approached with deliberate ambivalence as to its true center of value. "Revelation is not the development and not the elimination of our natural religion," he says, but its necessary "conversion and permanent revolution."[18] Where historic communities shaped by henotheistic faith seek the transcendent to ratify their unjust privilege, the God of Jesus Christ continually resists and protests the idols of nation and tribe. Therefore, "revelation is the beginning of a revolution in our power thinking and our power politics."[19] Henotheistic faith seeks only the good that will protect its tribal community over against the other, but Jesus Christ reveals the good which interprets and gives to others in relation to *the total community of being*, which includes all humanity and creation.

In *Radical Monotheism and Western Culture*, Niebuhr further developed this theme of social communities in relation to historic centers of value. According to Niebuhr, radical monotheism apprehends through conditioned historicity that God, the power of being, is also the redeemer of the center of value in history. Therefore, historic communities of moral concern are not inevitably closed societies or social groups but are called into trusting relation to the community of being through God's gracious action. Christian ethics are then matters of living trust and covenantal responsibility in dialogue with being.

In *The Responsible Self*, Niebuhr expands this model of responsibility by portraying human agents as *responders* to actions that impinge upon their total life context. Different centers of interpretation support differing ethical visions of the total interaction in which human beings respond in time. For example, where a white racist faith commitment predominates, people imagine themselves and others in the midst of moral interaction in primary relation to their white tribe and other loyalists to its cause of supremacy. Radical monotheistic faith imagines a broader ethical discernment where human action in social communities is trusting response to the total action of a gracious God in the cause of the kin-dom or beloved community for all. Yet for henotheistic centered faith, Niebuhr affirms, the prevailing vision of interaction and interpretative response to others and Other is as threat of nothingness and death.

In fact, this study shows the dominant white community in Elizabeth repeatedly interprets itself as threatened and perishing. The practical reasoning that follows is shaped by this desperate cause of keeping whiteness and privilege alive. From this perspective on value, white henotheistic devotion practices racial profiling and nihilistic violence toward the other (and

18. Niebuhr, *The Meaning of Revelation*, 17.
19. Niebuhr, *The Meaning of Revelation*, 139.

ultimately the Other) as manifestations of *bad faith*. This communal existential stance of distrust shapes practical reasoning regarding public life and civic values in service to its fear of death. As survival of the *white privileged community* is made the primary lens of interpretation, "secondary" values of human dignity, justice for all, constitutional rights of the accused, and due process are reinterpreted into this ethical matrix.

White privilege as ultimate value then hijacks religious discourse to cover its nihilistic violence. Without this clever religious cloak, the underlying pattern could be more easily exposed for what it is: brutal loyalty to whiteness as supremacy. Whiteness in this way also uses the authority of the state to sustain domination. As the police participate in this white survival ethic, their "protect and serve" trope is perverted into tribalism, and they become yet another social gang—albeit with greater power and justification for its violent practices.

7

Christian Social Witness

Christian reflection must help frame the responsibility that people have toward one another not only as individuals, but as members of social groups. In this narrative, I have gathered fragments on the structural forces of race and class by which the group in power creates division and negates the other to maintain domination. A crucial part of how this is accomplished in the post-civil rights context involves "violent innocence" through mystification and scapegoating.

This historical narrative seeks to learn from the experience and resistance of those who are being scapegoated. As some, such as Traci C. West, have argued, ethical theory must learn from concrete experience and practices from below, while theory shapes and informs practice. Christian ethics is most effective when it is both aware of concrete vulnerabilities and captivities to situated evil (such as violent innocence) and dedicated to the efficacy of Jesus Christ (God's grace) in liberating the real neighbor and self.

This learning builds on the critical-responsibility model of Martin Luther King Jr. I am arguing that a central task of Christian witness is *critical responsibility* for the neighbor. That is, to engage both in radically *critiquing* the social order while also responding to the neighbor here and now. To sacrifice *effectiveness* in loving the neighbor in the present is to divorce responsibility from Christ's commission to love the real neighbor "on the road to Jericho" (Luke 10). This neighbor seeks release and liberation not as pure religious or moral action. This neighbor seeks liberation in the form of effective action and salty practice, i.e., practice that stirs up existential courage in community.

The other pole of this dialectic is *radical criticism* of the social order which includes deconstructing subjugating assumptions of that order. That is, Christian reflection must analyze interlocking structures and patterns of violence that oppress the self and neighbor. To be *effective*, this *criticism* should be done concretely, that is, in ways that are socially and culturally comprehensible. Therefore, classes, polities, and nations are analyzed and addressed, as well as individuals.

POST-CIVIL RIGHTS RITUALS OF WHITE RACISM

In this historical narrative of New Jersey, we have glimpsed how white planters sowed seeds of destruction over four centuries ago. These social constructions of race were reifications laden with moral meaning. After the gains of the civil rights movement, these forces of white racism adapted and used *social rituals of violence toward the other, especially in criminal justice,* which distort communal identities and dehumanize public practices. The ability to retain domination via ritualistic mechanisms of negation under the mystification of law and order is *violent innocence*. It is a habitus of deceit by which forces of racial idolatry use state mechanisms to dehumanize and subordinate the other. Rooted in the historical sewer of white supremacy, it shames the non-white poor in particular. It manufactures rituals and games which are contrary to the meaning of human dignity before God.[1]

White supremacy and exploitation of the poor, theologically speaking, are fallen principalities, expressions of the last enemy, death. They play God and dehumanize others under the cloak of false innocence. This narrative of Elizabeth reveals how their bitter fruits crush human persons. As such, they deny "the liberating, humanizing, reconciling work of Christ, the promised one who has taken on human form."[2]

In the 1990s, the privileges of the top 10 percent of the population increased exponentially while decimation of the poor in America was occurring. During this time, the elite solidified control of over 75 percent of the nation's economic wealth, including 90 percent of all stock.[3] Decisions were made which shaped not only the political economy, but the criminal justice system and other social institutions which engendered sacrifice of

1. Bonilla-Silva, *White Supremacy*, 103–10.
2. Boesak, *Black and Reformed*, 104.
3. Hobgood, *Dismantling Privilege*, 4.

the other. This trend was seen in Elizabeth through deindustrialization, environmental racism, housing segregation, policing, and mass incarceration. The sword of state was far from a neutral force. Rather, its monopoly over "legitimate" coercion was used to enforce a racialized social order. State violence against the non-white poor was exemplified in the young man's brutal beating by the police near the church window. These post-civil rights "now you see it, now you don't" practices are glimpsed through the experience of those directly affected. As one young man severely beaten by the police said, "White people are going crazy today because they fear there is nothing for them but nothing."[4]

The implications of white nihilism are real, especially for the next generation. As the population of the nation approaches majority non-white status, the animosity latent in whiteness will raise its ugly head anew with increased violence. Followers of Jesus Christ are called to resist these forces with the gospel of radical neighbor love. Christians cannot retreat into sectarian enclaves of left or right that hide from the powers of racism and social misery. This means claiming the salty courage of unmasking and engaging this principality in all realms of life. The mirror of reflection and sword of agency must be wielded with truth-love.

Though the *bondage* of white racism is real, for Christians the *efficacy* of Jesus Christ in history (and beyond history) is real and ultimately decisive. This is revealed through everyday resistance in places like Elizabeth, which means in Hebrew "dedicated to God." Christians often underestimate the former (bondage of white racism) in the real church as well as the latter (efficacy of Christ) in pluralistic society. Denying situated hope in Christ to attain a leaven of justice for the neighbor in society, or to resist forces of greater injustice, is not helpful. Lack of participation strengthens the forces of white nihilism and weakens the forces of resistance to idolatry and social misery.

RESISTING THE ETHIC OF NON-PARTICIPATION

George Hunsinger and other theologians argue that sectarian trends of turning away from discipleship in society in the name of communal piety shuns a demand to discern differences between true and false words being lived outside the church. It places human lives at risk, as demonstrated in Germany in the 1930s and 1940s.[5]

This historical narrative teaches that dynamic boundaries between church and society can take a different course from which people think

---

4. Doug Murray, interview with author, Elizabeth, NJ, September 20, 2009.

5. Hunsinger, *Disruptive Grace*, 84–85.

they can discern. For example, Southern white church leaders denounced King for violating law and order through his practices of costly discipleship which led him to a Birmingham jail, while social justice seekers, who were both doubters and believers, engaged in courageous resistance with King. Some members of white churches support "law and order" incarceration today, while others outside the church institution resist these deadly practices. In other words, neighbor love is as neighbor love does.[6]

There is no dimension of life outside the realm of God's gracious command to love the self and neighbor. The true *koinonia* is where partnership is practiced on the road without constrictions of religious purity. This road is provisional and dangerous; it includes housing projects, police stations, prisons—all of life. Refusal of responsibility for the neighbor at hand is renouncing the sovereignty of God.

The sectarian ethic underestimates Christ's efficacy in prophetic witness in the pluralistic, modern world. The breakthroughs embodied by the civil rights movement were forged through courageous partnerships of diverse communities. Such breakthroughs of compassion will not be sustained by retreating to ecclesiastical fortresses or sectarian orthodoxies. The tendency to denounce liberal democratic practices, in fact, only reinforces sectarian walls of monologue. Some in the fold of orthodoxy reject participation in democratic practices of citizenship because such practices do not privilege the proclamation of Jesus Christ. In so doing, they reject the kind of pluralistic society that emerged historically as Christendom gave way to secularization. Such an ethic allows individuals and churches to maintain their identity as "Christian" while participating in rituals of racism in society. They are given religious fig leaves, so to speak, to deny reality.[7]

In contrast to the sectarian approach, Traci C. West in *Disruptive Christian Ethics* constructs a pluralistic method of resistance and hope that breaks through elitist assumptions about how ideas for ethics are generated. She affirms a social ethic that begins with the concrete experiences and conditions that trap socially marginalized people in society. This experience of the downtrodden rather than the powerful must shape universal ethical norms that are relevant to the entire society. Christian ethics should attend to concrete practices and experiences before the generic abstractions of the good and just. They should critically unmask and deconstruct multiple layers of degrading assumptions about gender, race, class, and disability which breed human exclusion. And they should analyze what is needed to

6. Rasmussen, *Earth Community, Earth Ethics*; see Matthew 25 for an eschatology and ethics that encourage this approach.

7. Stout, *Democracy and Tradition*.

resist and transform them. Doing so in practice includes learning from the experience and narratives of those who are marginalized and who resist. Ethical theory needs concrete practice to be authentic and truthful, and practice needs theory so that it may better confront and resist. Christian ethics should be in critical dialogue with both social theory and practice to reveal negative assumptions hidden in both, as well as strategies of hope for human justice and flourishing of creation.[8]

In the present time, Christians must seek to overcome the cynicism and division regarding social justice action that infects many. Cynicism and division are not allies of Christian discipleship. This study confirms that the sociocultural rituals of violent innocence greatly contribute to the cynicism which masks vice with virtue and enables duplicity in rhetoric by leaders. This double-mindedness engenders a Christianity that is serviceable to the powers that be, which binds to the status quo, rather than being transformational. The goal of Christian ethics is not to externally Christianize the social order. Christians must challenge and dialogue with pluralistic communities in shaping a shared public ethic. Truthful dialogue and action with the marginalized are core elements. Dialogue must occur between Elizabeth teenagers, for example, and those seeking core understandings of justice. Christian ethics must practice a method that helps Christians build a shared ethic with non-Christians, and find ways to break through the plate glass windows that reproduce oppressive conditions and tolerance for sustaining these conditions.[9]

RESPONSIBILITY: EXPANDING KING'S LEGACY OF RADICAL LOVE

Among the existential resources available today to garner resistance to white racism and nihilism, King's legacy of radical love for the neighbor and costly discipleship is among the best. This is demonstrated in his lived hermeneutic of Jesus' parable of the good Samaritan.

In this parable, the boundary between church and society is liminal. Jesus does not distinguish between two such realms in the command to love thy neighbor. In the parable's introduction (Luke 10:26), Jesus uses a technical term regularly used by the scribes or lawyers when consulting one another about a matter of the law: "What is your reading of it?" The lawyer gives the correct theoretical answer, the necessity of loving God and his neighbor (v. 27). He then asks the question, "Who is my neighbor?" (v. 29),

8. West, *Disruptive Christian Ethics.*
9. West, *Disruptive Christian Ethics.* See introduction and chapter 3.

which prompts Jesus into giving this parable which radicalizes the notion of neighbor on the road to Jericho.

Scholars agree that in the time of Jesus, the road from Jerusalem to Jericho was notorious for its dangers and was called the "way of blood" because of the violence perpetrated there. The behavior of the priest and the Levite toward the neighbor ("near one") in the ditch on this dangerous road is described in terms of myopic self-centeredness and theological-ethical vision. As servants of the temple, custodians of religious worship and interpreters of the law, their moral imagination was constricted by excessive concern with religious purity and the temple cult. This played itself out in practice with neither time nor risk for the other in the ditch. The ugliness of this neglect and denial of responsibility toward the other is exposed when, surprisingly, the despised Samaritan is introduced as the one concerned, attentive, and compassionate. The Samaritan practices love toward the other by delaying his journey, expending energy with the binding of wounds, and spending two days wages—with the assurance of more.

The presupposition of the parable is that the other in the ditch is there by no fault of their own, but by thieves and robbers—and the bulldozer forces they represent—who beat and stripped this man half dead.[10] Ceremonially unclean, socially outcast, and religiously a heretic (from the dominant Jewish perspective), the Samaritan's faith and practice toward the other in the ditch is oppositional to the actions of the lawyer and priest. Jesus alters the lawyer's "innocent" question of who is my neighbor to: Who proved to be neighbor? The implications of denial and imperative of responsibility are exposed for the lawyer—and hearers of the text. Jesus commands, "Go and do likewise."[11]

Dr. King, in his last public words spoken before he was murdered in the city of Memphis, appropriated this parable in teaching Christian ethics to the church and nation. He focused on the aspect of the Samaritan breaking through the racial barrier through "*dangerous unselfishness*." King said,

> You remember that a Levite and a priest passed by on the other side. They didn't stop to help him. And finally a man of another race came by . . . We rented a car and drove from Jerusalem down to Jericho. And as soon as we got on that road I said to my wife, "I can see why Jesus used this as the setting for his parable." It's a winding, meandering road. It's really conducive for ambushing. That's a dangerous road. And you know it's

10. Who are these robbers and thieves and the forces they represent, today? This book is in part an answer to that question.

11. Mays, *Harper's Bible Commentary*; Keck, *Luke*.

possible that the priest and the Levite looked over that man on the ground and wondered if the robbers were still around. Or it's possible that they felt that the man on the ground was merely faking, and he was acting like he had been robbed and hurt in order to seize them over there, lure them there for quick and easy seizure. And so the first question that the priest asked, the first question that the Levite asked was, "If I stop to help this man, what will happen *to me?*" But then the Good Samaritan came by, and he reversed the question: "If I do not stop to help this man, what will happen *to him?*"[12]

King then turns the text back to the hearers in Memphis,

That's the question before you tonight . . . Not, "If I stop to help the sanitation workers what will happen to all of the hours that I usually spend in my office every day and every week as a pastor?" The question is not, "If I stop to help this man in need, what will happen to me?" The question is, "If I do not stop to help the sanitation workers, what will happen to them?" That's the question.[13]

The parable is prophetically interpreted by affirming Christian discipleship as decisive in the *effective relationship and practice* of radically loving the other across racial and religious boundaries. Neighbor love is as neighbor love does in real pluralistic life. Courageous resistance to violence done to the other stirs up moral courage in political community to overcome evil with good incarnate in Christ, whether or not people explicitly acknowledge the divine name. Christian discipleship, as King taught and practiced, is about leadership in resisting evil and loving the real neighbor in pluralistic society—on the dangerous road, where there is risk—in anticipation of the reign of God. In the United States, this imperative of Jesus involves exposing and disrupting the thieves and robbers latent in post-civil rights whiteness to engage society's best possibilities for beloved community.

EXPANDING RADICAL NEIGHBOR LOVE

Based on his African American communal legacy, which was implicit in his social ethics, King's interpretation of neighbor love can be extended to all humanity. King wrote, "Moreover, I am cognizant of the interrelatedness of all communities and states. I cannot sit idly by in Atlanta and not

---

12. King, "I See the Promised Land," para. 27.
13. King, "I See the Promised Land," para. 28.

be concerned about what happens in Birmingham. Injustice anywhere is a threat to justice everywhere. We are caught in an inescapable network of mutuality, tied in a single garment of destiny. Whatever affects one directly, affects all indirectly."[14]

Mutuality by extension can be expanded to include "all that participates in being."[15] Responsibility for the other includes not only human persons and communities, but animal and plant life as well. As Larry Rasmussen exegetes along these contours in *Earth Community, Earth Ethics*, in relation to this same text, "As in the parable of the Good Samaritan, class, social standing, function in society, address and purity rules of all kinds have nothing to do with the definition of the neighbor." This expansion of neighbor love for what is at hand connects to the social ecology in places like Elizabeth, New Jersey. "In a word, the neighbor in a million guises is the articulated form of creation to whom justice, as the fullest possible flourishing of creation, is due."[16] And yet ecological ethics must not redefine neighbor love in a way that subordinates dignity and justice for human beings, especially the marginalized.

CRITICAL RESPONSIBILITY

H. Richard Niebuhr's approach to responsibility in relation to all that participates in being helps ground this expanded neighbor love ethic. Niebuhr's ideas should be understood in relation to his focus on the paradox of the historically conditioned yet free self in dialogue with being; that is, on the life of the community of faith interpreting the divine pattern in history, and the necessary reinterpretation or "permanent revolution" of religious symbols, metaphors, and narratives in lived historical experience. For Niebuhr, these religious symbols and practices are rooted in the Reformed tradition. For Niebuhr, Western intellectual traditions are in crisis because of consciousness that our thinking is historically conditioned and fragmentary. We not only live in time and space, time and space live in us. This engenders relativism regarding the social apprehension of ethical truth, contrary to the dominant traditions of theology in Western philosophy. Yet from the perspective of faith, or inner sacred history, Niebuhr paradoxically affirms the normative validity of these moral fragments. This is affirmed in the face of dominant traditions of radical empiricism, skepticism, and subjective idealism. "Relativism does not imply subjectivism and skepticism. It is not evident that the

14. King, "Letter from a Birmingham Jail," 128.
15. Niebuhr, *The Responsible Self*, ch. 1.
16. Rasmussen, *Earth Community, Earth Ethics*, 261.

man who is forced to confess that his view of things is conditioned by the standpoint he occupies must doubt the reality of what he sees."[17]

For Niebuhr, though they are fragments in history, they are fragments of value and transcendence—to which the whole self responds and interprets in community. This value points not only to the value of all humanity, but to all being. Thus, social ethics involves particular lived historical communities of interpretation, including those of trust (ethics of ultimate reconciliation) or distrust (ethics of survival) of being. For Niebuhr, the myriad forms of the ruling mythology of Death, as the unconquerable End of all personal and communal histories, has become dominant in the Western intellectual tradition. Nihilism is one consequence, vividly expressed in white racism and violence toward the racialized other. Yet historical communities of trust and dialogue are called to demythologize this overarching myth of Death and offer alternative ethos, narratives, and practices in concrete response-ability.

For Niebuhr, the problem of historicity for Western civilization is solved not through sectarianism or circumscribed subjective ideals, but through responses to divine presence mediated dialogically through historically conditioned language, culture, reason, and faith communities. As R. Melvin Kaiser asserts, Niebuhr's vision partly transcends Cartesian subjectivity and the Kantian critical idealist traditions in relation to historicity.[18] For Niebuhr, ethics are not circumscribed subjective ideals or aesthetics (Kant's second and third critiques), but placed at the center of human existence. For Niebuhr, a gracious pattern of radical love summons responsibility of the whole self in community, society and history to value all Being.

SOCIAL REPENTANCE IN AMERICA

No one is untouched by participation in original sin and the original social sin of white racism in America. As Richard Rohr and others teach, "Unless we transform our misery, we will transmit it."[19] A key theological issue related to repentance and transformation has to do with our faith in interpreting social experience. H. Richard Niebuhr's model of ethics portrays human agents as responders to actions that impinge upon their total life context. According to Niebuhr, different centers of interpretation support differing visions of the total life interaction in which human beings respond in time. For example, where a white racialized faith commitment predominates,

17. Niebuhr, *The Meaning of Revelation*, 13.

18. Keiser, *Roots of Relational Ethics*, xi.

19. Rohr, *A Spring Within Us*, 120.

people imagine themselves and others in the midst of moral interaction in primary relation to their whiteness and other loyalists to its cause.

Radical monotheistic faith imagines a broader spiritual-ethical framework where human agency in social communities is trusting response to the total action of a gracious God in the cause of beloved community for all human beings. Yet for henotheistic-centered faith, the prevailing vision of interaction with others and Other is the threat of nothingness and death. In fact, white supremacy today repeatedly interprets itself as under threat and perishing.

The practical reasoning that follows is shaped by the desperate cause of keeping whiteness alive at all costs. From this perspective on value, white henotheistic devotion inflicts violence and thanatos upon the racialized other (and ultimately the Other) as manifestation of bad faith. This communal stance of distrust of Being shapes practical reasoning regarding public life and civic values in service to its underlying fear of death. As survival of whiteness is made the ultimate concern, "secondary" values of human dignity, equal justice under the law, and constitutional and human rights are reinterpreted into this matrix. Whiteness as supreme value attempts to appropriate political and moral discourse to cover its underlying idolatry. As agents of the state actively participate in this idolatrous ethic, the "protect and serve" vocation of policing and criminal justice is perverted into *de facto* white tribalism, albeit with the authority and cloak of the sword of state.

Niebuhr articulates reconstructed faith on earth as trusting response to Being that precedes and transcends us and our tribe. Radical monotheism is a type of faith in which a person or group focuses its ultimate trust and loyalty in a transcendent center of value and power, that is neither a conscious or unconscious extension of personal or group ego, nor cause or institution. It involves loyalty to the principle of Being and to the source and center of all value and power. Faith on earth does not mean the negation of less universal or less transcendent centers of value and power—church, nation, class, race, tribe, gender—but it does mean their relativization and reordering. Monotheistic faith calls people to an identification with a universal community—with the Reign of God—which transfigures all other commitments. It leads to repentance, metanoia, and radical love—including loving one's neighbor, and even the enemy, as oneself. The only cure for the deep sickness of racism is finally this transforming faith and love which is "permanent revolution" on earth.

In relation to this movement of mourning and metanoia in America, a colleague the Rev. Dr. Christopher Michael Jones, pastor of First Baptist Church, Hillside shared the following vision for the church:

I can recall while spending time with Bishop Desmond Tutu, in Cape Town a few years ago him mentioning the one regret he had while chairing the Truth and Reconciliation Commission. In hindsight, he regretted the fact that very little time was given to implementing a season of national lament in South Africa . . . In Bishop Tutu's opinion, South Africa failed to develop the type of restorative justice that not only acknowledged the historical pain of the oppressed, but that could lead to the implementation of the type of social, economic, and political mechanisms which could restore true wholeness, justice, and equality to the oppressed more fully. As you already know, Apartheid has ended, but 80% of the wealth in South Africa still belongs to the Apartheid class.

I am questioning whether or not the church has a role to play in leading discussions on lamentation both locally and nationally being that repentance is a part of our Judeo-Christian faith tradition. Is there a need for a more robust discussion on the need for lamentation both locally and nationally as a preamble to discussions on repentance and reconciliation? Many will assume that the act of repentance will include the act of repentance which then creates the opportunity for hope and restoration. However, I rarely ever see a prophetic call to national lamentation explicitly stated when matters pertaining to white supremacy, repentance, and hope are discussed.[20]

HOPE ON EARTH

The legacy of Martin Luther King Jr. as expressed by Dr. Jones and other prophetic leaders exemplifies hope on earth in this time of reckoning. Resistance to violent innocence with hope involves mourning and making a difference for the real neighbor through broad based coalitions seeking *effective* practices of justice and love. The assertion in this ethical position is that a genuine difference can be made, not that actual "progress" is always being made. As Jeffrey Stout affirms, "You are still making a difference when you are engaged in a successful holding action against forces that are conspiring to make things worse than they are."[21] This position asserts that part of the difference being made is embodied in inclusive communities which practice the change envisioned.

20. Jones, email correspondence, May 14, 2021.
21. Stout, *Democracy and Tradition*, 58.

Hope grounded in being and loving practice is especially important in an era of fear and white backlash. It is one of the gifts the church can offer to pluralistic secular communities in the struggle for justice today. Hope goes to the heart of critical responsibility and intellectual passion for resisting white supremacy and planting seeds of justice and healing in our nation. Understood in this sense, hope through communities of engagement implicitly dispraises those who triumph sectarian resistance to secularism and restoration of the generic church of glory. The real church in dialectical hope with pluralistic society seeks a shared public ethic and restoration for the oppressed in dialogue with others, rather than Christian triumphalism or sectarian defeatism.[22]

This approach does not side with neoconservatives in seeking the restoration of Christendom over political community. Refusal of a secularized society is not theologically necessary for Christians because an ethic of responsibility affirms God's presence in every society, including our own, whether or not people acknowledge the divine name. It affirms that coexistence and dialogue with other religious communities is part of the divine revelation for our historical era. To not participate in this dialogue is heresy.

Sectarian religion and differences are often used to reify violence and legitimize social atrocity. Yet ethics practicing compassion in the context of pluralism can provide tools to resist violence and nihilism, ground practices of justice, and defend the dignity of all human beings. Genuine dialogue between religious and secular communities can provide strong countervailing resistance to the forces of hate and violence. I-Thou encounter with other living traditions has value in exposing texts of terror and expanding communal traditions from moral myopia. We need each other, as King envisioned. The underlying theological-ethical affirmation is that divine life is graciously present with diverse creation in this struggle for the flourishing of all being.

A central task of Christian reflection, then, is to discern how God's will concretely manifests itself in a given society and community at this point on the journey. Resentment of the secular state is one response to this question for American society. That is, secular political communities are against God's will because of their lack of explicit acknowledgement of Jesus Christ and non-pious participation in the institutional church. Yet if concrete humanity is created and redeemed through God's grace, then our secular society is not outside the realm of divine sovereignty and the "hidden Christ" is at work in all of life. Our society is a crucible of life and death where beloved community is assaulted, yet manifest and anticipated.

22. West, *Disruptive Christian Ethics*, intro.

As King affirmed, Christian communities in the United States have a theological hope and mandate to join with others in multiracial partnerships of struggle for justice and neighbor love over against the forces of white racism, economic exploitation, and militarism. To critically expand King's imagination today we must include the categories of gender, sexual orientation, ecology, and different-abledness in the vision of beloved community. This is how the historical efficacy of Christ works in the eschatological "now" to resist that which is directly opposed to the will of God, i.e., the demonic. It does not happen in sectarian retreat. On the contrary, insofar as churches do not enter into partnerships to embody inclusive community with others in the present moment, they regress into bubbles of nostalgia (often for the 1950s), triumphalism of the fantastical (Billy Graham-like revivals), and fortresses of exclusion by race, class, gender and different-abledness, which constrict moral imagination and betray neighbor love.

Cornel West calls on Christians to reclaim an ethic of radical democracy for just-love and rejects the sectarian approach to ethics. For West, social ethics is about prophetic frictions and moral agency in relation to specific structural and experiential constraints and possibilities in history. He consciously refrains from systematic theological construction—acknowledging the problems of historicity—but critically addresses concrete oppressions and prophetic possibilities in relation to embodied pluralistic traditions. West's historical consciousness connects the public intellectual calling for Christian ethics with an imperative to concretely transform the United States. Prophetic discipleship is one of existential commitment to real persons and real community in relation to God's whole creation. It is not one of triumphalism, but costly discipleship of the Crucified One who calls us to passionate engagement in God's world.[23]

Douglas Hall in *The Cross in Our Context* also affirms this model of radical participation which is at the heart of being Christian, "Discipleship of the crucified Christ is characterized by a faith that drives its adherents into the world with a relentlessness and a daring they could not manage on the basis of human volition alone."[24] There is in us that which evades this commitment "that following Jesus Christ entails." This evasion to challenging discipleship included King, especially in his early experience in Montgomery, Alabama. In the face of death threats, he sought escape from public leadership. Yet at his kitchen table in the middle of the night, he encountered a gracious Presence who affirmed, "Martin, stand up for justice and righteousness, and I will be with you." It should be noted that this

23. West, *Democracy Matters*, 161–68.
24. Hall, *The Cross in Our Context*, 182–83.

reluctance also included Jesus of Nazareth, in his humanity, who sought solitude from friends and prayed in Gethsemane that the cup of costly engagement with creation would be removed.[25]

This understanding of discipleship means renouncing a theology of glory which "without anguish, without doubt and vacillation, the triumphant church" already claims to know what is good and evil through abstract ethics "derived quite independently of actual human situations." It means living partnerships with the divine pathos for creation, "and therefore an inherently contextual theology, the incarnational theology par excellence." This means Christian ethics with "no great distinction between theory and practice, no hiatus between knowing and being/doing."[26]

This expansion of King's legacy of prophetic discipleship with others in the post-civil rights context requires that Christian communities allow radical love for neighbor to become central. It means becoming "prisoners of hope" with diverse partners to resist the forces which perpetuate misery. As Cornel West writes, "To be a prophetic Christian is not to be against the world in the name of church purity; it is to be in the world but not of the world's nihilism, in the name of the loving Christ who proclaims the this-worldly justice of a kingdom to come."[27]

Given the historical momentum of whiteness and violence at present in the United States, this will not be easy. The engagement of the Black church in multiracial partnerships in the service of love and justice ironically taught white religious conservatives to become more politically organized. Since the 1980s, they have learned to make alliances with power elites in society. This political aggressiveness of religious conservatism and white backlash accompanied the consolidation of white privilege in post-civil rights America. This pattern of backlash against the divine movement to transform our common life toward beloved community continues into the present, especially since 2016. As delineated in this narrative, a primary way it does is by embracing rituals and coding of white racism in relation to state-based violence and the criminal justice system that scapegoat the other and discourage resistance. This interpretative retrenchment perpetuates the "now you see it, now you don't" character of post-civil rights white racism. This coincides with the intellectual aggressiveness in public life of neoconservatives, neoliberal economists, conservative politicians, and

25. King, *Stride Toward Freedom*.

26. Hall, *The Cross in Our Context*, 183–85.

27. West, *Democracy Matters*, 162.

corporate controlled media. People who stand up for the racialized poor and other marginalized groups are often derided and scorned.[28]

Will predominantly white churches continue to accept this ethos of white nihilism for society? Cornel West asserts there has been an eclipse of justice and kindness in the nation that is terrifying. He asks what keeps Christians from moral outrage at the massive greed of corporate elites while millions of children live in poverty? "The movement led by King that forged the most significant democratic Christian identity of modern time now lies in ruins. Can these dry bones live again?"[29]

King affirmed radical love as solidarity of "I want you to be." There is, he asserted, an affirmation of the mystery of the other in relationships based on love and justice, an affirmation of unexplained and unfathomable differences. Relationships based on love recognize that others have a right to be. These relationships accept the sacredness of difference while affirming interconnectedness. This acceptance means that no one individual racial group or community captures or espouses an absolute truth. All struggle, in their own way, some outside of religious systems and some within them, to interpret mystery and transcendence.

The sacredness of the other is anathema for the unrelenting racial profiling of white nihilism, which cannot acknowledge the legitimacy of other ways of being. If other ways of being have moral validity, the hegemony of whiteness is shattered. There can be no alternative ways to think or to be. All alternatives must be crushed.

For the white community to overcome nihilism, it must leave its ghetto and learn multiracial engagement and discipleship in dialogue with otherness and so disrupt the rituals of whiteness and violence. This involves both criticism and affirmation. It means genuine grace, repentance, and openness to radical love of neighbor that embraces critical questioning and tragic-comic hope. We must not be afraid of facing the truth. The white church must join with prophetic Christians of all colors who practice humility and responsibility toward society. The church must build coalitions with prophetic Jews, Muslims, Buddhists, believers, seekers, and doubters. This requires moral hope and ethical dialogue with the other.

It also requires an ethical grounding in the pluralism of God. As Krister Stendahl affirmed, the church must learn to sing to Jesus with abandon, without telling negative stories about others. What one religious position says about another religious position often broaches the commandment "Thou shall not bear false witness against your neighbor" (Exod 20:16).

---

28. West, *Democracy Matters*, 166.
29. West, *Democracy Matters*, 166–67.

What white Christians say about the other is usually self-serving and violates this basic word.[30]

White Eurocentric Christians still cannot accept that it is not God's dream that everybody be like us. We don't need to degrade others to sing to Jesus with abandon. This is the profound lesson in a plural world for Christian theology and ethics in the twenty-first century. In 1 Corinthians 13, Paul has to deal with the question: How can diversity and pluralism become an asset instead of a liability? How can white churches learn to turn the statement around and say not, "How much diversity can we afford?" but, "How much unity can we afford?"[31]

Paul's eschatological image is that radical neighbor love is measured by how much creative diversity people can handle. As Stendahl observes, Paul had to learn it the hard way because in an earlier part of his ministry, he learned that by forcing things he could not get it his way. Paul knew firsthand of murderous postures toward the other. He finally accepts that now we see like an old-fashioned bad mirror, in a glass, dimly; now our knowledge is fragmented. It is when Paul thinks about diversity that he has to admit—don't be so sure about absolute truth. You have your insights, but you are just at the beginning. He ends by saying, so there remains those three: faith, hope, and love, and the greatest of these is faith. That's what he should have said as the apostle of faith—that everything depends on faith. But here, suddenly, there is a breakthrough in thinking about the Christ, and he says: and the greatest of these is radical love, inclusion of the other—not "insisting on its own way."[32]

SUMMARY: FRAGMENTS OF CRITICAL RESPONSIBILITY

The key fragments of this dialectical approach to Christian social witness includes several pieces. First, this approach trusts in God's power to fulfill universal moral purpose in the pluralism of all life. Next, it affirms the capacity for partnership between God and diverse humanity. Third, the central organizing method is nonviolent agency and collaboration with others in multiracial partnership. This includes radical love, by which inclusive communities practice effectiveness and truth toward the other as an expression of the reign of God, over against forces of violent innocence. Predominantly white churches in America are called to repent of white supremacy through

30. See Stendahl, "Why I Love the Bible."
31. Stendahl, "Why I Love the Bible," para. 27.
32. Stendahl, "Why I Love the Bible," para. 28.

costly grace and discipleship which include amending social and communal relations. We are called by God's grace to *participate* in the historic conflict at work in the United States. The central conflict today is between forces of violent innocence which degrade and divide and the forces of beloved community which make space for and affirm the other. Claiming agency and knowing hope means overcoming the temptation to deny this conflict through apathy and cynicism. Social repentance includes not only the agency of individuals and communities, but changing public policies and practices—seeking the shalom of the city wherein we dwell, for in its shalom shall be our shalom (see Jer 29:7).

MOURNING AND METANOIA IN AMERICA

Metanoia points to judgment that includes self, church, and nation. This historical narrative of breaking through the plate glass window in Elizabeth, New Jersey, implicates most of us, including myself. I underestimated my own complicity, conscious and unconscious, in white supremacy. The process of lamentation and transformation is ongoing. As part of the community of forgiven and forgiving sinners, justified by the grace of God, those who seek to follow Jesus have a direct responsibility to unmask injustice within and without. Only then can we begin to stir up hope in our communities and nation.

Insofar as the predominantly white church neglects this calling in the twenty-first century to live out metanoia in all realms of life, its faith succumbs to defeatism. It denies the challenge to be partners in God's work this day. It turns away from working out our salvation with awe and trembling before the possibilities in this historical era. Rather than transformation, the church succumbs to the conformity of false innocence by which the lesser (sinful) self gains the consent of the larger (true) self to avoid confronting social misery.

This historical narrative confirms that as long as white nihilism is hidden, it cannot be healed. Religious complicities in idolatry must be exposed to the light. This includes the "mantles of cheap grace" by which they are elegantly cloaked. Unless this task of deconstructing white racism is undertaken, the gospel of justification by grace is subject to distortion by tools of suppression. The gospel is used as a cloak against the demands of true healing. The pandemic of white racism is allowed to mutate, engendering sickness and death.

This analysis reveals that self-deception and self-righteousness are malignancies that fuel violent practices toward the other. These pharisaic patterns shape real churches and communities—as opposed to generic ones—which too often sanction sacrifice of the other. Therefore, the American church and society stand in need of radical surgery just at their points of self-deception and self-righteousness. In the United States, this prophetic task involves bringing to light white duplicity. It involves focusing intellectual passion and praxis on release from this demonic principality. For release from the bondage of violent innocence, both divine forgiveness and justice, unconditional love and prophetic criticism, are required. As Coleman Brown said, "The New Testament knows something we forget at peril to our social causes and hopes for the world: justice without mercy only breeds new animosity. But mercy without justice is not mercy!"[33] The real neighbor requires not purity, but responsibility. Responsibility requires breaking through the plate glass window daily with others.

The goal of investigating the question of how the Confederate flag got into the front plate glass window in Elizabeth came to involve aggressive labor in the fields of history, economics, sociology, critical white studies, and psycho-dynamics. This in turn led to deeper existential reflection and action. Persons and nations are social and timeful beings. The insights of critical thinking must be lived out with real communities in fragmented ways in history.

The cultures of denial are incredible strong in predominantly white communities in relation to the subject of white supremacy. It is the strongest plate glass window in America. Yet there are multiple plate glass windows of class, gender, sexual orientation, ecology, and different-abledness to break through. It takes intellectual passion along with truthful dialogue and praxis to break through the barriers. How could it be otherwise? Bearing to listen to others and to think dangerous thoughts are first steps. Greater truth in the many layers of self, community, and nation remain to be discovered and practiced.

The Confederate flag was placed in the front window of the church on Lincoln's birthday in 1963 precisely when Blacks were marching for justice. It stayed there for thirty years. Two young people were crossing the street near the church in 1998 and were brutally beaten by the police. Dynamics of history and culture are at work in churches and in policing. Yet they do not determine them. That white racism was and is "cultural" or "societal" does not justify fatalism. As the wise monk said to the searching young man in Brothers Karamazov (to paraphrase), "Remember you're just like everyone else. Only don't act like everyone else."[34] "You're just like everyone else" has

33. Brown, *Our Hearts Are Restless*, 151.
34. Dostoyevsky, *The Brothers Karamazov*, 354–55.

been my discovery for self and church. Yet one can hear the word, "Only don't act like everyone else."

How to heal hearts and amend actions? Before the answer comes a deeper question. That is, there is an "answer" in reframing the question, such as Jesus of Nazareth did in confronting the blind man sitting near the pool. He asked, "Do you want to be healed?" Do persons and communities in America want to be healed of white supremacy and hate?[35] That question I never really asked. Why didn't I ask? Probably fear. Fear that the answer would be, "No."

Yet then what—only more suffering?

In terms of justice in America, that is one conclusion. As Thomas Hardy said, "If the way to the better be, it involves looking at the worst."[36] We may have to see the decay of American empire yet more clearly before we amend our ways. We saw white terrorism on display on January 6, 2021, in the storming of the Capitol in Washington, DC. We saw a mob riot and murder as the constitutional transfer of power was being made from a white nationalist regime. In the process, the Confederate flag was put in the front window of American democracy. We saw over one million deaths in the COVID pandemic, many of which were avoidable. The norms of homelessness, lack of affordable housing and healthcare, economic injustice, opiate dependence, gender violence, suicide, gun violence, mass incarceration, racialized policing . . . are expressions of American addiction to thanatos and white supremacy in a time of reckoning.

Yet the gospel assures us that if sin abounds, grace abounds all the more. Grace is hidden in the judgment. How is this? Beholding the ugliness of racism and hatred in light of the gospel means beholding the trembling possibility of metanoia and what Paul calls, "godly grief" (2 Cor 7:10). They come together. "In Christ, God was reconciling the world to Godself" (2 Cor 5:19). The antidote to the poison lies in the poison. That which transfigures the ugly must first lift up and reveal the ugliness in order to change it. Yet to enter in, one must trust and experience there is something more than poison and ugliness. As the Black spiritual sings, "Were you there when they crucified my Lord? / Sometimes it causes me to tremble, tremble, tremble." This vulnerable, trembling of God's self-revelation appears first as danger and threat and one flees with great speed and device for one's very life. Yet the hope of transformation begins with the decision to arrest the flight, to

35. See Baldwin, *Notes of a Native Son*, 103: "I imagine one of the reasons people cling to their hates so stubbornly is because they sense, once hate is gone, they will be forced to deal with pain."

36. Quoted in Becker, *Escape from Evil*, iv.

stop the games of self-deception. It takes a miracle to truly begin—to hear in the heart the deeper question in spite of fear.

Do you want to be healed?

An honest evaluation of this historical narrative thus concludes that it is radically incomplete—a whole other severe movement in God's grace needs to follow, entitled *"America, Do You Want to Be Healed?"* Or *"America, Do You Want to Claim Your Promise?"*

SECTION III

Wisdom Fragments

Jesus Christ is the assurance that all of life, the life of every human and the rest of creation, originates in and ends in the life of God. Your life, or mine, or that of anybody, issues from the word of God. This is and remains the essential truth about you or me or anybody, no matter whatever else may seem to be true.
—William Stringfellow[1]

The words my father overheard in the Georgia barbershop in the summer of 1958 were prophetic. The Hebrew Congregation Temple, Atlanta's oldest synagogue and an active partner for civil rights, was bombed by white supremacists in October 1958. The building was damaged extensively by the dynamite fueled explosion. Five suspects were arrested after the bombing; none were ever convicted. Yet the bulldozer does not have the last word. When Jon Ossoff was sworn in as Georgia's first Jewish senator in January 2021, he held the Hebrew Bible that belonged to Rabbi Jacob Rothschild, the leader of that synagogue and a friend of Martin Luther King Jr. When Raphael Warnock was sworn in two weeks later as the first Black senator from Georgia, he was the first Black democrat elected to a Senate seat by a former state of the Confederacy.

Amidst the four-hundred-year pandemic of white racism, the narrative myths and daydreams of whiteness are being disrupted on the streets of the nation. A new generation of leadership is rising. When I went to rallies

1. Stringfellow, *Instead of Death*, 6–7.

in Elizabeth, Trenton, and New York in 2020 there were not hundreds, but thousands of demonstrators. We have not seen numbers like this since the civil rights movement. The names of George Floyd, Philando Castile, Sandra Bland, Eric Garner, Mike Brown, Tamir Rice, Alton Sterling, Freddie Gray, Amadou Diallo, Trayvon Martin, and others were lifted up. There are tragically many more children of God across the nation who died in similar ways, some of the names known only to God.

America is presently engaged in a battle for its soul, a kind of second Civil War. Some seventy-four million people or 46.8 percent of the electorate voted for Donald Trump in 2020. The Trump banners and equivalent are still evident in parts of New Jersey and Pennsylvania, along with the occasional Confederate flag. Voting rights in many red states are being eviscerated. In some public school districts, laws were passed forbidding the study of our racial history and its bitter legacy. Arrayed against the movement for racial justice and compassion in America is a toxic mix of Trump world nihilism, white supremacy, predatory capitalism, white evangelical Christianity, and the social ecology of right-wing media. The demographics of the nation are changing, and many whites are afraid of losing power and, beneath that, of nothingness. If the forces of white racism and oligarchy cannot effectively cling to power through "legally" suppressing the vote, then authoritarian rule is the next option. This is a genuine either/or moment in American history. Cognitive dissonance will lead either toward breaking into a more compassionate and just democracy or double downing on tyranny and a demonic police state.

Given the empirical reality of sin, Christians should not be afraid of facing the brokenness of our racial history, it should be a call for honest reflection, confession, transformation, and redemptive action. Healing the racial wound in America will not mean the damage never existed. It will mean the damage no longer has to dominate our lives and life together. Some of the hope is eschatological.

A friend of Thomas Merton, Jim Forest, once wrote, "What we see and what we fail to see defines who we are and how we live our lives. Our constant challenge is to be aware of the divine presence—and at the same time be alert to the demonic, to be able to tell the difference between that which safeguards life and that which destroys."[2]

I learned in my life and work that we can run, but we cannot hide from God. This is true in different ways for self, community, and nation. Grace is unrelenting. The unmasking and naming is part of the new life breaking in. Here in the trembling truth of self and other, the grace of God is hidden, at work. Here is discovery of new possibilities. Thus, the way opens, by little

2. Forest, "Lord, That I Might See," para. 14.

and by little. And leads to finding one's true voice, and more courageous if humble walking with the community of many colors and nations.

How shall we join our voices in walking prayer in this time of reckoning?

When Cornel West gave the charge in Elizabeth, he charged us all. He charged us to radically love our neighbor by centering the experience of African American people "who've been terrorized and traumatized and stigmatized for four hundred years in a land that likes to trivialize their suffering and overlook their humanity."

> It's a beautiful thing when you think of the Miles Hortons . . . the Anne Bradys . . . Abraham Joshua Heschel, and the Erik Foners in scholarship that put at the center of the modern experience the vicious legacy of white supremacy. You don't remain stuck there, but once you go through that lens you're gonna be able to more readily understand the suffering of others.
>
> Why? Because the degree to which Black people have been so hated and despised. We have no monopoly on that, not at all. But if you come in that way, you're going to understand working people a little bit better . . . poor people all around the world a little bit better . . . patriarchy and the sisters a little bit better . . . our gay brothers and lesbian sisters a little bit better, you're going to understand empire . . . and the wretched of the earth a little bit better . . .
>
> The great Reinhold Niebuhr used to say that any justice that's only justice soon degenerates into something less that justice. Justice must be rescued by something deeper than justice. And the only thing deeper than justice is love. And for a Christian like me, old school Christian, the only thing that keeps me going, is the blood at the cross, or I would snap, I'd go crazy, and I might do it anyway. I was a gangster before I met Jesus. And now I'm a redeemed sinner with gangster proclivities. The only thing keeping me is that love . . .
>
> So the kingdom of God, that we have the audacity to still align ourselves with, if that kingdom of God is within you, then everywhere you go, you ought to leave a little heaven behind. That's the charge: how much heaven are you going to leave behind in your short move from your mama's womb to tomb . . . How much heaven will all of us leave behind? More to come.
>
> But in the end Samuel Beckett is right, "Try, fail. Try again, fail again, fail better." That when they put us in the grave, even following the charge, we're still a relative failure because we fell on our faces; but most importantly we bounce back, because we

wanted to be part of that love train, that quest for the kingdom of God, that humility that our dear brother Professor James Cone was talking about at the center of the gospel which is inseparable from memory and inseparable from tenacity.

Charge to each one of us: how do we learn to love our crooked neighbor with our crooked hearts? Grace. Amazing grace. Empowers.[3]

Dottie Lockhart in South Boston asked, "What are we waiting for?" She then walked through the gauntlet and others followed. Her charge is existential. May we walk and keep walking in spite of threats of destruction, with Martin Luther King Jr., Valerie Russell, Coleman Brown, Ada Maria Isasi-Diaz, William Stringfellow, Robina Winbush, James Cone, Ella Baker, Thomas Merton, Daniel Berrigan, Ruth Baker, Steve Hartshorne, Newton Burkett Jr., Abraham Joshua Heschel, Sister Sue Murphy, the Niebuhr brothers, Phyllis Curtis, Otto Maduro . . . surrounded by a great cloud of witnesses on earth and in heaven.

"Then the Lord said to Moses [standing before the Red Sea], 'Why do you cry to me? Walk on . . .'" (Exod 14:15).

We don't find courage, courage finds us. Along with prophetic criticism, graceful witness for self and neighbor is decisive. Social witness has value in relation to real persons and communities with specific injustices. Walking existential prayer and organizing stirs up *moral courage and intellectual passion* for self and those who "dwell near" you, which transforms *existential relationships with the poor of the earth.* Breaking through the multiple plate glass windows of injustice in America will require heart and soul relationships. It will require perseverance and courageous community. This involves freeing up space for the other and Other. "For there is space aplenty."

In this final section, I acknowledge my limitations. I asked several people to offer prophetic fragments in this time of reckoning. What follows are selections from Mike Gecan, Archange Antoine, Karen Hernandez-Granzen, Richard Fenn, and Lorna Goodison. I give thanks to God for their gracious wisdom.

---

3. Quoted in LeighaCohen, "Cornel West and Chris Hedges."

8

Organizing and Justice
Racial Justice, Economic Justice, Social Justice

Mike Gecan, Senior Advisor, Industrial Areas Foundation

When Michael Granzen asked me to write a piece for his book, I said that I would be honored to do that, but gently warned him. I said that I believed that the quest for justice—racial as well as social and economic—was something that people *did*, not something that was the product of much talk. Over more than fifty years in the public arena, starting in 1966 in Chicago as a high school student taken to meetings of the struggling civil rights movement by our Jesuit instructors, through the late 1960s and early 1970s as a summer volunteer in the Contract Buyers League of Lawndale, and then into the mid-1970s and beyond as a professional organizer with the Industrial Areas Foundation, I have mostly worked in African American and Hispanic communities, with and for African American and Hispanic leaders, on the issues and struggles affecting their individuals, families, congregations, and communities. It has been a privilege—a blessing, as my Black clergy friends would say—to do so. I reflect every day on the leaders I met, the actions we ran, and the victories we scored. In spite of the warning, Michael urged me to write exactly what I thought and felt, which I was happy to do.

If there ever was a time and place where the realities of race and justice were most dramatic, most evident, most pervasive, it was South Africa in the summer of 1990. Nelson Mandela had just been released after twenty-seven years on Robben Island and was triumphantly touring the United States. Once Mandela was released, Bishop Desmond Tutu reached out to the rector of Trinity Church, New York, and urged him to invite two Industrial Areas Foundation organizers to fly to South Africa and conduct our training sessions for civic and clergy leaders there. In the previous seven years, undercover, funded by Trinity Church, the IAF had hosted South Africans recommended by Bishop Tutu in New York. These courageous leaders, almost all of whom had been imprisoned at one time or another, many of whom had been tortured, needed some rest and relaxation outside of the intense pressure cooker of oppression and surveillance created by the apartheid government. They flew to New York, where we found them housing, welcomed them to our training courses, and exposed them to the home-building strategy called the Nehemiah Plan, which we were advancing in Brooklyn. Bishop Tutu envisioned that the universals and skills of effective organizing would someday be needed in South Africa. Over the course of that period, the then-executive director of the IAF, Ed Chambers, made two trips to South Africa—undercover, of course.

When Ed got the call from Trinity, he called my colleague Arnie Graf and me and asked us if we would like to go. He said that the place was better obviously, but still unstable. The IAF had a number of top-flight African American organizers who would have been perfect for this assignment, but the odds that an African American organizer would be given a visa and be allowed in the country were low to zero. We were both thrilled by the invitation but had to check with our spouses. Arnie and Lucille, an African American, discussed the opportunity, but Arnie thought that it would not be prudent for her and their four children to go. My spouse, Sheila, was also supportive, so our entire family, including our three children—eight, five, and two—decided to go.

Even though apartheid had formally ended, the apparatus of the old regime still functioned in many ways. To get visas, I was grilled on the phone by a representative of the South African embassy in the United States. On our visa applications, Arnie and I described ourselves as "Anglican church growth consultants." The embassy officer was skeptical. He asked if Arnie was Anglican. I said, "No, Arnie is Jewish." He then asked if I was Anglican. I said, "No, I'm Roman Catholic." There was a long pause. "So I'm to understand that a Jew and a Catholic are visiting South Africa to advise Anglicans on church growth. Is that right?" The voice was measured, dripping with sarcasm. I assured him that was correct. There was another long silence. Finally, he asked the key question: "Where does the Industrial Areas Foundation get its money?" I said that we had originally been funded by the great businessman and retailer Marshall Field (which was true enough). "Surely,"

I said, sounding offended, "you have heard of Marshall Field." That seemed to stump him. For whatever reasons, he approved our visa applications.

A few weeks later, we landed in Johannesburg, after an all-night flight from London—Arnie, Sheila, our children, and I. As we walked through the airport, we noticed teams of heavily armed military—one white, one black—each team with a snarling German shepherd on a long leash. All through the airport, Black women were busily cleaning the windows, floors, and walls. For sport, the military teams would let the German shepherds lunge at the cleaning women—tugging back on the leash at the very last minute, just as the dog's teeth were about to snap into a woman's leg or thigh. The women would scream and cringe. My eight-year-old, Joe, watched this unfold and said to me, "Dad, you've got to do something!" And we told him that there was nothing in this country that we could do.

Outside, we waited for two hours for the van that would take us to an Anglican fellowship center midway between Soweto and Johannesburg. We were told that the delay was caused by the theft of the original van the night before. Once boarded, we drove on a massive superhighway toward what in those times was called a "black spot"—a community where, contrary to apartheid ideology, Blacks and Caucasians lived and worked together. Because it shouldn't exist, because it violated ideological purity, it was not recorded on official maps. It was just a unnamed spot of the map, not a recognized place. As we rode, most of the kids dozed off. Far ahead, I noticed a Black woman running across the highway—a common practice for those who lived in townships and wanted to avoid the circuitous, often three-hour bus rides to white areas. She was hit by a car, flung into the air, and crashed to the road. No car stopped. Vehicles simply veered past her dead body. Ours did, too. I turned and watched a long time, until her body was a small spot far in the distance. (Years later, I read a book, *Move Your Shadow*, by Joseph Lelyveld, about his experiences as a journalist in South Africa that includes an eerily similar scene.) When we arrived at the fellowship center, we learned that it had been shot up by security forces the week before, with no injuries, thankfully. That was our introduction to South Africa in the summer of 1990.

For the next two weeks, Arnie and I conducted training sessions for approximately fifty leaders there. Many of the lessons that we had learned and practiced in the United States seemed useful to these women and men. But two things stood out during that time. One was during the session on individual meetings. This is a fundamental part of our organizing approach—what we call our most radical tool. It is the belief that the best and most effective way to get to know and trust another person is to sit down with him or her face to face, one to one, and get a sense of who they are and what motivates them, while making sure that the other person has the chance to do the same with you. So we taught the theory of individual meetings and then, as we always did, asked pairs of people to try them in front of the rest of the group. Every single individual meeting we observed that day was fraught with stories of loss, violence, death, jail, torture, and, occasionally, betrayal. After every pair, we would have to take a break to relieve the tension and to shake out the images of the last individual meeting before we started the next one. We would take our cups of tea outside, into the stunning light of the South African winter afternoon, and quietly reflect on what we had just heard.

What struck us about these exchanges was, on the one hand, the brutal honesty people conveyed about the pain and suffering that they had endured at the hands of an avowedly racist totalitarian system and then, on the other hand, the lack of bitterness or cynicism. You might say, "Well, sure, they had won." But the emotions and expressions evident that day were not those of celebratory victors. They were the emotions and expressions of people who had endured and whose profound faith—religious, racial, and social—had sustained them through decades of oppression. Here we were being treated with consideration and respect by women and men who had encountered obstacles far greater than ours. Of course, everyone knew that we were there at the invitation of a national figure, Bishop Tutu, who, along with Nelson Mandela, was a gold-plated credential. But, still, the graciousness and generosity of those leaders, to us, to my wife, and, especially, to our children, overwhelmed us then and lives in our spirits to this day.

The second impression was made as we taught a session on action. In the United States, we talk about the purpose of action being a reaction. The reaction is a first step toward recognition. And recognition is the foundation for a public relationship of reciprocity and mutual respect. We didn't get further than talking about the purpose of action, when a hand went up. "Sir," a young man said, with the unfailing politeness of the group, "you say that the purpose of action is to get a reaction. But, in our country, we didn't need to act to get a reaction. We just needed to *be*. Just *being* created a reaction. What do you say to that?"

That young man was teaching us a lesson that afternoon. Being Black in South Africa—not doing anything special or different, not organizing, not going to City Hall, not confronting a landlord or police commander—was seen as an action by the whites who had dedicated their lives to organizing a system of relentless oppression. Now we—Arnie and his family particularly—obviously had some sense of this reality. But, for some reason, the comment from the young civic leader drove this theme home in a way that was indelible.

On our last day, the group held a religious service and thanked us for the work we did with them. Try to imagine yourself on a rocky hillside in South Africa, where humankind first stood up and walked in an unheated stone church, among fifty African leaders who had survived and overthrown apartheid and were just beginning to contemplate the creation of a redeemed country, listening to the astoundingly resonant singing of a great people. Those sights and sounds and faces remain vivid and resonant.

What does all this have to do with race and justice? Throughout those weeks and in the years since, I have been struck by how little the tough, mature, tested, seasoned leaders we have worked with—South Africans, Caribbean leaders in the UK and US, African American and Hispanic leaders here—have *talked* about race or wanted to talk about race. They were proudly Black. And we—Arnie and I, for instance—were white. We never lost sight of that and never took it for granted. But what those leaders on three different continents, over five decades, cared about, when it came to us or any other organizer of any race whom they met was contained in two questions, sometimes stated, more often implicit.

The first was: "Are you authentic? Are you for real?" And that was never resolved by what we said. It was answered, over time, sometimes over a very long time, by what we *did*. Did we pretend to care about a community? Or was this organizing gig just a stepping-stone to public office or law school, some think tank or foundation sinecure? When the going got tough, when there was danger, when the bricks and fists and clubs rained down, as they sometimes did, did we hang in? Or did we flee?

The second question was: "Can you be helpful? Can you be useful?" If we passed the first test—yes, we were genuine—that made us a decent person, perhaps. But if we didn't have insights and skills that could be helpful and useful, there was no reason to spend time organizing with us. Good intentions, decent values, were necessary, but not sufficient. Those good intentions had to be paired with talent and experience and a way of operating in the public arena that would lead to impact and progress.

That's what those South African leaders cared about, we sensed. Those are the same two questions those leaders would have asked of any organizer, of any race, who walked through the door of that conference room.

That's what the leaders in Lawndale in the late 1960s and early 1970s cared about—leaders like Clyde Ross and Charlie Baker and Ruth Wells— African American family leaders and home buyers who had been exploited by contract sellers and who wanted restitution. Could the young Jesuit who helped them put together their organization, Jack Macnamara, and the wide-eyed students who volunteered to assist them help them reverse the pattern of abuse and exploitation that had saddled them with contracts that

made them seek second and third jobs just to maintain their monthly pay-
ments? Ultimately, after years of struggle, after cold days trying to block
sheriffs' deputies from evicting families, after endless pickets of financial
institutions that provided cover for the rapacious contract sellers, after
thousands of hours in a city office building poring through title searches,
and after hundreds of Wednesday night community meetings, they won
and received restitution. It's rare for this kind of long-term, on-the-ground
organizing and protracted action to attract notice. But the work of Ross
and Baker and Wells and all the other contract buyers of that period was
featured three times—in a penetrating 1974 essay in *The Atlantic* by the late
James Alan McPherson; in a brilliant book, *Family Properties*, published in
2009 by Rutgers historian Beryl Satter; and in Ta-Nehisi Coates's remark-
able essay, "The Case for Reparations," also published in the *Atlantic* exactly
forty years after McPherson's piece.

And that's what the leaders of East Brooklyn—living in the beginning
of the end of civilization, as a group of mayors from other cities, touring
the devastated acres in the late 1970s, called the area—wanted to know. Icie
Johnson, Sarah Plowden, Domingo Lind, June Jones, Rev. Ernest L. White,
Carmellia Goffe—some of the extraordinary leaders of that era in that community were all quietly, even silently, asking. Were their organizers for real?
And could they be useful as these leaders imagined, designed, fought for,
and implemented a plan to rebuild their entire community? They rarely
talked about race. They embodied it. They didn't have to make the point
that their communities had been left in a state of neglect—"benign neglect,"
as the establishment smugly called it then—and shrinkage. It was obvious.
It was unhidden. It was deliberate and public policy. These leaders *knew* the
neglect was not benign and the shrinkage was not planned and that the reality was profoundly racial. What they weren't yet sure of was how to reverse
those trends and prove all the pundits and academics wrong. It took them
more than three decades. But that's what they did.

In every one of these settings—and a dozen more that I don't have
time and space to describe here—proud and powerful African American
and Hispanic leaders risked their lives, organized and fought for justice with
several white allies and partners who had earned their trust, and achieved
results that no amount of talk or theory would produce. Race was explicit
internally—totally understood, totally integrated into their drive for change.
They didn't need anyone to tell them *why* they had been exploited and oppressed. But they used that realization to design sophisticated and winning
strategies, not to make the larger world feel guilty.

I've written elsewhere that hope is visceral and physical. It's a muscle,
not a slogan, not a conversation, not a theory. So is racial justice. That muscle

gets stronger with daily use or atrophies when not exercised. My hope is that this book inspires readers to exert themselves—to *do* justice—in the public arena relentlessly and effectively at this critical point in our still-unfolding history.

9

Leadership. Liberation. Justice.

Rev. Archange Antoine, Political Director of New Jersey Clergy Coalition for Justice, Moderator of the Student Government Association at Princeton Theological Seminary

Rev. Michael Granzen is a man of the people, a prophetic leader with a deep history of commitment to partnering with oppressed and marginalized people in demanding justice from those in power. I learned about his work with the community after exposing a white supremacist group in the Elizabeth Police Department called the Family. They had a long history of planting drugs and falsely arresting Black, Brown, and poor people. Eventually, as a result of his partnership with community leaders, the FBI helped dismantle the Family. It was a huge win, but the culture of white supremacy and police violence persist against Black and Brown people.

It was three of us who grew up as kids in the city of Elizabeth. We committed ourselves to college and always returned to encourage our friends and other youths to go to college. We saw college as a solution to avoiding the street life. I went to Rowan University, and my other friends went to the University of New Haven and Jersey City University. After taking finals, we would return to our old neighborhood and share the good news of college, parties, and new friendships. One evening, we saw Elizabeth police officers, and because of the violent history, we knew it was time to leave. We went inside our car. They approached our car, unlocked the doors, dragged us out of the car, body-slammed us against the vehicle, violated our constitutional rights, and falsely arrested us under trumped-up charges of obstruction of public passage. They did not know we were college students until after we were inside the police station. We vowed to fight the case, despite our immigrant families' hesitancy. Our families have witnessed several decades of state violence under a brutal Haitian dictator. They did not like to challenge the police. We were also too poor to hire a lawyer, but we knew we were on the right side of justice. After demanding to go to trial with our public defenders, the prosecutor decided to drop all charges. I requested they drop the fees too. We won! But we were in pain, and we knew the culture of policing would continue. Years later, I took all my lived experiences and my victory against the police department and channeled my energy into faith-based community organizing with Jews, Christians, and Muslims fighting against systemic racism.

Rev. Granzen and I would meet a few years later, and I was thankful for his work to expose the racist network in the Elizabeth Police Department. Together, we would serve in several multiracial and multi-faith organizations focused on addressing racial, immigrant, and economic justice in New Jersey. We used our faith in God to challenge public officials, police unions, the attorney general, and even the governor. We celebrated when we won on issues and cried together when we lost, but we know we were doing God's work. These experiences have allowed me to bring a new perspective to the people I have served as a professor, public official, business owner, community organizer, and minister.

Now my responsibility is to ensure dedication by our congregations, institutions, and communities to some fundamental principles that will help us address systems of injustice and transform our nation for the betterment of all God's people. These are seven points I encourage everyone to adopt in their social justice and public work.

First, we must create a culture in our homes and immediate circles where bigotry, discrimination, and racist behavior never go unaddressed. If you are not willing to do the close work, you can't do the public work.

Second, prophetic voices must continue to stand up and speak out against systems that deprive innocent people of human rights. Our voice must be unapologetic and truthful to penetrate people's hearts and keep those in power on notice.

Third, we need a commitment to advancing public policy on the local, county, state, and national levels. More importantly, we need to learn effective lobbying efforts to push elected officials and decision-makers.

Fourth, community organizing must be a tool for building power with marginalized communities. People must be committed to long-term power-building efforts alongside victims of exploitations and oppression.

Fifth, the faith community must call racism sin, and our institutions must call for repentance, restitution, and reparations. We must combat bad theology that justifies supremacy and state violence.

Sixth, we must develop psychological solutions for the psychological problem of racism and white supremacy. Legal, policy, and organizing strategies are good, but ineffective against groups of people who suffer from a superiority complex, inferior thinking, or irrational fear.

Seven, raising money and gaining access to resources is essential to supporting the movements, campaigns, and strategies in the long-term. The money should work toward liberating efforts, not used as a tool to repress the voices of the people, especially the poor and marginalized.

IO

The Kin-dom Coming in the Joyful Worship of the God of All People

Rev. Karen Hernandez-Granzen, Pastor, Westminster Presbyterian Church, Trenton

PCUSA Woman of Faith Award for Racial Justice

Little did I know that, since my conception, the Holy Spirit had been preparing me for intercultural ministry. I am a multiracial, multicultural, and bilingual Nuyorican (a Puerto Rican born in New York) and, as such, native Taina, white European Spaniard, and Black African. I have been an urbanite all my life, having lived and/or served in New York City, Los Angeles, San Francisco, Chicago, and Trenton. I'll never forget receiving Westminster Presbyterian Church's Congregational Information Form (CIF) in September 1994. I was in the midst of studying for my ordination exams at McCormick Theological Seminary in Chicago. I bowed my head and tears flowed when I read the CIF, because I sensed in my heart and spirit that God was calling me to Westminster. Even before meeting the congregation in Trenton, New Jersey, I prayed earnestly that the older members would see the fruit of their labor before they died. The following quote from the CIF revealed Westminster's commitment to become a multiracial and multicultural worshiping congregation.

We are a "vintage" congregation of people, many of us born and raised in Trenton . . . a predominantly white congregation, a small band of disciples who still believe that Presbyterians belong in the city . . . we are the battleground . . . the mission field is our backyard . . . those of us who remain have chosen to be on the frontline. Some of us are excited about being on the cutting edge, some of us struggle with letting go of the old, most of us believe that our roots are planted at the corner of Greenwood and South Walter and should not be transplanted to the suburbs. We know that our future is dependent upon building membership, especially the youth membership. We know that we are not the same community that existed when most of us lived in the neighborhood and were not church "commuters" as we are today. We are aware that we can never be what "was" and that the church we hope to grow will be of a mixed complexion which reflects the "now" of our church neighborhood. We are God's people, called to spread the "Good News" so that all people can find a personal relationship with the Lord and become a part of the fellowship of believers. We who remain in the city believe that "thy Kingdom come, thy will be done, on earth as it is in Heaven."

When I was installed as the pastor of Westminster, I was honored to have Dr. Justo González, my professor and mentor, preach. Although he was preaching to an urban congregation within the Presbyterian Church (USA), his sermon challenged and continues to challenge every mainline or non-denominational homogeneous congregation be it white, Black, Latino, or Asian:

While the encounter with many peoples and cultures is intellectually and emotionally enriching, it is also painful, and many people feel justified to resent it. As the old certainties provided by more limited horizons are challenged by people coming out of different experiences, many respond in fear and bitterness . . . We must confess that we are all tempted to privilege our own people, our own tribe, our own language, our own nation.

I submit to you that this will be one of the most difficult aspects of Christian ministry in this country in the decades to come. It will be so difficult that many will be content with preaching and with believing a supposed gospel that does not challenge our exclusivisms and our tribalisms. And yet, faithfulness requires that we continually put forth the vision of John of, "a great multitude that no one could count, from every nation,

from all tribes and peoples and languages" (Rev. 7:9), whom
God also loves.[1]

González preached this sermon so that Westminster would not continue our
transformation process naively. Over the years we have learned that radical
transformation takes *Kairos* (God's time), *kronos* (chronological time), genuine compassion, open and ongoing communication, and *mucho* patience.
Westminster's congregational transformation from a homogeneous white
vintage congregation into a congregation that embraces all of God's people
has been and continues to be a long, at times arduous, and ongoing process.

By God's grace and faithfulness, Westminster has truly become an
intercultural worshiping community. Westminster was a 100 percent homogeneous white "vintage" congregation on the verge of closing, but now,
by the grace of God, our membership reflects the mixed complexion of our
neighborhood. As of December 31, 2020, our membership of a hundred
people was comprised of 21 percent European Americans, 66 percent African Americans, 7 percent Hispanic/Latinx, and 4 percent multiracial, and
2 percent Asian. Every Sunday, our joy-filled worship services embrace our
children's leadership, as well as traditional, contemporary, multicultural,
multilingual, and multimedia worship resources. At the end of worship service, we "share the peace" in four languages within a unifying circle as we
glimpse the image of God in all our faces.

As I share excerpts of Westminster's transformational story into an
intercultural church, I will not focus on simply objective facts, but on the
"historic," on those stories that have informed our present and future identity. It is important to acknowledge the lens we use when we read history.
Our congregation's mantra is: "We've Come This Far by Faith Leaning on
the Lord and Each Other." Therefore, my primary goal is to acknowledge
God's faithful and guiding presence. I want to share the stories of the great
cloud of witnesses that have gone before us, because as the prominent South
American philosopher, Ortega y Gasset, said, "Each generation stands on
the shoulders of its predecessors like acrobats in a vast human pyramid."[2]

When Westminster began its transformation into an intercultural congregation in the 1980s, the PCUSA defined that process as a redevelopment
process; a radical redirection of its ministry in light of changes in needs or
circumstances among its membership, the community to be served, or both.
Lyle E. Schaller, author of numerous books on church growth, stated that
redevelopment is a very challenging process. It is considered more difficult

1. González, "A Tale of Two Scrolls."
2. Quoted in González, *The Story of Christianity*, xiii.

than starting a new church because present and future ministries can be stifled by those who say, "But this is the way we've always done it."

Even though the exodus of the white/Anglo community from the city to the suburbs had been occurring for decades throughout all of the cities in our nation, and had been documented by our denomination in the early 1950s, Westminster still perceived its decline as a unique situation. In 1945, there were twelve Presbyterian churches in Trenton; now in 2016, there are only three. Of those three remaining churches, Westminster is presently the only congregation that is fully incarnating the broadest meaning of being an intercultural ministry.

As early as March 23, 1952, the Presbytery of New Brunswick called a joint strategy meeting to discuss the results of a survey revealing the demographic changes in Trenton with all of the trustees and elders of all the city churches. Twelve years later, in 1964, the presbytery's urban work committee invited all active officers to participate in a discussion of "The Church in the Changing City." At a congregational meeting in 1965, Pastor Zink expressed the following:

> We must face realistically the fact that our church neighborhood is changing rapidly in a racial way. This is evident as you walk the streets and as you see the boys and girls going to and from school. It is evident in those neighborhood programs in which our church is involved: released-time religious school, the study hall, the baby keep well clinic, the pre-kindergarten project and, I believe, also in our Boy Scout troop. We dare not close our eyes to this fact nor our doors to these people in our neighborhood. Christ has called us to minister to all. Not with a noisy crusade but in a quiet and loving way, we must let these people know that they are welcome in the name of Christ.

Our denomination's resource on redevelopment reveals that churches which experience change and decline often follow the stages of personal grief related to loss: the emotions of denial, anger, guilt, blaming, and finally acceptance. Our denomination also has witnessed that often the first pastor who fully "takes the wool off" the eyes of a congregation in order to help it meet the changing needs of its membership or community often becomes a scapegoat, because most congregations would rather continue in denial and avoid facing the challenge.

Even before Westminster's pastor, Rev. Dana Livesay and leaders knew about the PCUSA's "Five Dynamic Forces of Congregational Redevelopment" Westminster was implementing then. On October 18, 1987, Rev. Livesay implemented the Dynamic Force of "Coming to Terms with the Past, Present, and Future." At that time, he presented to Westminster's session the following "a to g" list of possible alternatives, as a response to the realities of declining membership and dwindling resources in the wake of suburban flight:

a. continue ministry as usual to present membership;

b. reach out to the community and become more integrated;

c. continue ministry to present members, but at the same time become a home for a new church development that would reach out to the community but be a completely separate church;

d. merge with another church and remain within our building;

e. close the church;

f. close the church and become the home of a new church development;

g. choose proposal (a) and seek to merge with another church and use their building.

It was a major awakening and challenge to Westminster, a Presbyterian church in the city, that things could not remain the way that they were. Yet, even at the risk of losing more members, Westminster chose option "b" to embrace its community by being open to radically changing the racial-ethnic composition of its congregational and pastoral leadership.

Rev. Livesay also implemented the dynamic force of "Re-entering the Community" through faith-based community organizing. Westminster took its first step toward redevelopment when it reentered its racially changed community through active involvement in the Interfaith Organizing Committee (IOC). Ms. Kathleen O' Toole was the IOC staff person who served as an "enabler" facilitating church members to build community among themselves. The church later reached out to the neighborhood community by participating in listening campaigns through "house meetings." This wasn't simply a clergy-driven initiative. Some of the members, who were led by the Holy Spirit, were trained and later became actively involved in faith-based community organizing.

Experimental and innovative ministries and clustering ministry models, such as "The Shared Ministry Experiment" led by Rev. Patti Daley, Rev. Jacqueline Lewis, Rev. John Nelson, and the Trenton Presbyterian Cluster of Churches' Trenton Youth Connection (TYC) ministry, also enabled Westminster to clarify God's mission and vision for Westminster's ministry in the Wilbur Community of Trenton. Westminster members realized that in order to reveal our commitment to ministering to our diverse community, our congregation would have to call a racial-ethnic pastor. Rev. Jacqueline Lewis became the first racial-ethnic pastor. I followed Rev. Lewis in 1995.

After gathering helpful suggestions from the congregation, the Session of Westminster Presbyterian Church at its congregational meeting on March 10, 1996, unanimously voted to adopt the following mission and vision statements as presented by the leadership team. These statements reflected the feedback gathered from the congregation. When Elder Willard R. Carson Jr., then a sixty-five-year member, made the motion, and Elder Paul Drum, then a twenty-one-year member, seconded the motion to adopt them, we paused to celebrate a truly historic event for our church and thanked God for God's faithfulness:

MISSION STATEMENT
A House of Prayer and Praise for People of All Nations

VISION STATEMENT
As a part of the Body of Christ we are a multiracial, multicultural and multigenerational congregation where:
—the Word of God is central.
—spiritual growth is nurtured.
—loving, compassionate fellowship is fostered.
—traditional and contemporary styles of worship are embraced.

As Ambassadors of "God's Kin-dom," we are in partnership with the community and other neighborhood churches to seek the welfare of the city through providing:
—programs and advocacy for social and racial justice.
—a safe haven and educational opportunities for children, youth and their families.
—recovery programs which nurture health and wholeness.

This mission statement was inspired by Genesis' affirmation that we are all created equally in God's image, Pentecost's declaration that the body of Christ is called to be united by the Holy Spirit in the midst of its rich diversity, and Revelation's images of the City of God where all tribes, nations, peoples, and languages will worship God. We again affirm that this is not without challenges, but we believe that this is where God continues to challenge us as Presbyterians who believe that we are called to "abide in" and "seek the welfare of the city."

In 1998, during our centennial anniversary year, the various events, celebrations, and the publication of our *Centennial History of Westminster Presbyterian Church* also helped Westminster come to terms with its past, present, and future. Westminster, in November 2000, became the first official Radical Redirection Ministry of the New Brunswick Presbytery. One of the most memorable events in our church history occurred in September 2006, when Westminster, along with four other churches, received former PCUSA's Multicultural Network's First Prize award for our "Multicultural Church Story." Although Westminster can no longer give financially to our denomination to the extent that we have in the past, we can and do share our God-given gifts and wisdom by leading workshops and providing worship leadership. Our staff and leaders share the wisdom that we have gathered with other churches and leaders who are considering transforming into a multicultural worshiping community and/or reentering their communities by providing programs for children and youth. In 2014 and 2015, Westminster's leaders played pivotal leadership roles in the Inaugural Urban Ministry Conference and the Interim and Transitional Ministry Conference held at Princeton Theological Seminary.

There are many challenges to creating intercultural churches. I have witnessed to my dismay how the suburbs have helped perpetuate so-called separate-but-equal worshiping communities of suburban whites and people of color in the inner cities. Many remnant white congregations that have remained in the city also have maintained so-called separate-but-equal relationships with neighborhood churches that are comprised of people of color. I find it very disturbing that many Christians, whites and people of color alike, are not convicted by the fact that despite Martin Luther King's prophetic critique proclaimed over fifty years ago, that Sunday morning continues to be the most segregated time in our society, and the church the most segregated institution.

C. S. Lewis, in his book *The Great Divorce*, described a vision of hell as a place where people move continually away from one another because they just cannot get along with each other. They choose instead to abandon their houses and entire blocks and neighborhoods and to build new houses at the periphery of hell, thereby creating an ever-expanding vacant center, with houses at the periphery and with the center abandoned behind them.[3] Joseph Barndt says that Lewis's description of hell could actually be a description of white flight from the city after WWII and the emergence of suburbs in the United States (and today's exurbs). He goes on to say that with suburbs came the demand for transportation systems to separate suburban whites from people of color in the inner cities. When I lived in Los Angeles, I drove the multilane and multilevel system ironically called "freeways." These have contributed to suburbanites' experiencing feelings of

3. Lewis, *The Great Divorce*, 18.

isolation and have even led some to minimize the effects of the commute by turning to alcohol and tranquilizers.[4]

Joseph Barndt's book *Dismantling Racism: The Continuing Challenge to White America* remains a valuable resource for our discussion on intercultural ministry. I appreciate his book because it reminds us that we can't talk about intercultural churches without first talking about racism, and in order to truly engage in introspection and intergroup dialogue, it is essential to use language that doesn't attack or produce defensiveness. Barndt analyzes the dehumanizing effects racism has on all of us—"people of color and white people alike—indoctrinated and socialized in such a way as to be made into 'prisoners of racism.'" He notes that every anti-racist leader, from Frederick Douglas to Martin Luther King Jr., emphasized how both white people and people of color are debilitated by racism, and that the goal is liberation for all people.[5]

Barndt utilizes creative and disturbing images to re-sensitize white Americans who have become anesthetized to the pain of living in a prison. He writes that

> white people, too, live in a racial ghetto. Although we may have built the walls ourselves, the resulting isolation and its effects are equally harmful. We live in a ghetto, on a reservation, in a separated, cut-off state of existence. We are racially, institutionally, and culturally segregated from people who are not white. Our communities are sterile, homogenous places of look-alike, dress-alike, act-alike conformity.[6]

People of color also anesthetize themselves from the pain of racism. Hyun K. Chung's description of Asian women's experience is also descriptive of what many other people of color experience. Asian women have defended themselves from the constant and sustained experiences of "shame, guilt, and self-hate by numbing themselves, thus creating a pseudo-safety of non-feeling." This behavior is dysfunctional because the oppressed are stripped of their power to resist. This numbing process is called the "separation sin" because it causes persons to be "separated from themselves, each other, and the God of Life."[7]

Joseph Barndt's image of hell comes to mind when I think of mainline urban European American churches who have not enthusiastically welcomed the "mission at their doorstep" opportunity when their

4. Barndt, *Dismantling Racism*, 54.
5. Barndt, *Dismantling Racism*, 6–7.
6. Barndt, *Dismantling Racism*, 6–7.
7. Chung, *Struggle to Be the Sun*, 41–42.

neighborhood racial-ethnic demographic composition changed. Instead, many respond to declining church membership due to "white flight" by fleeing to the suburbs, abandoning church buildings and leaving behind God's beloved communities.

My husband, Michael Granzen, in this book provides substantial evidence of the "conspiracy of silence" that exists in the predominantly white church in regard to open and sincere discussion of issues about race. Robert Terry, an analyst and educator on racism and racial justice, puts it succinctly: "To be white in America is not to have to think about it,"[8] and I would add, not to have to talk about it. Barndt asserts that European American congregations have become complacent and comfortable in their "white ghettoized churches in white ghettoized neighborhoods," no longer questioning whether this situation is a scandal to the gospel.[9]

The Book of Order of the Presbyterian Church (USA) contains strong "shall" statements on inclusiveness. Our constitution states that a "congregation shall welcome all persons who in trust God's grace in Jesus Christ and desire to become part of the fellowship and ministry of his Church" (F-1.0403); "No person shall be denied membership for any other reason not related to profession of faith. The gospel leads members to extend the fellowship of Christ to all persons. Failure to do so constitutes a rejection of Christ himself and causes a scandal to the gospel" (G-1.0302).

Yet, instead of being scandalized by how some racially exclusive churches contradict our witness to the Lord's gift of unity, the tendency is to rationalize the existence of these churches by stating, "This is just human nature," or by quoting church growth experts who claim that homogeneous communities are the most effective strategy for optimal church growth, or by clinging to the notion that being a good steward of God's resources means investing primarily in new church developments and redevelopments now known as transformation churches that are racially specific because their "successful" growth potential is much greater and the church is guaranteed a greater outcome from their investment. Mainline European American Christians have explicitly or implicitly expected Native Americans, African Americans, Hispanic/Latinx Americans, and Asian Americans to leave their cultures at the door of the sanctuary as they enter a Eurocentric-style worship service and thereby experiencing "cultural circumcision."

We must become aware of the fact that culture has a dictatorial power that influences our thoughts and behavior by creating unconscious, built-in

8. Terry, "The Negative Impact on White Values," 120.

9. Barndt, *Dismantling Racism*, 140.

blinders that become hidden and unspoken assumptions.[10] For instance, there is a hidden and unstated assumption prevalent in the dominant culture of the United States, and that is that "white/Anglo" is not an ethnic group.

Minority cultural groups are called ethnics, thereby implying that they are different from the norm because of their race and culture, the norm being the culture of the white/Anglo. Church historian and theologian Catherine González, in "The Diversity with Which We Begin," states that this unspoken assumption denies the fact that the white/Anglo worship style is influenced and controlled by their culture. Denying this reality prevents "the unraveling of cultural processes," and thus the white/Anglo worship style becomes superior and the norm.[11] The emphatic declaration "This is not Presbyterian!" made by many Presbyterians, white and people of color alike, is more often than not a reference to some element of worship that is not Eurocentric. The other hidden and unspoken assumption is that minority cultures have a uniformity that doesn't actually exist. For instance, the term Hispanic American denies the differences that exist among Hispanics from the Caribbean and Central and South America.[12]

Due to the complex, dictatorial power of culture, we all must desperately cling to the faith-knowledge that the Holy Spirit is continually transforming our conscious and unconscious conformity to the oppressive elements of this world by renewing our minds (Rom 12:2). We can make a choice to personally engage in the renewing process of our minds by exposing ourselves to Scripture. Justo González's "grammar for reading the Bible in Spanish" suggests we read Scripture in the vocative voice: "The purpose of scripture is not so much to interpret it as to allow it to interpret us and our situation."[13]

The title "The Acts of the Apostles" is truly a misnomer, because the body of Jesus Christ cannot accomplish its mission without the power of the Holy Spirit. Since the church's inception at Pentecost, the Holy Spirit revealed that the church of Jesus Christ would be "multilingual and multicultural, [since] at Pentecost God sanctioned linguistic and cultural pluralism."[14] Based on this interpretation, "Babel was a monument to the arrogance of one people; Pentecost on the other hand should lead to the humiliation of anyone who thinks their language is superior to others."[15]

---

10. Hall, *Beyond Culture*, 220.

11. C. González, "The Diversity with Which We Begin," 71.

12. C. González, "The Diversity with Which We Begin," 71.

13. González, *Mañana*, 86.

14. Malcolm, "The Christian Teacher," 53.

15. Malcolm, "The Christian Teacher," 53.

As recorded in the Gospels, Jesus set the stage for the type of church the Holy Spirit would empower by personally incarnating a ministry to the unwelcome strangers, the inferior untouchables of his society, i.e., an intercultural church. Luke 4 illustrates how Jesus, even at the risk of losing his own life, revealed God's clear preference for the poor, the captives, the blind, the oppressed, and even for the ritually unclean and culturally different Gentiles.

The Holy Spirit orchestrated the process needed to transform Peter's mind about the Gentile people and his exclusive understanding of the mission of the church. For us to truly grasp why a transforming process was indispensable, we need to be reminded of how Peter's religious training and cultural conditioning influenced his perception of Gentiles. Anticipating Peter's understandable reluctance, the Holy Spirit commanded Peter to go with Cornelius's men because, as Peter said so tactlessly upon entering Cornelius' home, "it is unlawful for a Jew to associate with or to visit a Gentile" (Acts 10:28). Most law-abiding Jews such as Peter would avoid even more any contact with a Roman centurion, since the Roman Empire encouraged their people to mix their religions.[16] Peter's next statement, "God has shown me that I should not call anyone profane and unclean," reveals his previous hidden opinion about Gentiles (Acts 10:28). The process began with a vision that was interpreted three times in order to make absolutely sure Peter understood; proceeded to an actual *cara a cara* ("face to face") encounter with God's children, which quickly gave him an opportunity to implement this new divine insight; and ended with the undeniable evidence of the Holy Spirit's presence and approval when the God-fearing Gentiles received the gift of the Holy Spirit, spoke in tongues, and worshiped God!

Through this process Peter, the great teacher of the gospel, actually became a learner: when he encounters Cornelius *cara a cara*, he declares with conviction: "I truly understand that God shows no partiality, but in every nation anyone who fears [God] and does what is right is acceptable to [God]" (Acts 10:34–35).

In order to create an intercultural church, white people, as well as people of color in our church, need to experience a transforming and renewing of their minds in order to be freed from the debilitating effects of internalized oppression. Internalized oppression manifests itself in many ways, such as "system beating, blaming the system, anti-white avoidance of contact, denial of cultural heritage, and lack of understanding of the political significance of differences."[17]

16. González, *Hechos*, 176.
17. Batts, *Modern Racism*, 11.

Realizing Westminster's God-given mission and vision to become an intercultural congregation by moving from a Eurocentric to a multicultural style of worship has required the delicate embrace of contemporary and traditional styles of worship. During our thirty-plus years of transformation, we have had periodic "worship wars" and other conflicts. Westminster has accepted that, given our diversity, conflicts are a given. When I became the pastor, I asked the congregation to adopt two norms in order to deal with conflicts in a healthy way: "care-fronting"; that is, caring enough about relationships so that conflicts are never avoided, but rather dealt with loving truth-telling,[18] and the Latino idiom, *hablar sin pelos en la lengua*, i.e., "speak without hair on your tongue." The metaphor means do not swallow your voice.

Frederick Buechner's quote, "The place God calls you to is the place where your deep gladness and the world's deep hunger meet,"[19] reminds me of what I often say after each of Westminster's several city-wide events, where hundreds of children and families are loved and served: "I am joyfully exhausted."

I truly believe that because Westminster and I embraced our God-given call to become an intercultural missional congregation with a passion and dedication to seek the shalom of the city, despite our relatively small size and limited resources, God has equipped us to be a cutting-edge leader in Urban Ministry in the PCUSA and beyond. Through our thirty-plus church nonprofit and private cooperation partnerships, we are actively and effectively engaged in addressing several of our nation's most challenging issues:

1. low quality public school education;

2. mass incarceration;

3. ministering to reentry/returning citizens and their families;

4. reaching out via the Bethany House of Hospitality to young adults who feel disenfranchised by the traditional church, yet still called to serve the City of Trenton;

5. and assisting immigrants to acquire English proficiency in order to support the education of their children and to secure gainful employment.

I believe that the Holy Spirit has been orchestrating Westminster's transformation process into an intercultural, beloved community of God. We have witnessed the Holy Spirit's presence and affirmation when Euro-American members no longer feel comfortable worshiping in an all-white, Eurocentric church, and when people of color overcome their internalized oppression

18. Cf. Augsburger, *Caring Enough to Confront*, 10.
19. Buechner, *Wishful Thinking*.

and are empowered to share their diverse gifts in worship with integrity and joy.

Urban centers are not forever damned because of their multiracial and multicultural diversity; they are forever blessed! "And I saw the holy city, the new Jerusalem, coming down out of heaven from God, prepared as a bride and a bridegroom adorned for each other. And I heard a loud voice from the throne saying, 'See, the home of God is among mortals. God will dwell with them; they will be God's peoples'" (Rev 21:2–3). Intercultural ministry is challenging, but it can also be very enriching and transforming for white people and people of color. Cities provide the "sacred space" whereby, as John S. Dunne wrote, "cultures can know and touch each other as never before, persons can be aware as never before of what was from the beginning always real: their common humanity and the many manifestations of the one ultimate mystery."[20]

20. Knitter, *No Other Name*, 211.

II

The "Rigors of a Time yet to Come"

Richard K. Fenn, Professor Emeritus, Christianity and Society,
Princeton Theological Seminary

Americans have on occasion imagined that their nation is exemplary, like ancient Israel: "a city set upon a hill" to give light to the other nations of the world. Our biblical inheritance once linked us through memory and devotion to the Israelites who, once fated to be slaves in Egypt, endured the trials of the wilderness to found a universal city radiant with divine glory. Peoples whose fate had been determined by the bonds of race, blood, and soil, once they found themselves on American shores, would find their destiny. Living to the full extent of their capacities, and through their sacrifices, they would share in the nation's glory. Therefore, the legitimacy of American institutions, of our legislatures and our courts, of schools and our communities, has depended on the extent to which they honor and foster the personhood of each individual human being. In return, hundreds of thousands have died to make these promises come true: many of them without ever having fulfilled their dreams or having lived to the full extent of their capacities.

Americans therefore live with a social contract that puts the nation's legitimacy on continuous trial. Reinforcing the American social contract and giving it existential force has been a culture that fosters the fulfilment of the self—of the soul—in a lifetime of self-offering. American heroes have been saintly or prophetic. In the past year, for instance, Americans have been revisiting moments that have posed a critical test of who we are, the focus of Blacks and whites has been on a single human being whose spiritual trial forged the destiny of the nation as a whole. Americans have revisited the day when John Lewis had nearly died on the bridge to Selma. For a moment, as Lewis lay stricken, looking upward at a man prepared to bring a pipe down on his head. A moment later, he could still breathe; a protestor had pushed his assailant out of the way. Years later, on the day before he entered a hospital to die of cancer, John Lewis spoke of having visited the Black Lives Matter Plaza outside the White House, where Black and white protestors had been pepper sprayed and forcibly shoved aside to make way for the president and his retinue on their way to be photographed outside St. John's Episcopal Church. Now that same plaza witnessed to the truth that Black lives do indeed matter. As Lewis put it: "That is why I had to visit Black Lives Matter Plaza in Washington, though I was admitted to the hospital the following day. I just had to see and feel it for myself that, after many years of silent witness, the truth is still marching on."[1] Now, the central figure is not a Martin Luther King or a Medgar Evers, whose assassination brought an abrupt end to the civil rights movement. It is no longer a John Lewis risking his life on the bridge into Selma, Alabama, or a James Lawson engaging in nonviolent resistance in order to make public facilities as accessible to Blacks as they long had been to whites. Now, it is a Black man named George Floyd begging for breath as he was dying under the knee of a white policeman staring blank-faced into the camera of a bystander. Now, however, as tens of thousands have been marching in the streets, they are shouting, "I can't breathe."

American democracy is legitimate if and only if it sanctifies the irreducible, essential, and ultimate value of the individual person. Otherwise, some are more entitled than others to life, to liberty, and to the pursuit of happiness. However, hundreds and thousands of them, both Blacks and whites, know that they have been ignored, abandoned, or sacrificed to the old gods of race, blood, and soil. The Black Lives Matter movement has given the lie to the notion that America is a nation with "justice for all." An angry mob waving the Confederate flag has invaded the Capitol building, with some of its members intent on capturing and executing the two leaders next in the line of succession to President Trump.

The old stories of an exemplary and heroic nation, freed from slavery, tested in the wilderness, favored by the deity and destined for glory, no longer ring true. Indeed, the stories we have told ourselves about America's destiny to be "the first new nation" among the nations of the word—a beacon of liberty and justice to those still straining under the burden of old bondage

1. Lewis, "Together," para. 2.

have always been proleptic: a way of talking as if the longed-for future had already arrived; a rhetorical promissory note that has justified sacrifices for a future that has yet to arrive and in the meantime created debts that can never be paid.

To sustain the American dream, therefore, we need to tell ourselves stories of those who have engaged in radical self-giving even in the face of death. That is why Americans continue to memorialize and revere the lives of those whose personhood represents a victory over their fate: an existential point of departure liking their own destiny with the nation itself. During the sixties, when James Lawson developed Satyagraha ("soul force") to open drinking fountains, bathrooms, and lunch counters to Blacks, he was indeed "scared to death"—as he revealed in his tribute to John Lewis, who himself told us, shortly before his death, that he thought he was about to die on that bridge into Selma. Fight, spiritual trial, existential struggle for the soul of the nation: these are also the terms of the national struggle. They apply with equal force to the spiritual trial of each American soul to face its own capacity not only for good, but for evil.

These stories challenge the ways in which we, as Americans, have protected ourselves from the fear of death while reassuring ourselves of our own uniqueness or superiority. As James Baldwin put it fifty years ago: "Perhaps the whole root of our trouble, the human trouble . . . is that we will sacrifice all the beauty of our lives, will imprison ourselves in totems, taboos, crosses, blood sacrifices, steeples mosques, races, armies, flags, nation, in order to deny the fact of death, which is the only fact we have."[2] As Dietrich Bonhoeffer once reminded us, in his *Letters from Prison*, it is only a God pushed to the margins who can help us now. We find that God in all our Gethsemanes: in all souls who begging for more time, sorrowful unto death, and longing for someone to watch with them.

James Baldwin had found a darkness in "the nature of the American psychology which, in order to apprehend or be made able to accept it, must undergo a metamorphosis so profound as to be literally unthinkable and which there is no doubt we will resist until we are compelled to achieve our own identity by *the rigors of a time that has yet to come*."[3] When Baldwin was writing, however, there was still a sense that the end was still a way off. The time would come, however, when what Americans held sacred would no longer be able either to protect them from death or to shield them from the truth about themselves. Only then would the nation itself confront

2. Baldwin, *The Fire Next Time*, 92.
3. Baldwin, *Notes of a Native Son*, 37; emphasis added.

death without the protections offered by the institutions, the beliefs, and the symbols that assure us of our uniqueness, our superiority, and our authority.

Early in the Trump administration there were signs that the rigors of just such a time of spiritual struggle had already begun. In his inaugural address, Trump announced the advent of a new era in the life of this country: ending its darkness and enlightening all those who could indeed see the light. The fight, however, had only just begun. There were enemies still to be identified and expelled from the deep-state, dangerous immigrants who would defile and destroy our way of life, and experts and politicians whose opinions took little account of the lives of the real people, the *volk*. Hitler, as we remember, also spoke of Germans as engaged in precisely such a spiritual struggle; he spoke of the nation's fight to free itself from the fate it had endured so that it could once again offer national devotions to the old gods. It would not be long before a mob would invade the nation's Capitol, intent on killing any official or legislator who opposed them. Some carried the flags of the Confederacy or wore the insignia of Nazi Germany; at least one who carried the American flew it upside down over a banner proclaiming the name of Trump. Armed with automatic weapons, handcuffs, rope, and a guillotine, they all had been commissioned by the president of the United States to save their country from Congress. The flags and the crosses, the emblems of our sense of racial and national superiority, were no longer protecting us from death but had become the emblems of a vengeful and murderous hatred.

In a little-noticed but damning and authoritative announcement scarcely two weeks after Donald Trump's inauguration as president, the Council of Bishops in the African Methodist Episcopal Church unanimously declared:

> Since his inauguration on January 20th, less than 10 days ago, now President Trump has taken actions which have divided and polarized the nation even more, showing insensitivity and callous disregard for the rights and wellbeing of countless millions of American citizens, and harming our national security around the world. The Council of Bishops of the African Methodist Episcopal Church, the first protestant denomination formed on American soil, had hoped that the Trump Administration would alter the views and policies espoused during the presidential campaign, but is disappointed and troubled by the decisions and actions taken during the early days of this administration, and vow to do all that we can to see that these decisions and actions do not last. We ask that every member of this denomination, and people who are committed to justice and righteousness, equality and truth, will join with us to thwart

what are *clearly demonic acts*. Indeed, the words of the Apostle
Paul to the believers at Ephesus apply today, "For we wrestle not
against flesh and blood, but against . . . *the rulers of the darkness*
of this present age, against *spiritual wickedness in high places*."[4]

Clearly, the African Methodist Episcopal Bishops had understood exactly
how evil were the forces of darkness, long latent and systemic in American
society, but now far more visible in what amounted to public lynching by
the forces of law and order.

The times were therefore both more dangerous and more frightening;
the time had come for the long overdue confrontation and exposure with
the powers of darkness. Spiritual wickedness in high places was legitimat-
ing the local assertion and display of the murderous hatred that had long
divided whites and Blacks. For over two centuries, Blacks have known what
it means for their own lives to be dismissed, diminished, and discarded:
to live in a country that would always ignore them when it was not pouring contempt on their very existence. Baldwin remembered that during the
WWII, white soldiers had shown more respect for their German prisoners
than for their Black comrades-in-arms; his white fellow soldiers even told
their German prisoners that Blacks were subhuman. Baldwin also knew
what it was to be hauled into the basement of the local police precinct and
there beaten for offenses he had not committed. More devastating was the
prospect of living a life that could never fulfill its potential precisely because
the white community withheld the very opportunities that were necessary
if any individual were to be able to realize the full extent of her capacities.
There was no doubt that Blacks suffered what Baldwin called "a necessary
dimension": the fatefulness of being born Black. It was the necessity imposed by being Black in a nation that has captured and enslaved them, a
nation that continues to regard them as unnecessary and expendable.

The American promise simply did not apply to being Black. The fate
of being a descendant of Ham precluded any other destiny than forever to
be guilty of a crime that one has not committed. If Black lives mattered,
therefore, they mattered to whites who needed to find an embodiment of
their own darkness. Unable to love another, whites needed someone to hate.
On the one hand, as Baldwin pointed out, the Negro's "depth of involvement
and unspoken recognition of shared experience . . . creates a way of life,"[5]
but unlike the Jews, they lack "centuries of exile and persecution" and their

4. Council of Bishops, *Episcopal Statement*; emphasis added.
5. Baldwin, *Notes of a Native Son*, 30.

tradition of reflecting on "the strength which endured and the sensibility which discovered in it the high possibility of a moral victory."[6]

However, as America becomes a nation running out of time, there is very little time left either for Blacks and whites to confront their fates or to lay hold of their destinies. Americans, Black and white, now have to choose between their fate and their destiny. That possibility could shape the common destiny of both whites and Blacks: the "We" of whom Baldwin once spoke as if it had already come into being. Now, as white supremacists storm the Capitol, the time has come to hear once again Baldwin's mandate that Americans, both white and Black, face and explore their own darkness. We now endure what for James Baldwin were only the "rigors of a time yet to come."

If we are separate our destiny from what has long been our fate, we will have to immerse ourselves in our old stories. As Louis Ruprecht reminds us, "In the telling of the mythos, in the fleshing out of Fate's skeleton, a distinctive character emerges, a Destiny emerges."[7] Americans have not entirely forgotten the agonies embodied in their religious traditions. A small majority of Americans have just elected a president who speaks of reclaiming the soul of this country and who promises to be "whole-souled" in his commitment to unify the country around its highest ideals; he himself is a devoutly Catholic Christian.

To discover our destiny in the midst of our fate, we will need to have some sense of what we mean by "God": the term many of us use to name our origin, our nature, and our destiny. As James Baldwin put it, "If the concept of God has any validity or any use, it can only be to make us larger, freer, and more loving."[8] Charles Peguy, on the other hand, imaged the myth of history, Clio, as dictating that "the total liberty of man must have had an infinite price in that affair of yours, and obviously, quite obviously, the intention was that everything should be done out of love in your system, and that love should only move in a full, complete, and well-balanced liberty."[9] To paraphrase Ruprecht in the passage just quoted, it is only in our ancient myths that we will be able to sense what may have been—or may yet become—our destiny. If it is not to rule over all creation, or to be a light to enlighten the other nations of the world, or be purified in the final fires that leave behind only the few found sufficiently pure or faithful to serve the purposes of the divine, it may well be what the Catholic theologian once discerned in a conversation with the muse of history.

6. Baldwin, *Notes of a Native Son*, 36–37.
7. Ruprecht, "Mark's Tragic Vision," 2–3.
8. Baldwin, *The Fire Next Time*, 4.
9. Peguy, *Temporal and Eternal*, 158.

No power other than love can open the gates to a world where neither skin color or protective masks can obscure and hide the presence of the real, particular, and personal presence. It is love that ignores or strips away whatever comes between souls. Now, if love is ever to "swing wide" the gates to an open society, whites, too, will need to make a comparably radical, open-hearted, and unconditional self-offering in the face of exclusion, oppression, and death.

In the passage already quoted, Ruprecht is speaking of the story of Jesus in Gethsemane, and it is crucial for us especially at this time, for it does not lend itself to a myth of the chosen and exemplary nation, destined to draw all other nations to itself or to rule with unfettered sovereignty over all other people; nor does Gethsemane tell the story of one whose humiliation and death on the cross prefigures a resurrected King of the Cosmos who will triumph in the End. On the contrary, it reveals to us what it means to struggle to realize one's destiny when all that is certain is one's fate: the intensity of spiritual trial in the time remaining when faced with finality. The moment is fateful; how one lives in it will determine whether one's death is a mere capitulation to fate or a final approach to one's destiny. As in any Kairos, what is clearly a point of no return becomes a point of departure for all that is yet to come. The end becomes both a turning point and a new beginning.

Gethsemane is thus the consummate critical moment: the Kairos that marks the difference between all that has come before and that will come afterward. In the story of Gethsemane, time itself is transformed, as the eternal becomes once and for all enmeshed in the temporal. It is the future of God that is at stake and not of humanity alone. Translated into the terms of secularity, a comparable Kairos for this nation would be one in which its destiny is not only revealed and shaped, but the nation will also have taken an irrevocable step toward its destiny.

CONCLUSION

At the core of American identity, then, is the conviction that our way of life, our institutions and values, and our place in history is that America stands and falls on how, as a nation, we honor the unconditional and ultimate value of the individual person. The nation's legitimacy, then, is fractured when any individual's right to be and to become a fully constituted and realized person is undermined, thwarted, or threatened by social policies or practices. That is precisely James Baldwin's point when he argues that, as a nation, America has no real place for the Black. To be a Black is to be deprived of the rights and stature of personhood: Blacks being easily disregarded and devalued when they are not being demeaned, debased, or simply discarded. The nation now is engaged in a spiritual trial that requires us to face and to understand the powers of darkness and the "spiritual wickedness" endemic in American society. The widespread degradation of our collective life during the administration of Donald Trump—the violation of our democratic standards and practices, the hundreds of thousands of deaths that could have been averted had the president sought to distribute masks, protective equipment, medicines, and vaccines, the loss of our capacity to ensure either the sanctity of the vote or public health and safety, have brought the nation to a point of no return. We know and can name evil when we see it, but few have had the moral courage of the bishops of the A.M.E. Church to denounce it.

The time has come for precisely this belief in Christ as the consummate and universal human person. Here is Pasternak again: "Human personhood as a divine attribute elevates the prosaic ordinariness of human life everywhere by connecting it to the very essence of God."[10] The doctors, nurses, and technicians who overcame their exhaustion, fear, and depression were offering themselves: their souls and bodies were sacraments of that divine essence; so are the victims of police violence gasping, "I can't breathe," and the tens of thousands chanting, "Black lives matter."

That America is founded on a principle that calls into question the value of every institution or practice that fails to honor the human person does not separate America from other nations or make America special. This is what might be called a "civilizational" fact. You can find it on the streets of Moscow when tens of thousands of Russians protest, saying, "I exist." That is the power of the movement led by Navalny, the value of whose personhood, even when he is being beaten, jailed, or poisoned, threatens the legitimacy of the Kremlin. That is why we can find in the Russian writer Boris Pasternak a tribute to the sanctity of personhood that could as well have been written by James Baldwin himself:

> Jesus's importance lies not in his being the Son of God or the second person of the Trinity (that is, his divine attributes), but rather in how he, in his humanity, affirms the worth of human personhood as an attribute of the divinity . . . [and reflects] Pasternak's own interest in personalist philosophy at this time . . . Pasternak confessed that the "general spiritual picture" of the brotherhood of the English personalists—"its conceptual contours, those aspects through which symbolism and Christianity

10. Pasternak, letter from December 1945, quoted in Givens, *The Image of Christ in Russian Literature*, 184.

are present in it"—coincides in surprising fashion with what is happening with me. It is dearest to me now.[11]

The sanctity of the human being, the dignity and worth of the human personality, and the significance of human personhood are key components of both personalist philosophy and Pasternak's Christology in his novel.

---

11. Pasternak, letter from December 1945, quoted in Givens, *The Image of Christ in Russian Literature*, 182.

12

This Is a Hymn

Lorna Goodison, Poet Laureate, Jamaica

Professor Emerita, English Language and Literature and African Studies, University of Michigan

This Is a Hymn

For all who ride the trains
all night,
sleep on sidewalks and park benches;
beneath basements
and abandoned buildings

This is a hymn.

For all those whose homes
are the great outdoors,
the streets their one big room;
for live men asleep in tombs.

This is a hymn.

For bag women
pushing rubbish babies

in ridiculous prams;
dividing open lots
into elaborate architects' plans.

This is a Hymn.

Mansions of the dispossessed,
magnificence of desperate rooms,
kings and queens of homelessness,
die with empty bottles
rising from their tombs.

This is a hymn

For all recommending
a bootstrap as a way
to rise with effort
on your part.
This is a hymn

may it renew
what passes for your heart.

This Hymn

is for the must-be-blessed;
the victims of this world
who know salt best.
The world tribe
of the dispossessed,
outside the halls of plenty
looking in.
This is a benediction.
This is a hymn.

One day in late August 1986, I saw a tall Black woman stride up to an ATM machine outside the Harvard Co-op in Cambridge, Massachusetts, and put in a bank card which was promptly ejected from the machine. The woman tried the card three more times; each time it was rejected, until the machine took possession of the card and refused to give it back, even after the woman hammered hard on the keypad and pounded on the metal sides. I was standing a few feet away and I never heard the woman utter even one word during the entire time that all this was taking place. When she turned to walk away,

I caught a closer look at her and observed that she was dressed in an outfit that would have been considered smart business attire back then, except that her well-tailored "power suit" was now badly in need of cleaning, and her leather pumps looked as worn out as the designer handbag out of which she'd fished the now redundant bank card.

I have never been able to forget that woman, who was more than likely once considered a real somebody. Maybe someone who'd attended Harvard University and who used to have a good job and a bank account from which she was accustomed to withdrawing money, maybe at that same ATM that had so unceremoniously spat her card back at her, before it grabbed it and locked it away forever.

"There but for the grace of God," I thought to myself that day, as I made my way back to the Bunting Institute where I was blessed enough to have been on a fellowship that year. Then a few days after I saw that woman, I was walking along Brattle Street in the middle of the day, trying to figure out the way to the Harvard Divinity School, when I met Michael Granzen. Actually, what happened was that as I was proceeding along Brattle Street, I looked up ahead and saw a man bending down and carefully placing an empty soda can, not in, but behind, a trash can. When he straightened up, I noticed that he was wearing a Union Seminary T-shirt, and I thought to myself surely this is someone who would be able to point me in the direction of the Harvard Divinity School; which, as it turned out, Michael had recently graduated from, and where he happened to be heading that day. On the walk there, I asked him why he had been so carefully placing an empty soda can behind, as opposed to in, the trash bin; and he explained that he'd done this so that the people who collected and sold empty soda cans did not have to sort through the garbage to get to them. I knew at that moment that I'd found myself in the company of someone who is what some older Jamaicans would describe as "not a usual person." As I found out more about him and his profoundly life-changing work with the homeless community in Cambridge and his parish at Fourth Presbyterian Church in South Boston, I became convinced that he was way more than a not usual person. I became certain that Michael Granzen is one of the ones appointed to help take care of the world.

I credit my friendship with him, begun that day on Brattle Street, with helping me to accept the fact that I too have a duty of care for the world, that I too could speak for those who have no voice, for those who have had their voices taken from them.

All that fall of 1986, I kept thinking of the woman at the ATM machine. I felt guilty that I had not tried to help her. I should have offered to give her some money. I should have said something. I should have done something, something like what Rev. Mike did when he placed that empty soda can where a fellow human could get at it while still maintaining some semblance of dignity. So one day I wrote the poem "This Is a Hymn," and I dedicated it to Michael Granzen, my good, good friend lo these thirty-odd years who showed me that day on Brattle Street how an act as seemingly simple as saving a fellow human being from the further indignity of sifting through trash to get at an empty soda can is a kind of benediction. A kind of hymn.

Bibliography

Acuff, Annalise, and Kathryn Hardison. "Update: Names Released of Those Accused of Sexual Abuse in Jefferson City Diocese." *Columbia Missourian*, November 8, 2018. https://www.columbiamissourian.com/news/local/update-names-released-of-those-accused-of-sexual-abuse-in-jefferson-city-diocese/article_0ca13052-e389-11e8-9f36-d3d6a3afe1c8.html.

Adler, Claire. "A Review of New Jersey Prison Theater Cooperative's Caged." *Pen America*, June 18, 2020. https://pen.org/a-review-of-new-jersey-prison-theater-cooperatives-caged/.

Aho, James. *This Thing of Darkness: A Sociology of the Enemy*. Seattle: University of Washington Press, 1994.

Alexander, Michelle. *The New Jim Crow*. New York: New Press, 2010.

Alters, Diana. "A Walk of History, Healing." *Boston Globe*, September 8, 1986.

Amnesty International. *Threat and Humiliation: Racial Profiling, Domestic Security and Human Rights in the United States*. Ridgefield Park, NJ: Globe Litho, 2004.

Augsburger, David. *Caring Enough to Confront: How to Understand and Express Your Deepest Feelings Toward Others*. Ventura: Regal, 1981.

Badham, Roger. *Introduction to Christian Theology*. Louisville: Westminster John Knox, 1998.

Baldwin, James. *The Fire Next Time*. New York: Vintage, 1992.

———. *Notes of a Native Son*. Boston: Beacon, 1984.

———. "On Being White and Other Lies." *Essence*, April, 1984.

———. *The Price of the Ticket*. New York: St. Martin's, 1985.

Barlow, Andrew. *Between Fear and Hope: Globalization and Race in the United States*. New York: Rowman and Littlefield, 2003.

Barndt, Joseph. *Dismantling Racism: The Continuing Challenge to White America*. Minneapolis: Augsburg Fortress, 1991.

Batts, Valerie. *Modern Racism: New Melody for the Same Old Tunes*. EDS Occasional Papers. Cambridge: Episcopal Divinity School, 1998.

Becker, Ernest. *Escape from Evil*. New York: Free Press, 1975.

Bell, Derrick. "A Commission on Race? Wow." *New York Times*, June 14, 1997. https://www.nytimes.com/1997/06/14/opinion/a-commission-on-race-wow.html.

———. *Faces at the Bottom of the Well: The Permanence of Racism*. New York: Basic Books, 1992.

Bennett, Lerone. *Shaping of Black America*. Chicago: Johnson, 1975.

Bensman, David, and Roberta Lynch. *Rusted Dreams*. New York: McGraw-Hill, 1987.

Bertram, Eva, et al. *Drug War Politics: The Price of Denial*. Berkeley: University of California Press, 1996.

Bluestone, Barry, and Bennet Harrison. *The Deindustrialization of America*. New York: Basic Books, 1983.

Boesak, Allan. *Black and Reformed: Apartheid, Liberation and the Calvinist Tradition*. Maryknoll: Orbis, 1984.

Bollas, Christopher. *Being a Character*. New York: Hill and Wang, 1992.

Bonilla-Silva, Eduardo. *Racism Without Racists*. Oxford: Rowman and Littlefield, 2003.

———. *White Supremacy and Racism in the Post-Civil Rights Era*. Boulder, CO: Lynne Riener, 2001.

Bowlby, Chris. "Vladimir Putin's Formative German Years." BBC News, March 27, 2015. https://www.bbc.com/news/magazine-32066222.

Brooks, Roy. *Racial Justice in the Age of Obama*. Princeton: Princeton University Press, 2009.

Brown, Coleman. "Baccalaureate Address." Ursinus College, Collegeville, PA, 2007. Unpublished manuscript.

———. *Our Hearts Are Restless, Till They Find Their Rest in Thee: Prophetic Wisdom in a Time of Anguish*. Eugene, OR: Cascade, 2020.

Bruni, Frank. "Am I My Brother's Keeper?" *New York Times Magazine*, May 12, 2002.

Buber, Martin. *I and Thou*. Translated by Ronald Gregor Smith. New York: Scribner, 2000.

Buechner, Frederick. *Wishful Thinking: A Theological ABC*. San Francisco: HarperOne, 1993.

Bullard, Robert. *The Quest for Environmental Justice*. San Francisco: Sierra Club, 2005.

Bullard, Robert D., et al. *Toxic Wastes and Race at Twenty*. Cleveland: United Church of Christ, 1997.

Burrow, Rufus, Jr. *God and Human Dignity*. Indiana: University of Notre Dame, 2006.

Buss, Terry, and Redburn Stevens. *Mass Unemployment: Plant Closings and Community Mental Health*. Beverly Hills: Sage, 1983.

Byron, Tammy K. *"A Catechism for Their Special Use": Slave Catechisms in the Antebellum South*. PhD Dissertation, Minnesota State University, 2008.

Calligaro, Lee. "The Negro's Legal Status in Pre-Civil War New Jersey." *New Jersey History* 70 (1967) 167–80.

Carr, Howie. *The Bulger Brothers: How They Terrorized and Corrupted Boston for a Quarter Century*. New York: Grand Central, 2007.

Carr, Leslie. *Color-Blind Racism*. Thousand Oaks: Sage, 1997.

Carter, Dan T. *The Politics of Rage: George Wallace, the Origins of the New Conservatism, and the Transformation of American Politics*. Baton Rouge: Louisiana State University Press, 1995.

Cashin, Sheryll. *The Failure of Integration: How Race and Class Are Undermining the American Dream*. New York: Public Affairs Council, 2004.

Checker, Melissa. *Polluted Promises: Environmental Racism and the Search for Justice*. New York: New York University Press, 2005.

Chung, Hyun C. *Struggle to Be the Sun Again*. New York: Orbis, 1990.

"Club Formed to Back Dunn, Mayoralty Race Hinted." *Elizabeth Daily Journal*, December 9, 1963.

Coalter, Milton, et al., eds. *The Mainstream Protestant Decline: The Presbyterian Pattern*. Louisville: Westminster John Knox, 1990.

Coffin, William Sloane, Jr. "A Politically Engaged Spirituality." *Yale Divinity School News*, April 28, 2005. https://divinity.yale.edu/news/politically-engaged-spirituality-comments-william-sloane-coffin-jr.

Cohen, David Stephen. *The Ramapo Mountain People*. New Brunswick: Rutgers University Press, 1994.

Coleridge, Samuel Taylor. "Work without Hope" (1825). *Poetry Foundation*. https://www.poetryfoundation.org/poems/43999/work-without-hope.

Cone, James. *A Black Theology of Liberation*. Maryknoll: Orbis, 2010.

———. *The Cross and the Lynching Tree*. Maryknoll: Orbis, 2011.

———. *God of the Oppressed*. Maryknoll: Orbis, 1997.

———. *Martin and Malcom and America: A Dream or a Nightmare?* Maryknoll: Orbis, 1991.

Connerton, Paul. *How Societies Remember*. Cambridge: Cambridge University Press, 1999.

Cooley, Henry S. *A Study of Slavery in New Jersey*. Baltimore: Johns Hopkins University Press, 1896.

Council of Bishops. *Episcopal Statement*. Chicago: African Methodist Episcopal Church, 2017.

Cowan, Rosemary. *Cornel West: The Politics of Redemption*. Malden, MA: Polity, 2003.

Cox, Oliver Cromwell. *Caste, Class and Race*. New York: Doubleday, 1948.

Crew, Spencer R. *Black Life in Secondary Cities*. New York: Garland, 1993.

Cunningham, John T. *Colonial New Jersey*. New York: Thomas Nelson, 1971.

Davies, Alan. *Infected Christianity: A Study of Modern Racism*. Montreal: McGill-Queen's University Press, 1988.

Davies, Susan E., and Paul Teresa Hennessee. *Racism in the Church*. Cleveland: United Church, 1998.

Davis, David Brion, *Inhuman Bondage*. New York: Oxford University Press, 2006.

Davis, James H., and Woodie W. White. *Racial Transition in the Church*. Nashville: Abingdon, 1980.

Dawson, Kathy. "Practical Theology, Opening the Doors with the Local Congregation: A Situated Conversation between Dietrich Bonhoeffer, Howard Gardner, and the Fourth Presbyterian Church, South Boston, Massachusetts." PhD dissertation, Princeton Theological Seminary, May 2002.

De La Torre, Miguel. *Doing Ethics from the Margins*. Maryknoll: Orbis, 2004.

Delgado, Richard, and Jean Stefanic, eds. *Critical White Studies*. Philadelphia: Temple University Press, 1997.

Dickinson, Emily. "The Master." In *The Complete Poems*, edited by Thomas Johnson, 156. Boston: Little, Brown, 1960.

Dickson, David. "US Underworld Linked to Illegal Toxic Waste Disposal." *Ambio* 10, no. 4 (1981) 189–90.

Dostoyevsky, Fyodor. *The Brothers Karamazov*. Translated by Constance Garnett. New York: Lowell, 2018.

Dray, Philip. *At the Hands of Persons Unknown: The Lynching of Black America*. New York: Modern Library, 2002.

DuBois, W. E. B. *Black Reconstruction in America: 1860–1880*. Cleveland: Meridan, 1964.

———. *Dusk of Dawn*. New York: Harcourt Brace, 1940.

Dyson, Eric Michael. *I May Not Get There With You: The True Martin Luther King Jr.* New York: Free, 2000.

"Elizabeth Drive Begun by Klan." *Elizabeth Daily Journal*, January 7, 1966.

Elkins, Stanley. *Slavery: A Problem in American Institutional and Intellectual Life.* Chicago: University of Chicago Press, 1959.

Escholz, Sarah. "The Color of Prime-Time Justice: Racial Characteristics of Television Offenders and Victims." In *Racial Issues in Criminal Justice*, edited by Martin D. Free Jr., 59–72. Westport: Praeger, 2003.

Farrow, Anne, et al. *Complicity: How the North Promoted, Prolonged, and Profited from Slavery.* Hartford: Ballantine, 2006.

"Father Carter Urges Bias Foes to End Midtown Marches." *Elizabeth Daily Journal*, September 23, 1963.

Feagin, Joe R. *The New Urban Paradigm: Critical Perspectives on the City.* Boston: Rowman and Littlefield, 1998.

———. *Systematic Racism: A Theory of Oppression.* New York: Routledge, 2006.

———. *The White Racial Frame: Centuries of Racial Framing and Counter-Framing.* New York: Routledge, 2010.

Feagin, Joe, and Vera Herna. *White Racism.* New York: Rutledge, 1995.

Fessler, Pam. "HUD: Growth of Homelessness During 2020 Was 'Devastating,' Even Before the Pandemic." *NPR*, March 18, 2021. https://www.npr.org/2021/03/18/978244891/hud-growth-of-homelessness-during-2020-was-devastating-even-before-the-pandemic.

Forest, Jim. "Lord, That I Might See." *Jim and Nancy Forest*, November 30, 2019. https://jimandnancyforest.com/2019/11/lord-that-i-might-see-talk-at-the-bishops-peace-dinner/.

Frankenberg, Ruth. *The Social Construction of Whiteness.* Minneapolis: University of Minnesota Press, 1993.

Free, Martin D., Jr., ed. *Racial Issues in Criminal Justice.* Westport: Prager, 2003.

Freire, Paulo. *Pedagogy of the Oppressed.* New York: Continuum, 2000.

Gans, Herbert. *The War Against the Poor: The Underclass and Antipoverty Policy.* New York: Basic Books, 1995.

Gelbspan, Ross, and Diane Tracy. "Hundreds Arrested in Boston Protest." *Boston Globe*, May 8, 1985.

Geller, William, and Hans Toch. *Police Violence.* New Haven: Yale University Press, 1996.

Gigantino, James. *The Ragged Road to Abolition.* Philadelphia: University of Pennsylvania Press, 2015.

Gillett, Ezra Hall. *History of the Presbyterian Church in the United States of America I.* Philadelphia: Presbyterian Board, 1873.

Gillette, Howard, Jr. *Camden after the Fall.* Philadelphia: University of Pennsylvania, 2005.

Girard, Rene. *Violence and the Sacred.* Baltimore: Johns Hopkins University Press, 1977.

Givens, John. *The Image of Christ in Russian Literature, Dostoevsky, Tolstoy, Bulgakov, Pasternak.* Ithaca: Cornell University Press, 2018.

Goldman, Benjamin, and Laura Fitton. *Toxic Wastes and Race Revisited.* Washington, DC: Center for Policy Alternatives, 1994.

González, Catherine C. "The Diversity with Which We Begin." *Reformed Theology and Worship* (Spring 1987).

González, Justo L. *Hechos. Comentario bíblico hispanoamericano.* Miami: Editorial Caribe, 1992.

———. *Mañana: Christian Theology from a Hispanic Perspective.* Nashville: Abingdon Press, 1990.

———. *The Story of Christianity.* Vol. 1. 2nd ed. New York: HarperOne, 2010.

———. "A Tale of Two Scrolls." Unpublished sermon. Trenton, New Jersey, 1995.

Gordus, Jeanne, et al. *Plant Closings and Economic Dislocation.* Kalamazoo, MI: W. E. Upjohn Institute for Employment Research, 1981.

Granzen, Michael. "Housing Matters." *Massachusetts Law Reform Institute* 4 (April 1990) 6–7.

Green, Charles. *Manufacturing Powerlessness in the Black Diaspora.* Oxford: AltaMira, 2001.

Griffin, Paul R. *Seeds of Racism in the Soul of America.* Cleveland: Pilgrim, 1999.

Grutner, Charles. "Mafia Secrets Revealed in Federal Court by Transcript of FBI Bugging." *New York Times,* June 11, 1969. https://www.nytimes.com/1969/06/11/archives/secrets-of-mafia-are-revealed-in-transcript-of-fbi-bugging-mafia.html.

Haggerty, Joan B. "Elizabeth Police Top in Civil Control." *Elizabeth Daily Journal,* June 28, 1969.

Hall, Douglas. *The Cross in Our Context: Jesus and the Suffering World.* Minneapolis: Augsburg Fortress, 2003.

Hall, Edward T. *Beyond Culture.* New York: Doubleday, 1976.

Halle, David. *American's Working Man: Work, Home and Politics among Blue Collar Property Owners.* Chicago: University of Chicago Press, 1984.

Harding, Vincent. *Martin Luther King: The Inconvenient Hero.* Maryknoll: Orbis, 1996.

Harris, David. *Profiles in Injustice.* New York: New, 2002.

Hartshorne, M. Holmes. *Hartshorne Speaking: Words of Hope and Meaning.* Hamilton, NY: Colgate University, 1998.

Harvey, Jennifer, et al., eds. *Disrupting White Supremacy from Within.* Cleveland: Pilgrim, 2004.

Hatfield, Edwin F. *History of Elizabeth, New Jersey.* New York: Carlton Lanhan, 1868.

Hauerwas, Stanley. *Character and Christian Life.* San Antonio: Trinity University Press, 1975.

———. *A Community of Character.* Notre Dame: University of Notre Dame Press, 1981.

Hauerwas, Stanley, and Romand Coles. *Christianity, Democracy and the Radical Ordinary.* Eugene, OR: Cascade, 2008.

Hedges, Chris. "Blue Shadows in Elizabeth." *New York Times,* May 13, 2000.

———. "The Play's the Thing." *TruthDig,* December 16, 2013. https://www.truthdig.com/articles/the-plays-the-thing/.

———. "Terrorizing the Vulnerable." *Common Dreams,* April 27, 2017.

Herbst, John, ed. *New Jersey: The Afro-American Experience.* Newark: New Jersey Historical Society, 1981.

Herman, Judith. *Trauma and Recovery: The Aftermath of Violence—from Domestic Abuse to Political Terror.* New York: Basic Books, 1997.

Heumnn, Milton, and Lance Cassak. *Good Cop, Bad Cop: Racial Profiling and Comparative Views of Justice.* New York: Peter Lang, 2003.

Hinks, Peter P. *To Awaken My Afflicted Brethren: David Walker and the Problem of Antebellum Slave Resistance.* University Park: Pennsylvania State University Press, 1997.

Hobgood, Mary Elizabeth. *Dismantling Privilege.* Cleveland: Pilgrim, 2000.

Holbert, Steve, and Rosa, Lisa. *The Color of Guilt and Innocence: Racial Profiling and Police Practices in America.* San Ramon: Page Marque, 2008.

Hood, Robert E. *Begrimed and Black.* Minneapolis: Fortress, 1994.

hooks, bell. *Killing Rage.* New York: Henry Holt, 1995.

Hunsinger, George. *Disruptive Grace: Studies in the Theology of Karl Barth.* Grand Rapids: Eerdmans, 2000.

Hwang, Syni-An, et al. "Childhood Asthma Hospitalizations and Ambient Air Sulfur Dioxide Concentrations in Bronx County, New York." *Environmental Health* 59 (May 2004) 266–75.

James, Williams. *The Varieties of Religious Experience.* New York: Mentor, 1958.

Jamieson, Kathleen Hall. *Dirty Politics: Deception, Distraction, and Democracy.* New York: Oxford University Press, 1992.

Jargowsky, Paul A. *Poverty and Place: Ghettos, Barrios and the American City.* New York: Russell Sage Foundation, 1997.

"JFK at Lowest Level since Inauguration: Reason Civil Rights Factor." *Elizabeth Daily Journal*, November 12, 1963.

Kaiser, R. Melvin. *Roots of Relational Ethics: Responsibility in Origin and Maturity in H. Richard Niebuhr.* Atlanta: Scholars, 1996.

Keck, Leander E. *Luke.* New Interpreter's Bible Commentary. Nashville: Abingdon, 1995.

Kennedy, Randall. *Race, Crime, and the Law.* New York: Pantheon, 1997.

Kierkegaard, Soren. *Either/Or: A Fragment of Life.* Translated by Alastair Hannay. New York: Penguin, 1992.

———. *Fear and Trembling and The Sickness Unto Death.* Translated by Walter Lowrie. Princeton: Princeton University Press, 2013.

———. *Writings.* Edited and translated by Howard V. Hong and Edna H. Hong. 26 vols. Princeton: Princeton University Press, 1978–2000.

Kim, Janice J., et al. "Ambient Air Pollution: Health Hazards to Children." *Pediatrics* 114 (2004) 1699–1707.

King, Martin Luther, Jr. *I Have a Dream: Writings and Speeches That Changed the World.* Edited by James Melvin Washington. San Francisco: Harper, 1992.

———. "I See the Promised Land." *United Church of Christ*, April 3, 1968. https://www.ucc.org/what-we-do/justice-local-church-ministries/justice/faithful-action-ministries/racial-justice/sacred-conversation_dr-kings-last-sermon/.

———. "Letter from Birmgingam Jail." In *The Radical King*, edited by Cornel West, 127–46. Boston: Beacon, 2016.

———. *Strength to Love.* New York: Harper & Row, 1963.

———. *Stride toward Freedom.* New York: HarperCollins, 1956, 1987.

———. *Where Do We Go from Here: Chaos or Community?* New York: Harper & Row, 1967.

Kirp, David, et al. *Our Town: Race, Housing, and the Soul of Suburbia.* New Brunswick, NJ: Rutgers University Press, 1995.

"Klan Leader Living in Elizabeth." *Elizabeth Daily Journal*, December 14, 1965.

Knapp, Charles. *New Jersey Politics during the Period of the Civil War and Reconstruction.* Geneva: W. F. Humphrey, 1924.

Kovel, Joel. *White Racism.* New York: Columbia University Press, 1984.

"Ku Klux Klan Takes $25 Gift to Church." *New York Times,* May 16, 1922. https://www.nytimes.com/1922/05/16/archives/ku-klux-klan-takes-25-gift-to-church-white-robed-men-march-to.html.

Kunkel, Fritz. *In Search of Maturity: An Inquiry into Psychology, Religion, and Self Education.* New York: Scribner, 1943.

Lamott, Anne. *Help, Thanks, Wow: The Three Essential Prayers.* New York: Riverhead, 2012.

Lehr, Dick, and Gerard O'Neill. *Black Mass: Whitey Bulger, the FBI, and a Devil's Deal.* New York: PublicAffairs, 2012.

LeighaCohen. "Cornel West and Chris Hedges: Ordination Services for Chris Hedges." YouTube video, 20:06. October 10, 2014. https://www.youtube.com/watch?v=XaVav16Zz-M.

Lewis, C. S. *The Great Divorce: A Dream.* London: HarperCollins, 2002.

Lewis, Jacqueline L. *The Power of Stories.* Nashville: Abingdon, 2008.

Lewis, John. "Together, We Can Redeem the Soul of Our Nation." *New York Times,* July 30, 2020. https://www.nytimes.com/2020/07/30/opinion/john-lewis-civil-rights-america.html.

Lipsitz, George. *The Possessive Investment in Whiteness.* Philadelphia: Temple University Press, 1998.

Litwack, Leon F. *Been in the Storm So Long: The Aftermath of Slavery.* New York: Vintage, 1980.

———. *How Free Is Free? The Long Death of Jim Crow.* Cambridge: Harvard University Press, 2009.

Loetscher, Lefferts. *A Brief History of the Presbyterians.* Philadelphia: Westminster, 1978.

Lott, Eric. *Love and Theft: Blackface Minstrelsy and the American Working Class.* Oxford: Oxford University Press, 1995.

Lubiano, Whneema, ed. *The House That Race Built.* New York: Pantheon, 1997.

Lukas, J. Anthony. *Common Ground: A Turbulent Decade in the Lives of Three American Families.* New York: Vintage, 2012.

MacDonald, Michael Patrick. *All Souls: A Family Story from Southie.* Boston: Beacon, 1997.

MacManus, Edward. *Black Bondage in the North.* Syracuse: Syracuse University Press, 2002.

Malcolm, I. G. "The Christian Teacher in the Multicultural Classroom." *Journal of Christian Education* 74 (1982) 48–60.

Marable, Manning. *The Great Wells of Democracy.* New York: Basic Civitas, 2002.

———. *How Capitalism Underdeveloped Black America.* Boston: South End, 2000.

Massey, Douglas, and Nancy Denton. *American Apartheid: Segregation and the Making of the Underclass.* Cambridge: Harvard University Press, 1993.

Mauer, Marc. *Race to Incarcerate.* New York: New, 2006.

Mays, James L., et al., eds. *Harper's Bible Commentary.* New York: HarperCollins, 1988.

McDermott, Monica. *Working-Class White: The Making and Unmaking of Race Relations.* Berkeley: University of California Press, 2006.

McVeigh, Rory. *The Rise of the Ku Klux Klan: Right Wing Movements and National Politics.* Minneapolis: University of Minnesota Press, 2009.

Merton, Thomas. *Conjectures of a Guilty Bystander.* New York: Image, 2014.

Mills, Charles W. *The Racial Contract.* Ithaca, NY: Cornell University Press, 1999.

"Mob in Elizabeth Union." *Elizabeth Daily Journal,* December 1, 1969.

Moltmann, Jurgen. *Resurrected to Eternal Life: On Dying and Rising.* Minneapolis: Fortress, 2021.

Morgan, Edmund. *American Slavery, American Freedom.* New York: Norton, 1975.

Morrison, Toni. *Playing in the Dark.* Cambridge: Harvard University Press, 1992.

Mortimer, K. M., et al. "The Effect of Air Pollution on Inner-City Children with Asthma." *Respiratory Journal* 19 (2002) 699–705.

Moss, Simeon. "The Persistence of Slavery in a Free State (1665–1866)." *Journal of Negro History* 35, no. 2 (July 1950) 289–310.

Murray, Andrew. *Presbyterians and the Negro: A History.* Philadelphia: Presbyterian Historical Society, 1966.

"New Jersey Puts 5000 in Washington DC March." *Elizabeth Daily Journal,* August 28, 1963.

Newman, Katherine S. *Falling from Grace.* Los Angeles: University of California Press, 1999.

Niebuhr, H. Richard. *The Meaning of Revelation.* New York: MacMillan, 1941.

———. *Radical Monotheism and Western Culture.* New York: Harper & Brothers, 1960.

———. *The Responsible Self.* Louisville: Westminster John Knox, 1999.

Niebuhr, H. Richard, and Richard R. Niebuhr, eds. *Faith on Earth: An Inquiry into the Structure of Human Faith.* New Haven: Yale University Press, 1989.

Niebuhr, Reinhold. *The Children of Light and the Children of Darkness.* New York: Scribner, 1944.

———. *Justice and Mercy.* Edited by Ursula M. Niebuhr. New York: Harper & Row, 1976.

———. *Moral Man and Immoral Society.* New York: Scribner, 1933.

———. *The Nature and Destiny of Man.* Vol. 2. New York: Scribner, 1955.

O'Connor, Elizabeth. *Cry Pain, Cry Hope.* Waco: Word, 1987.

O'Connor, G. T., et al. "Acute Respiratory Health Effects of Air Pollution on Children with Asthma in US Inner Cities." *Journal of Allergy Clinical Immunology* 121, no. 5 (May 2008) 1133–39.

Omi, Michael, and Howard Winant. *Racial Formation in the United States.* New York: Routledge, 1994.

"Organized Crime in Elizabeth." *Elizabeth Daily Journal,* August 5, 1969.

Ottley, Roi, and William Weatherby. *The Negro in New York.* Dobbs Ferry: Oceana, 1967.

Parish, Joe. "Environmental Update." *Elizabeth Gazette,* July 10, 1997, 1–2.

Plato. *Apology.* In *The Collected Dialogues,* edited by Edith Hamilton and Huntington Cairns, 3–26. Translated by Hugh Tredennick. Princeton: Princeton University Press, 1989.

PCUSA. *Constitution of the Presbyterian Church (U.S.A.).* Louisville: Office of the General Assembly, 2013.

———. *Extracts from the Minutes of the General Assembly, 1818.* Philadelphia: Bradford, 1818.

Perkinson, James W. *White Theology: Outing Supremacy in Modernity.* New York: Palgrave MacMillan, 2004.

Peterson, Ruth D., et al., eds. *The Many Colors of Crime: Inequalities of Race, Ethnicity, and Crime in America*. New York: New York University Press, 2006.

Phillips, Howard. *The Politics of Rich and Poor: Wealth and the American Electorate in the Reagan Aftermath*. New York: Harper Perennial, 1991.

Pingeon, Frances D. "Slavery in New Jersey on the Eve of the Revolution." In *New Jersey in the American Revolution*, edited by Williams C. Wright, 48–64. Rev. ed. Trenton: New Jersey Historical Commission, 1974.

"Police Bar Violence as Youth Rush Bias Marchers." *Elizabeth Daily Journal*, September 20, 1963.

"Police Haul Away Pickets." *Elizabeth Daily Journal*, August 7, 1963.

Rasmussen, Larry L. *Earth Community, Earth Ethics*. New York: Orbis, 1996.

Reich, Robert B. *The Work of Nations*. New York: Vintage, 1992.

"Republicans Win State Legislature and Union County Freeholders." *Elizabeth Daily Journal*, November 11, 1963.

Roediger, David R. *How Race Survived U.S. History*. London: Verso, 2008.

———. *The Wages of Whiteness: Race and the Making of the American Working Class*. New York: Verso, 1991.

Rohr, Richard. *Everything Belongs*. New York: Crossroads, 2003.

———. *A Spring Within Us: A Book of Daily Meditations*. Albuquerque: Center for Action and Contemplation, 2016.

Rosaldo, Renato. *Culture and Truth*. Boston: Beacon, 1993.

Rothenberg, Paula S. *White Privilege*. New York: Worth, 2002.

Rothschild, Emma. "Reagan and the Real America." *New York Review of Books*, February 5, 1981, 12–18.

Ruprecht, Louis A., Jr. "Mark's Tragic Vision: Gethsemane." *Religion & Literature* 24, no. 3 (Autumn 1992) 1–25.

Ryan, Joe. "Jacinta Fernandes." *Newark Star Ledger*, December 31, 2006.

Safi, Omid. "The Saint I Never Met: Daniel Berrigan." *On Being*, May 5, 2016. https://onbeing.org/blog/the-saint-i-never-met-daniel-berrigan/.

Schwartz, J. Dockery, et al. "Acute Effects of Summer Air Pollution on Respiratory Symptom Reporting in Children." *American Journal of Respiratory Critical Care Medicine* 150 (1994) 1234–42.

Sennett, Richard, and Jonathan Cobb. *The Hidden Injuries of Class*. New York: Vintage, 1973.

Smith, Robert C. *Racism in the Post-Civil Rights Era: Now You See It, Now You Don't*. Albany: State University of New York Press, 1995.

Smothers, Ronald. "Thomas Dunn, 76, Longtime Elizabeth Mayor." *New York Times*, February 13, 1998. https://www.nytimes.com/1998/02/13/nyregion/thomas-dunn-76-longtime-elizabeth-mayor.html.

State of New Jersey. "Air Toxics in New Jersey: 2005." *Department of Environmental Protection*, January 28, 2020. https://www.nj.gov/dep/airtoxics/unionavg05.htm.

Staudenraus, P. J. *The African Colonization Movement, 1816–1865*. New York: Octagon, 1961.

Stendahl, Krister. "Why I Love the Bible." *Harvard Divinity School Bulletin* 35, no. 1 (Winter 2007). https://bulletin.hds.harvard.edu/why-i-love-the-bible/.

Stout, Jeffrey. *Democracy and Tradition*. Princeton: Princeton University Press, 2004.

Stringfellow, William. *An Ethic for Christians and Other Aliens in a Strange Land*. Eugene, OR: Wipf & Stock, 2004.

———. *My People Is the Enemy: An Autobiographical Polemic*. Eugene, OR: Wipf & Stock, 2005.

———. *A Simplicity of Faith: My Experience of Mourning*. Eugene, OR: Wipf & Stock, 2005.

Sullivan, Ronald. "Gallagher Pleads Guilty to Tax Evasion." *New York Times*, December 22, 1972. https://www.nytimes.com/1972/12/22/archives/gallagher-pleads-guilty-to-tax-evasion-congressman-admits-he-held.html.

Swift, David Everett. *Black Prophets of Justice: Activist Clergy Before the Civil War*. Louisiana: Louisiana State University Press, 1989.

Takaki, Ronald. *A Different Mirror: A History of Multicultural America*. Boston: Little, Brown, 1993.

Terry, Robert. "The Negative Impact on White Values." In *Impacts of Racism on White Americans*, edited by Benjamin P. Bowser and Raymond Hunt, 119–51. Newbury Park, CA: Sage, 1981.

Thandeka. *Learning to Be White: Money, Race, and God in America*. New York: Continuum, 2000.

Thayer, Theodore. *As We Were: The Story of Old Elizabethtown*. Elizabeth: Grassman, 1964.

Tillich, Paul. "Knowledge through Love." In *The Shaking of the Foundations*, 108–17. New York: Scribner, 1955.

Townes, Emily. *Womanist Ethics and the Cultural Production of Evil*. New York: Palgrave MacMillan, 2006.

US Census Viewer. "Elizabeth, New Jersey Population: Census 2010 and 2000 Interactive Map, Demographics, Statistics." Generated by Michael Granzen, February 11, 2022. http://45.79.181.212:8080/city/NJ/Elizabeth.

Van Ausdale, Debra, and Joe Feagin. *The First R: How Children Learn Race and Racism*. Lanham: Rowman & Littlefield, 2001.

Volf, Miroslav. *Exclusion and Embrace*. Nashville: Abingdon, 1996.

Washington, Ethel M. *Union County Black Americans*. Mount Pleasant: Arcadia, 2004.

Websdale, Neil. *Policing the Poor*. Boston: Northeastern University Press, 2001.

Weis, Lois. *Class Reunion: The Remaking of the American White Working Class*. New York: Routledge/Falmer, 2004.

Wellenius, G. A., et al. "Particulate Air Pollution and Hospital Admissions for Congestive Heart Failure in Seven United States Cities." *American Journal Cardiology* 97, no. 3 (2006) 404–08.

Wellman, David. *Portraits of White Racism*. New York: Cambridge University Press, 1993.

West, Cornel. *Democracy Matters*. London: Penguin, 2004.

———. *Race Matters*. Boston: Beacon, 1993.

West, Traci C. *Disruptive Christian Ethics: When Racism and Women's Lives Matter*. Louisville: Westminster John Knox, 2006.

Wilmore, Gayraud S. *Black and Presbyterian*. Philadelphia: Geneva, 1998.

Wilson, William Julius. *When Work Disappears: The World of the Urban Poor*. New York: Vintage, 1996.

Wish, Naomi Bailin, and Stephen Eisdorfer. "The Impact of Mount Laurel Initiatives: An Analysis of the Characteristics of Applicants and Occupants." *Seton Hall Review* 77 (April 1997) 1268–71.

Witcher, Gregory. "Dorchester House Is Helping Homeless Find the Way Back." *Boston Globe*, November 18, 1985.

———. "Tent City Group Departs with Hope for a Home." *Boston Globe*, June 12, 1984.

Wright, Giles R. *Afro-Americans in New Jersey*. Trenton: New Jersey Historical Commission, 1988.

Wright, Marion Thompson. *The Education of Negros in New Jersey*. New York: Arno, 1971.

Wright, William, ed. *New Jersey in the American Revolution: Political and Social Conflict*. Trenton: New Jersey Historical Commission, 1974.

Zilversmit, Arthur. *The First Emancipation: The Abolition of Slavery in the North*. Chicago: University of Chicago, 1967.

Made in the USA
Columbia, SC
13 June 2022

61679528R00140